theatre & the body

Theatre&
Series Standing Order: ISBN 978–0–230–20327–3 paperback

You can receive further titles in this series as they are published by placing a standing order. Please contact your bookseller or, in the case of difficulty, write to us at the address below with your name and address, the title of the series, and the ISBN quoted above.

Customer Services Department, Palgrave Macmillan Ltd.
Houndmills, Basingstoke, Hampshire, RG21 6XS, England

theatre &
the body

Colette Conroy

palgrave
macmillan

First published 2010 by
PALGRAVE MACMILLAN

Palgrave Macmillan in the UK is an imprint of Macmillan Publishers Limited, registered in England, company number 785998, of Houndmills, Basingstoke, Hampshire RG21 6XS.

Palgrave Macmillan in the US is a division of St Martin's Press LLC, 175 Fifth Avenue, New York, NY 10010.

Palgrave Macmillan is the global academic imprint of the above companies and has companies and representatives throughout the world.

Palgrave® and Macmillan® are registered trademarks in the United States, the United Kingdom, Europe and other countries.

ISBN: 978–0–230–20543–7 paperback

This book is printed on paper suitable for recycling and made from fully managed and sustained forest sources. Logging, pulping and manufacturing processes are expected to conform to the environmental regulations of the country of origin.

A catalogue record for this book is available from the British Library.

A catalog record for this book is available from the Library of Congress.

10 9 8 7 6 5 4 3 2 1
19 18 17 16 15 14 13 12 11 10

Printed and bound in China

contents

series editors' preface

The theatre is everywhere, from entertainment districts to the fringes, from the rituals of government to the ceremony of the courtroom, from the spectacle of the sporting arena to the theatres of war. Across these many forms stretches a theatrical continuum through which cultures both assert and question themselves.

Theatre has been around for thousands of years, and the ways we study it have changed decisively. It's no longer enough to limit our attention to the canon of Western dramatic literature. Theatre has taken its place within a broad spectrum of performance, connecting it with the wider forces of ritual and revolt that thread through so many spheres of human culture. In turn, this has helped make connections across disciplines; over the past fifty years, theatre and performance have been deployed as key metaphors and practices with which to rethink gender, economics, war, language, the fine arts, culture and one's sense of self.

Theatre & is a long series of short books which hopes to capture the restless interdisciplinary energy of theatre and performance. Each book explores connections between theatre and some aspect of the wider world, asking how the theatre might illuminate the world and how the world might illuminate the theatre. Each book is written by a leading theatre scholar and represents the cutting edge of critical thinking in the discipline.

We have been mindful, however, that the philosophical and theoretical complexity of much contemporary academic writing can act as a barrier to a wider readership. A key aim for these books is that they should all be readable in one sitting by anyone with a curiosity about the subject. The books are challenging, pugnacious, visionary sometimes and, above all, clear. We hope you enjoy them.

Jen Harvie and Dan Rebellato

foreword: unanswered questions

> Presence.
> Being present, over long stretches of time,
> Until presence rises and falls, from
> Material to immaterial, from
> Form to formless, from
> Instrumental to mental, from
> Time to timeless.
>
> Marina Abramović / Ulay, *Nightsea Crossing*, 1981

I strongly believe that the most powerful tool today in performance is the artist herself.

Years ago at the Documenta exhibition in Kassel, Nam June Paik was supposed to give a piano concert at a Fluxus performance. He took a microphone and said that it was going to be a very boring concert ('please leave the room'). He repeated his appeal for 45 minutes, and finally people started to leave. In the end he was fantastic. It was boring indeed, but it made me realize how afraid we are of doing little or nothing, and yet it is precisely that doing nothing that opens the door to different perceptions. The performer uses the public like a mirror and vice versa.

In Western cultures, it is necessary to have some trauma, some terrible tragedy in your private life, to be able to make a mental leap; perhaps somebody dies, or you have an operation, or you clinically die and then recover. In Eastern cultures altered states of minds are often a matter of education and bodily practice. Sufi dancers, for instance, turn in concentric circles, increasing the speed of the outer circles until those in the inner circles enter a trance. They play with sharp swords in a very restricted space so that any wrong move could cause the death of somebody. For them, there is no past or future, only a present that is like a trampoline from which you can make the mental jump into another state of consciousness.

Thinking of all those things, there are still so many unanswered questions related to performance practices.

How should the performer prepare for the performance?
What kind of diet should they have?
What kind of liquids should they take?
What kind of physical exercise should the performer have to do to prepare?
What kind of mental exercise should the performer have to do to prepare?
When should you be naked and when should you be dressed?
What is performance?
What is the performance body?
What is the difference between performance and theatre?

How do you start and how do you end performance?

What about documentation?

Are the photographs taken of the performance a work of art themselves or just documentation?

What is your responsibility to your audience?

Why is performance still an alternative art form?

If the performance is performed again, what are the rules?

How do you sell the performance and what are the rules?

Why is performance an art form that will never die and will always reappear in different moments of history?

What is the role of the audience?

Silent voyeur or active participant?

What happens to a performance if something unpredictable takes place?

Can performance elevate the spirit of the performer and the audience?

Why is it so important to stage pain and danger in the performance?

What about time?

What about repetition?

What about risking your own life?

Marina Abramović is an internationally acclaimed artist, born in Yugoslavia and resident in New York, who has often taken her own body as the medium for a series of intense live artworks (many of them made in collaboration with fellow artist Ulay) exploring the limits of the body, the ethics of spectatorship, the interplay of pain and repetition in performance. They include Rhythm 0 *(1974),* Lips of Thomas *(1975),* Breathing In – Breathing Out *(1977),* The Lovers: Walk on the Great Wall *(1988), and* The House with the Ocean View *(2002).*

theatre & the body

Sarah Bernhardt's body

The following passage from Sarah Bernhardt's posthumously published manual *The Art of the Theatre* (*c*.1924) offers advice for anybody considering a career in acting:

> To summarize, those entrusted with the admission of potential dramatic artists, ought to take special note of the bodily proportions of aspirants, and refuse to admit little women with big heads or lads with long bodies, supported by short and bandy legs – even as comic actors. It is better for the laughter to be the result of their studies rather than that of their physical imperfections. For I refuse the title of artist to those who owe their reputations to a physical deformity. I regard them as buffoons. (p. 49)

Bernhardt (1844–1923) is a fascinating figure. She is probably the most written-about actor in the history of theatre. She was known for her technical mastery of acting as well as her histrionic and emotional performances. Bernhardt devotes the first 80 of the 224 pages of her manual to a consideration of the natural vocal and bodily qualities required for success as an actor. She claims that only the physically perfect and well proportioned should even consider acting as a career. She pre-empts the objection that some physically imperfect actors succeed in their chosen career with the contention that these performers are not artists.

Her advice offers a clear distinction between the artistry produced in training and the simple exploitation of the unusual body. Her opinion appears to emerge from a wish to see skilled performance on stage and from the notion that unintended acts are meaningless. Intention is important to Bernhardt. If we laugh at an actor's absurd gait, it matters that she or he has *adopted* this gait. If we laugh at the way that he or she walks, then we are not responding to acting. The audience must be able to separate the voluntary from the involuntary. For Bernhardt, acting involves the adoption of an unfamiliar range of actions from the basis of a familiar body.

Bernhardt continued her career into her seventies, even after the amputation of a leg. She was a disabled performer when she wrote her acting manual. The amputation left Bernhardt with extremely limited mobility and suffering terrible pain. Her determination to continue to work obliged her to develop a number of strategies of coping and concealment. She was cast against both sex and age, and, if we were to adopt her own aesthetic criteria, we could say that she continued to use her reputation to pass as an actor rather than as a deformed 'buffoon'. One obituarist wrote: 'Sarah was a weird figure of stageland, especially in her later days ... when, maimed and incomplete, she masqueraded her age into youth, her femininity into the masculine and her ugliness into beauty.' The tension between Bernhardt's advice to aspiring actors and her practice isn't just an example of hypocrisy. It introduces an important set of ideas about audiences, actors and the cultural idea of the body. *The Times* of the very early 1920s published numerous paparazzi-style photographs of Bernhardt, taken as she was being carried into hotels. Photographers really wanted a shot that showed she had had a leg amputated.

In an article about Bernhardt's vaudeville career, '2-A-Day Redemptions and Truncated Camilles' (1994), Leigh Woods writes that while Bernhardt struggled against pain, poverty and physical limitation, her audience came to regard the specific form of her body as spectacle in itself. Vaudeville is a satirical form of theatre, interspersed with songs, that sometimes includes variety acts. As a form of popular entertainment it was a long way from the classical and dramatic roles that had made up the high points of Bernhardt's career. In Bernhardt's case, the 'big scenes' that had made her famous were taken out of the context of the plays they came from, and the aging actor went through a process of playing out the heightened dramas of tragic death in extract form. The celebrity of the actor and the fact that she had had her leg amputated were reasons Bernhardt could earn her living in playing out her own death.

Woods notes that Bernhardt's famously colourful and frequently scandalous private life added to the pleasure that the audience took in watching her play out climactic death scenes. Woods suggests that the audience may have seen the punishment of the 'fallen woman' on stage simultaneously in the fiction of the play and in the real suffering of the elderly celebrity amputee. The prurient interest in Bernhardt as amputee is perhaps reflected in the disturbing urban legend that P. T. Barnum, the freak show proprietor, offered to buy Bernhardt's amputated leg from her. I cannot find any credible source for this story—all versions cite other versions in an endlessly uncorroborated way—but I find in the story's circulation an explicit cultural connection between acting and the framing and presentation of human oddity in freak shows. Four main strands emerge from this example, and these strands, introduced briefly below, run throughout my approach to theatre and the body.

Four ways of thinking about theatre and the body

First of all, there are conventions of presenting and viewing bodies on stage. Questions about what sorts of bodies may appear on stage, questions about who may play which part, are important to the way we understand and make theatre. The connections and distinctions between characters and actors have a profound effect on the making and the watching of theatre. Ideas about the relationship between the inert body and its movement or action are crucial to the ways that we watch and appreciate theatre and performance. Notions of artistry and skill are understood differently in different contexts, so the training of actors, the writing of drama and the directing of theatre use and articulate different ideas about the relationships between theatre and the body.

Second, the body is a site of power, and a site where power can be questioned and explored. Bernhardt succeeds in passing on her powerful opinion about *suitable* bodies because of the fame that her years of success have brought her. Her celebrity confers a degree of power that enables her to regard her body as different from the body of a young or aspiring actor. And yet this celebrity also causes the public gaze to fall upon her bodily difference. The amputation of her leg attracts the curious gaze of a popular vaudeville audience, as well as the readers of *The Times*. Both Bernhardt's acting manual and her experience of paparazzi-style prurience alert us to the fact that audiences look at bodies for all sorts of reasons. Great artistry and freakishness seem to belong to different critical universes, but here they are seen together in the same story.

Third, the body can be used as an analytical strategy or vantage point. The relationships between performance and culture can tell us much about both. The Bernhardt example offers several perspectives: Bernhardt's thoughts about acting bodies, others' comments on and analyses of Bernhardt's performances, Leigh Woods' theory about Bernhardt and vaudeville, the connection between Bernhardt and the freak show. The series of ideas expressed around this specific body reveal the working of power upon the body in culture and society. The analysis of the performing body also tells us something about the spectating body. Whenever I watch or analyse a piece of theatre I occupy a physical perspective, and I rely on my own physical body as the vantage point of my analysis. So my analysis is always subject to the restrictions or possibilities that my own body imposes or opens up. The 'ideal' spectator exists only as an abstract idea.

Fourth, in the Bernhardt story, there is a distinction to be made between 'the body' and 'bodies'. Bernhardt supposes that there is an ideal body for an actor — a neutral medium of communication that can be trained and that can simply stand for a character without distracting the audience's attention. Bernhardt's idea of the body, however, is an abstraction. There is an important distinction to be made between the body as an idea or an ideal and bodies as real physical objects that vary hugely from each other. For Bernhardt, *the body* is an idea, and *bodies* that necessarily differ from this may distract the audience from the artistry involved in acting.

I imagine that you could use the word 'body' correctly in more than two hundred sentences if I asked you to, and I accept this means that you understand this ordinary word perfectly well. I don't intend to try to convince you otherwise, because I do not want needlessly to complicate a straightforward idea, but I do want to suggest that the body, as it is used in the analysis of human culture and behaviour, is a necessary simplification. I'd like this book to offer choices as to how you simplify ideas about bodies, and to provide a starting-point for the investigation of the connections between theatre and the body.

This book looks critically at the notion of the body as a paradigm – a conceptual framework – for the understanding of human relationships with the world. It also looks at the connections between the body and theatre, and at the ways in which we use theatre to explore and articulate ideas about the experiences of bodies. This subject is vast, and throughout I have tried to use examples that highlight the main patterns of thought and argument that contribute to this area of study. In selecting the material, my main aim has been to find ways of opening this area up for further investigation and to find ways that help to explain the connections between theatre and the body. Throughout the book my analytical tools are examples from theatre and from plays. You will see that many of the ideas and arguments contradict each other, and at all levels of critical and performance-based work there is surprisingly little consensus on how to think and write about bodies and theatre.

This area of investigation is a lively and contentious one; philosophy and critical theory meet the three-dimensional experience of theatre and performance, and just beneath the surface of the whole debate lie the discourses of medicine and science. Students of theatre and drama sometimes lack the knowledge and confidence to draw upon these discourses, with the result that we frequently defer to science without subjecting it to critique or analysis. This seems to be part of the necessary separation of specialists into different fields: the scientific community deals with facts and physical bodies, and the artistic community deals with abstract thought and the world of pleasure, fiction and aesthetic responses. The result of these conceptual distinctions is that we find it difficult to connect our theorising, spectating and acting with our cultural and scientific understanding of the shape and form of the body. Theatre can offer many examples that help us to conceptualise difficult ideas, not just about performance but about society and culture as well. Since theatre offers a cultural space for the meeting of multiple disciplines it is useful to look beyond texts that are specifically about theatre.

Many commentators on contemporary performance concentrate on events that explore extreme uses of the performer's body. Such performances exploit the limits of human endurance or pain; they seek to expose bodily vulnerability or explore the boundaries of the lived body. These extreme performance practices are motivated by the same sort of questions that I ask throughout this book, but the examples I use are mostly from plays. Theatre is fundamentally concerned with the human body, and it also allows us to ask what we mean when we talk about bodies. I want to show that it is perfectly possible to think about bodies in dramatic texts and plays, and this has motivated my choice of examples. There is a dazzling array of critical works about live and performance art, about installation work, about performance and pain, about physical theatre work, and about all other types of performance (and you will find some of these analyses listed in the further reading section). This book will introduce you to some questions that will make it easier to read this further work, and it will assist you to develop your own analysis of any kind of theatre or performance work you happen to encounter.

Bodies and meaning

Conventions of abstraction

If we think about the process of learning about bodies, we can see a distinct difference between the way that bodies are depicted in anatomical diagrams and the way that we learn as children to depict bodies in crayon drawings. One learns to draw a recognisably human form not by drawing what one sees but by learning the conventions through which one can represent the body. In both examples, the 'real' version is too complex for the communication of a specific, limited set of ideas. Each depiction relies on a series of conventions through which we learn to use the term 'body'. You might remember from school textbooks that there is a surprising lack of variety in the outline of the anatomical drawings – it is difficult to think that any one person is *really* that shape. The outline is not in itself important; it is a generalisation that allows the diagram to be understood as a simplified illustration of one aspect of human bodies. The diagram refers to a set of ideas and not to a specific body. It would seem absurd to point at myself and say 'This is (or I am) the body'.

The body is necessarily abstract, but it is an abstraction based on the idea of a fleshy, palpable class of objects in the world. What happens when we use an abstract concept for the development of analysis? Is a body *part* of a person? We would think so, because we can talk about 'my body'. And yet it is not possible to separate myself from my body. These questions are important, but they will carry us only so far in our understanding. The different uses of the term 'body' are absolutely crucial, because they carry with them assumptions and theories. These theories are often grounded in ideological or political perspectives.

At this point, you might intelligently object that bodies are *real objects*. They operate in real space, and they are made of real matter. This is an important idea, and this wish to find a real and material object to talk about has in part motivated the current interest in the body as a paradigm. This has been a backlash against some rather abstract theories of subjectivity and an attempt to get down to a discussion of something that is real – or at least physical – or at least material. In emphasising the idea that bodies carry meaning along with them, I am trying to guide the argument gently but decisively away from the idea that in theatre we use bodies simply to copy the actions of other bodies. Perhaps there is an extent to which we think we do this, but I believe that the practice of theatre-making and theatre-watching is usually more interesting than that.

Some of the ideas in this book appear abstract and extremely distant from the real bodily experiences of walking or eating or sleeping. This remoteness is sometimes used as a reason not to analyse concepts or theories. After all, it might seem like nonsense to suggest that the presence or existence of the human body can be disputed, or that its obvious materiality can be deconstructed, or that its observable shape and form can be critically interrogated. When we work within theatre and performance studies, the discipline continually provokes us to bring ideas back to the physical experiments and the dramatic fictions of performances. At the same time, the discipline appears to demand a process of critical enquiry that emerges from our own experiences of watching or acting. It seems to me that these critical and analytical processes are important responses to theatre and that theatre as a cultural form offers some significant ways of framing and understanding the body.

Theatrical bodies

If you contemplate the different uses of bodies in theatre, you might see the practical impact of some of these ideas. The methodologies of the Stanislavski 'system' are sometimes seen as the basis for acting in mainstream European and North American theatre and film, and much of current actor training is strongly influenced by this approach. In this excerpt from the preface to *An Actor's Work*, the Russian actor and theatre director Konstantin Stanislavski (1863–1938) compares the inner creativity of the artist's mind with the physical body that must be developed to release the mind's creativity:

> Acting is above all inward, psychological, sub-conscious. The best thing is when creation occurs spontaneously, intuitively, through inspiration. ... However, before attaining the beguiling heights of inspiration, we have to deal with the conscious technique for achieving it. We are faced not only with the actor's invisible, creative mind but also his visible, palpable body. That is real, material, and to work on it you need the 'drudgery' without which no art is produced at all. (p. xxvi)

If you are familiar with traditions of actor training, Stanislavski's explanation may be well known to you. It may be that the habit of seeing the body as material to work on seems accurate and obvious. It is important to remember that Stanislavski's work is based on a highly theorised account of the relationship between the body, the mind and the theatre.

A contrasting approach can be found in this example from 1972. The actor Billie Whitelaw was cast in the role of Mouth in the first production of Samuel Beckett's play *Not I* (Lincoln Center, New York). In her autobiography, *Billie Whitelaw ... Who He?* (1995), she describes the role: 'All that *Not I* consists of is a mouth; that's all the audience can see of the actress – no body, no face, nothing except a mouth half-way up, on an invisible raised stage' (p. 123). As well as the obscuring of the body, the actor needs to be entirely still. The mouth needs to be lit with a tiny pinprick of light from a spot, but it needs to be bright enough for an audience in the theatre to see and focus upon the mouth. The stillness required was an enormous feat of athleticism. Whitelaw draws attention to a distinct difference between Beckett's instructions and her expectations of the role as an actor: 'His "Don't act" instruction necessarily caused me some difficulty. An actor is usually hired precisely for the personal things he will bring to a piece' (p. 120).

The removal from the actor playing Mouth of all freedom and all self-determination is an important element of the play. Beckett (1906–89) was an important proponent and innovator of theatrical modernism. He worked directly against realist conventions, experimenting boldly with ideas of form and rejecting notions of realist character and setting. His ideas about bodies are not directly compatible with Stanislavski's.

Of course, the differences between Beckett and Stanislavski can't be reduced to the fact that they think differently about the body. The appearance of the body on stage, the experience of preparation and training for the actor, the experiences of empathy and engagement all emerge from different philosophical and theoretical perspectives. Making theatre requires the practitioner to develop a rigorous and coherent set of ideas about what he or she is doing when the body appears as character onstage. Two things are suggested by these examples: first, that theoretical perspectives on the body are a significant part of the process of making theatre; second, that it is helpful, or maybe even necessary, to understand the reasons for thinking in a certain way about the relationship between the body and the form of theatre.

I have already mentioned that I think theatre is a place where we can examine the operation of bodies and explore the meanings of bodies. Simon Shepherd expresses the intrinsic connection between theatre and the body in his book *Theatre, Body and Pleasure* (2006). He argues that '[t]heatre is a practice in which societies negotiate around what the body is and means' (p. 1). Bodies are elements of theatre. The shape, form, resonance and movement of the actor's body are used as creative elements within the art form. The body of the audience member is physically present in the same room as the acting body. Theatre is founded on the dynamic interplay between actor and audience, and between the two the entire set of communication strategies, mimetic games and temporal and spatial experiences that make up theatre are played out. But, as well as being a part of the analytical corpus of theatre, bodies and their actions may appear within theatre as objects of analysis. That is to say, bodies may be thought of as texts.

The ideas and examples discussed in this book help us to think about human bodies in a number of ways and to understand the limitations and the implications of these ways of thinking. In theatre we need to be able to use ideas as possibilities – that is, without necessarily believing in them. We also need to develop series of connections without necessarily claiming that 'this is how the world is'. I think that if a performance is any good, and if we are to have fun as spectators, we play with hypotheses, nightmares, wild fantasies and endless other possibilities when we watch a piece of theatre. We do this not because we like to waste our time in idle speculation (although we might) but because it is a necessary and compelling and important way of dealing with our relationships with other people, and even our relationships with our own bodies. You will find that I have chosen to look in detail at what is often called the mind/body problem, at ideas about the embodiment of gender and at ideas that connect notions of intention and consciousness to the concept of the body. These are theories that provide opportunities to develop an exploration of theatre and the body through a process of asking questions.

What sorts of question are provoked by the notion of the body? The body seems to have shifting boundaries. What is included in the body, and what is excluded? Are my spectacles a part of my body? Is his wheelchair a part of his body? How are internal or interior experiences such as emotion, pain, pregnancy or illness shown on the body? In what ways can we think about the body as a text? Is it a raw material or a tool? And, as an example of the difficult and vexing theoretical questions that occupy us, how do we understand the relationship between the body and the mind? Perhaps you already think that I am unlikely in such a short book to offer answers to all the questions I raise, and you would be quite correct. In fact, my argument takes us away from the task of answering specific questions about embodiment and the theatre. Instead, I argue that these are questions we return to frequently in all our cultural actions and that in theatre we are obsessively, and productively, engaged in ideas and actions that explore the connections between theatre and the body.

Bodies and language

The philosopher Ludwig Wittgenstein (1889–1951) explored the possibilities of language as a means of understanding. To understand the meaning of certain concepts, we need to do more than look the word up in a dictionary. Dictionaries merely describe language use. To gain an understanding of, for example, the colour blue, we can investigate the speed of light and measure the pattern of refraction as light passes through a prism, we can read lengthy discussions of the

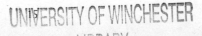

pigments that produce a particular shade of paint, or we can investigate the effect when blue light hits the retina. Although these investigations might be interesting, none of them would give us an understanding of the concept.

Wittgenstein suggests that we don't usually trouble ourselves with the sorts of circuitous investigations that can tell us nothing about the use of a term such as 'blue'. If you want to communicate the concept 'blue' to another person, you simply identify a blue object, and you point at it, saying 'This is blue.' If you point only at a blue pen you might accidentally communicate the idea that blue *is* a pen, so you have to find a number of other objects that are blue – the sky or a piece of clothing, for example. You might also point to a red pen, a red piece of clothing, and explain that the difference between the objects is a difference of colour. In this way you teach your listener to apply the word to a certain *aspect* of a number of different objects, and in this way you communicate the concept of the colour blue.

The body is not a concept that you can learn about by pointing at one body. Indeed, I would argue that it is not a *concept* at all. When you point at a body, you must always point at a specific body in a specific place, and the complexity of the body means that you are pointing at a complex system, not at an object. If you point at a person walking down the road and say 'That is a body', you are misleading us, and also possibly being impolite. It sounds silly to say 'I am a body'; it is more usual to say 'I have a body', and yet this seems to tie us to a distinction between our selves and our bodies. (This distinction will be examined critically later in this section.) To refer to a group of your colleagues as 'a room full of bodies' seems rather rude because it reduces them to the status of an inert mass, collections of cells, or structures of flesh and bones. The body is not the same as 'a person' or 'an individual' or even 'a human being'. I can talk about 'my body' in such a way that it sounds as though I own it, and as if there is such a thing as 'I' without the body. But is there a difference between *my* body and *the body*?

Consider a few contexts in which one might use the term 'body':

> Body and soul
> Body and mind
> A body of evidence (a collection of documents etc.)
> A charitable body (an organisation or group of
>   people working for charity)
> A body of work or a body of water
> An out-of-body experience
> A dead body (a corpse)
> My body/your body (something we own)
> Somebody/anybody (deprived of identity)
> Selling your body (being paid for sex)

My list suggests that I use the term 'body' as a way of structuring or organising thoughts about the human being. Bodies of water and bodies of evidence are masses of a substance – collections. Bodies of work and charitable bodies are ways of referring to multiple items. 'Body' is an expression of coherence out of disparate elements. Here's a commonplace observation about theatre spectatorship: we become spectators by physically attending a performance. We sit in the same room as the actors, and we look at the actions they perform with their bodies. We laugh or cry or yawn. But do we think or analyse or reflect with the body? Commonplace understandings of spectatorship suggest that some of our responses are related to our bodies and that others are related to the mind. Experiences of empathy may be very physical – think about an audience's response when a character is kicked in the crotch or when something even more violent occurs. How might we begin to think or to talk about these sorts of spectatorial response?

Human bodies

In the introduction to *Volatile Bodies* (1994), feminist philosopher Elizabeth Grosz accuses Western philosophy of exhibiting 'a profound somatophobia' (p. 5), by which she means hatred and fear of the body. She highlights Plato's characterisation of the body as a prison for the mind or the soul. This image is one of the foundational conceptions of the understanding of mind and body. The separation of mind and body is a highly influential way of thinking, an example of a *dualist* doctrine. Dualism is a form of analysis that holds that an entity can be divided into two separate but related parts, such as mind/body or body/soul or nature/culture. Within dualist thinking, the notion of the body carries within it a separation from other aspects of humanness. The opposing of body and mind or of body and soul demonstrates a theory of embodiment that posits the body as present, accessible and touchable. This depicts the body as a sort of envelope for those aspects of the self that are specific or unique to the individual and that cannot be touched. In many world religions, the belief is that the soul is released from its corporeal prison when the body dies.

Most world religions uphold a difference between the mortal body and the immortal soul. Religions that teach belief in an afterlife suggest that there is a sphere where the spirit or soul, minus the body, continues its existence in some way. The body dies and the soul goes to heaven or hell. Bodies are considered corruptible, decaying and impermanent, and subject to base appetites. Bodily desires such as the need for food, material comfort and sex are seen as the factors that chain us to the physical world. The transcendence of bodily desires is regarded as a perpetual and necessary struggle.

The separation between body and soul is the primary argument of Christopher Marlowe's play *Doctor Faustus* (*c*.1593). Faustus, an accomplished scholar, sells his soul to the devil in exchange for the knowledge of magic. The play presents the fleshy reality of the seven deadly sins. Pride, Covetousness, Wrath, Envy, Gluttony, Sloth and Lechery are paraded by Lucifer. They are comic and grotesque, and they represent the sins of the body that can lead the soul to be condemned. The distortion of human form in performance connects metaphorically with the unseen twisting and deforming that sin causes to the soul.

The connection between the twisted form and the form of the mind is explored metaphorically in Freud's writing, as we will see below. In *Doctor Faustus*, the seven deadly sins are sent away to hell and are followed soon after by Faustus himself, who has sacrificed his immortal soul for a brief lifetime of power and knowledge. Faustus' vanity has led him to exchange a brief physical life of pleasure for eternal damnation. The body leads us astray. Traces of this separation between body and soul are still present in culture. Theatre struggles with the idea of representing or imagining the soul or spirit without the use of the human form, and this indicates that this most abstract idea is still imagined through the body – through precisely that which it is not.

The political philosopher Hannah Arendt (1906–75), in her book *The Human Condition* (1958), suggested that in the pre-industrial past, much of philosophy and political theory has tried to explain what it is that makes us specifically human. It has seemed important that the human being be conceptually separated from the animal. Perhaps this is the act that is performed by referring to a 'human being'. As with 'body', the category 'human' acts as a specification of what one is not. As 'humans' we are self-determining: we can recognise, analyse and make choices about our own existence and identity. We are not limited to existing in response only to our bodies. The importance of self-determination and the process of freeing us from our bodily wants can be seen as processes of abstraction, in which we develop a set of actions and capabilities that are not related to the need to propagate the species and to sustain life. This basic distinction between the fully human and other beings is an important one.

Arendt uses the example of the fifth century BCE, the time of the Greek playwright Sophocles, when thinking and contemplation are regarded as the activities of free citizens. Slaves and women are not really human, because they live lives of the body, just as animals do. Women live their social role through their body; their whole existence is bound up in reproduction, and there's little choice in that. Slaves are compelled, by the threat of violence or starvation, to work. Neither woman nor slave is free from the needs of the body, and so neither attains the status of full human. For the ancient Greeks, freedom is expressed through the ability to think and to choose, rather than simply to act and to respond. At this point, the body and the presumed capacity to think become a means of making social and political distinctions. The process of thinking and speaking about women as if they were bodies persists in some attitudes and actions to this day. Today, however, denying a woman the right to become an airline pilot because she might get pregnant at some point would be seen as outrageous. The reproductive potential of an individual is regarded as a private matter, and one that is subject to choice and to self-determination.

This distinction makes it seem that, in Arendt's analysis, the ancient Greeks had a different set of ideas about agency and self-determination and that they interpreted the mind/body distinction differently than we do in the twenty-first century. Indeed, it sounds as though Arendt is saying that ancient Greek citizens lived a life of the mind, whereas slaves and women lived a life of the body. So how did the ancient Greeks see the distinction between mind and body?

In her book *In and Out of the Mind* (1992), Ruth Padel examines ancient Greek tragedy in search of representations of the way that fifth-century BCE Greek society thought about mind and body. First, she argues that the theatre was a valuable and culturally important place to think about human beings' interactions with the world:

> Tragedy is the concentrated, intense genre that the community prized, for which they shut up shop, came to their uncomfortable theatre, and sat still for days on end. Its ways of looking at human beings and human relations with the outside world must have had some bearings on that community's inner life. (p. 6)

You will notice that the experience of the body could be disregarded. Having transcended the experience of bodily discomfort, the audience members were able to get on with the task of thinking. We are very used to supposing that thinking happens in the brain. Padel suggests that thinking was represented as a bodily activity in Greek culture. In this model, the guts are where the mind resides. Evidence of thinking emerges from the guts' susceptibility to feelings of nervousness, anger or excitement and the individual's ability to feel the innards in motion:

> Sophocles refers to a controversy, current when he was young, about what part of the body we think with. ... In ordinary fifth-century life, when people wondered what was going on

inside someone, what mattered was that person's *splanchna*, 'guts'. ... Psychology in tragedy's world has practically nothing to do with the head. (pp. 12–13).

According to this analysis, thinking is unquestionably a bodily experience; it is simply a different form of action. It is the analysis of freedom, and not the knowledge of biology, that separates us from the fifth-century BCE Athenians. The question of *where* thinking takes place is important because thinking seems to be an invisible activity, but humans must think audibly or visibly if they are to communicate with each other at all, let alone create theatre. A 'gut feeling' for us is an animal instinct.

For twenty-first-century society, the question of what makes us consider another to be human is associated not with the particular form of body but with a number of factors that vary according to context. The category of humanity is frequently connected to our capacity to think and to feel emotion towards other people. The habit of referring to unrepentant murderers as 'animals' is an expression of the way that a human being has transgressed the standards of human emotion and behaviour. Conversely, our ability to attach values and ideas to others is a process of conferring the status of human on other people.

Case study: *A Day in the Death of Joe Egg*

In Peter Nichols' play *A Day in the Death of Joe Egg* (Citizens' Theatre, Glasgow, 1967), Sheila and Bri have a profoundly disabled daughter, Joe. The play explores how the two parents live with a child who is 'a kind of living parsnip'. Profound ethical problems of consciousness and embodiment are explored in the play, and the question of what constitutes a person is a continuous theme. Joe has a healthy body but is badly brain damaged; there's a question of whether she is a *person* at all. Issues of care and euthanasia and ideas about a liveable life, dignity and modern medicine are all played out in *Joe Egg*. The play shocks its audience because it shows the boundaries of human-ness. Joe is a human being, with a human body, but there is absolutely no connection with others, and there seems therefore to be no thought. Is Joe just a body? Is it possible to be just a body? The play gets much of its comedy from Bri and Sheila's process of playing *as if* Joe could think and feel as we feel. They make up responses for her and treat her as if she were speaking to them. Although the character is a child, she is used as a puppet in a number of sequences, but this is a process of trying to confer a personality on the child:

> Bri: The lady in the bus said you'd been good. Sat by the driver, did you?
> Joe: Aaaah!
> Bri: There's a clever girl.
> Joe: Aaaah!
> Bri (as though he understood): Saw the Christmas trees?
> Joe: Aaaah!
> Bri: And the shops lit up?
> Joe: Aaaah!

Bri: What d'you say? Saw Jesus? Where was he,
where was Jesus, you poor softy? (p. 17)

The audience knows that Joe can neither understand nor speak. The words that Bri and Sheila invent for her are often very funny, underlining the deficiencies of Joe's treatment by medical and welfare professionals. However, it is clear that the parents can't relate to each other or to Joe without creating this comic dialogue with the powerless and utterly dependent child. The whole play sets up tensions between ready interpretation of the human body as a speaking and thinking subject and the discrepancy between human subject and human object.

The connection between body and mind is an important ethical issue. Theatre is concerned, seriously and obsessively, with this area of inquiry. Richard III is frequently cited as an example of an immediately recognisable villain. His evil mind is shown on stage by his twisted and deformed body. Whether the character is evil because everybody has responded to his twisted body with repugnance, or whether the deformed body is an outward manifestation of his evil mind, is a decision to be taken by directors. The decision will depend on how a director theorises the relationship between mind and body. Sigmund Freud (1856–1939) wrote about the character in his paper 'Psychopathic Characters on the Stage' (1905). Psychoanalysis is concerned with how what is hidden and inaccessible comes to have an impact on the world, and also with how the world and the rules that dictate material behaviour come to have an impact on the psyche. In psychoanalysis, as in theatre, there is a form of analysis that connects bodily action with thought. As the architect of psychoanalysis, Freud was extremely interested in the act of reading and interpreting the actions of individuals, and also in the way that our emotions are physically manifested. His concept of the uncanny is a useful example because it offers a visceral or corporeal response to anomalous bodies.

The uncanny

Uncanniness is the feeling that something is disturbingly not quite right, that it is not understood fully, that it may or may not have subjectivity. Subjectivity is the condition of having autonomy and a perspective on the world. Humans have subjectivity, but inanimate objects do not. Our ability to live in society, and also part of the ability to watch theatre, is based on the fact that when we look at other people we imagine that their subjective experiences are analogous to our own. Where this basic identification is thrown into doubt, we get a creepy sensation of uncanniness. Evil walking or talking dolls, severed heads, unmotivated laughter and demonic possession in horror movies are all attempts to tap into the uncanny. The physical effect of the uncanny is a sense of uncertainty and fear as spectators wonder whether they understand what they see. Freud suggests that uncanniness is a physical response to a disturbance of expectations about the human body and human capacity. Disembodied limbs, the idea that something has life when it shouldn't, a face at a window – all these images produce an unpleasant sensation of discomfort. The notion that suddenly our habitual ways of reading a body don't work, or a body that changes our expectations about its capacity or appearance, produces in the spectator a distinctive thrill of horror.

Freud connects this experience to the discovery of sexual difference in infancy. In a 1925 essay, 'Some Psychical Consequences of the Anatomical Distinction between the Sexes', he writes about the male child's distress upon discovering the girl's lack of a penis. Before this discovery, the boy assumes that everyone has a body like his, including a penis. When he sees that he is mistaken, the little girl's lack of a penis causes him to feel 'a horror of the mutilated creature or triumphant contempt for her' (p. 336). A sense of uncanniness emerges from the exclusion of the little girl from the class of similar objects. For the little boy, women are no longer the same as he is. This moment, and the shock of understanding that he is not the same as all other people, causes the male child to associate himself with people who are like him (other boys and men). According to Freud, this moment invests the little boy in the system of patriarchy, in which men hold and share power over women. But the sensation of the uncanny recurs throughout life, serving as a reminder of this moment of traumatic recognition.

In *Joe Egg* and in Freud's notion of the uncanny, we see a process of questioning the human status of the stage figure. *Joe Egg* has us laughing at helplessness while asking questions about the status of the disabled child. Freud discusses the unpleasant yet thrilling sensation of throwing the human status of the individual into doubt. Both these responses show the spectator responding physically to the contemplation of bodies on stage.

Bodies and power

I'd like to develop the idea that theatre can cause us to question the human status of fictional characters, and to move towards an analysis of the way that bodies are used to explore the effects of power.

Case study: *Our Country's Good*

Our Country's Good was written by Timberlake Wertenbaker and first performed in 1988 at the Royal Court, London. It is based on Thomas Keneally's novel *The Playmaker*, written the year before, and it covers the establishment of a convict colony in Australia in 1787. At the centre of the action is the attempt by Lieutenant Ralph Clark to direct the convicts in a production of George Farquhar's Restoration comedy *The Recruiting Officer* (1706). *Our Country's Good* exploits the tension between the dehumanising effect of the regime of punishment in the 1780s and the possibilities that are opened up in the act of creating a performance. The inception of theatre as a representation of culture and learning in a deportation colony is controversial. The convict cast are not initially obvious actors, because their bodies are starved and diseased, and disciplined only by the brutal repressive regime and its summary justice. The bodies and attitudes of the convicts are assessed and appraised by the soldier–director. He believes that performing the play will act on the bodies of the convicts, changing them through the act of acting:

> I asked some of the convict women to read me some lines, these women who behave often no better than animals. And it seemed to me, as one or two – I'm not saying all of them, not at all – but one or two, saying those well-balanced lines of Mr Farquhar, they seemed to acquire a dignity, they seemed – they seemed to lose some of their corruption. (Act 1, scene 6)

Our Country's Good is concerned throughout with the points of contact between state, culture and bodies. The convicts and the Aboriginal people of Australia are figured as bodies. The convicts have been physically removed from their homes and social contexts as a way of punishing them for fairly minor crimes such as petty theft. The political act of thinking of the continent as empty and unclaimed, the transmission of disease from the English to the Aboriginal people, the starvation, the free sexual licence, the depictions of corporal punishment and the continual threat and presence of capital punishment make this into a text about the social value and visibilities of bodies. The play shows bodies subjected to two sorts of discipline: first, the repressive and violent rules of law and colonisation; second, the laws of interpersonal relationships and culture which emerge through the metaphor of the theatrical performance. The convicts engage in the play because there is little else to do.

Ralph Clark directs the play because he is hoping for pro-
motion. And yet the conventions and the dynamics of the
play create another form of social interaction by opening up
a series of linguistic and mimetic possibilities.

It would not be at all true to suggest that the theatrical performance offers a utopia or an escape. Starvation is
still a possibility; summary justice and punishment by flog-
ging and hanging remain as perpetual physical threats to
the convict–actors and their play. Within the narrative, the
process of resisting and overcoming the threats gives the
performance importance. Theatre makes apparently powerless criminal bodies into intending, acting human beings
without arguing through philosophy and politics. As with
reading or listening to music, one cannot engage in theatre
without paying a specific sort of attention. Unlike reading
or music, however, theatre is necessarily a public disciplinary regime: you act out the impact of your self-discipline
and knowledge. The desire to perform publicly or to be seen
to act is the drive towards self-discipline and social cohesion
for the convicts. The act of rehearsing and performing the
play is seen by the officers as an attempt to inculcate culture
and morality among the convicts.

If *Our Country's Good* shows the vulnerability of the
human body to the discipline of the state, it also offers the
model of transformation through the embodiment of the
drama. The process of voluntarily learning and enacting
Farquhar's play subjects the convicts to a sense of inner discipline that is repeatedly challenged by the brutal exercise
of power by the officers. The heightened dramatic language

is the counterpoint to the images of violence and criminality. The language confers a dignity on the animal-like bodies of the convict–actors. To speak the culturally recognised words and to participate in theatre can change the convicts into members of a society. Language is seen to have the power to make bodies into subjects instead of objects.

The work of the French poststructuralist philosopher Michel Foucault (1926–84) might contribute to this discussion.

Michel Foucault

Foucault talks about the body as a discourse. A discourse is a system of language use that carries with it the operation of power by seeming to represent a particular set of ideas. One element of the discourse of the body is the way the body comes to seem obvious and real, and the way that ideas about it come to be seen as instantly and obviously physically verifiable. Sex and gender, science, race and medicine all operate as discourses. The boundaries of the discourse determine the ways in which the world can be thought about and analysed. The discourse sets the rules for linguistic representation through concepts such as disciplinary boundaries and notions of truth or proof. When one analyses discourse, one analyses the way that power operates within a specific system.

Foucault suggests that the body is used as a way of placing human beings within a regulatory system. Foucault's *The History of Sexuality* (1979), for example, examines the assumption that increasing knowledge of bodies and sexuality leads to increased liberation and self-determination. Instead, he argues, knowledge of bodies and the process of describing and categorising sexual practices are subtle ways of subjecting them to power and social control. In investigating the foundations of self-determination and looking at how individuals emerge as subjects in a network of discourses, writers such as Foucault have questioned the basis of identity and the process of embodiment. In *Our Country's Good*, there is a distinction between the violent imposition of power on the convicts and the process of persuading them to embody the position of subject of power voluntarily. Acting as a character and acting as a member of society place the individual body within a regulatory discourse.

The body is an important area of philosophical investigation, and it is also an interesting way to think about humans and their lives as physical beings. It is useful to ask what we gain from using the body as an analytical strategy. Why analyse bodies rather than *people* or *humans*? The body is a way of thinking about the points of connection between the person and the world. It is a way of thinking about the flesh or matter or morphology or biology of a person, and about how that conflicts with, connects with or constitutes culture. The American philosopher Judith Butler points out that the notion of the body is an abstraction that carries with it other regulatory systems, such as gender. In her essay 'Performative Acts and Gender Constitution' she points out that however abstract the body may be, it carries along with it the expectation that real or material bodies are gendered: 'Considering that "the" body is invariably transformed into his body or her body, the body is only known through its gendered appearance' (p. 406). In turn, gender can be regarded as a regulatory abstraction.

Who may play whom?

In *Our Country's Good*, the act of casting is foregrounded in a metatheatrical way. The act of acting is seen as educational: the creation of a culture is important to the colony. The act of speaking the words changes the actor. There is a transformative quality here because the play offers a way of organising unruly, undisciplined bodies into a common goal or culture. The issue of who may play whom and what it means to be an acting body is of huge importance. The act of acting is transformative because of the processes that must be undertaken in order to embody a character. The play suggests that the act of acting is a political use of bodies.

That the destitute and starving convicts can play genteel and military characters and that their rehearsal process involves them 'playing' actors indicates that there is a vastly flexible and readable use of representation and imitation in theatre. In his book *The Semiotics of Theatre and Drama* (1980), Keir Elam discusses the idea that in theatre any stage vehicle can stand, in principle, for any other. He cites structuralist writer Jindrich Honzl's influential argument that there are 'no absolutely fixed representational relations' (p. 13). This is so with space: there's no need to show space pictorially or architecturally on stage. Instead, one can indicate space gesturally, verbally or acoustically. The real space of a stage does not *resemble* the fictional space of

a battlefield, but it stands for it, symbolically. In the case of actors and characters, it is convention, and not resemblance, which determines the answer to the question 'Who may play whom?' Honzl says: 'If what matters is that something real is able to assume [the character] function, the actor is not necessarily a man; it can be a puppet, or a machine, or even an object' (Elam, p. 13).

Within realist theatre traditions, certain conventions exist that determine which actor may play which character. There is also a series of conventions that determine the sorts of body we expect to see on stage, even in non-realist plays. Although it is important to Shakespeare's play that the character Othello is north African, the director needs to cast the play so that the character and his actions and the way he is treated by other characters are comprehensible to a twenty-first-century audience. The fictional cultural and racial differences between Othello and Iago must be marked in the process of casting. Would it be reasonable to say that an actor didn't 'look like' Othello or Iago? Such an assertion would seem like nonsense: the characters are fictional. There is no 'real' person for them to resemble. But because there is a long cultural tradition of casting the parts, it seems that the expectations, based on tradition, have become part of the conventions by which the performance is made legible.

The audience carry with them expectations about the conditions for representation. The process of renegotiating these conventions has been an important part of theatrical innovation in avant-garde and post-dramatic performance.

Audiences make use of a series of unwritten theatrical conventions that are introduced by the context, style and manifest intentions of a performance. There's no reason whatsoever that the character Hamlet should not be a wheelchair user – and, indeed, the disabled actor Nabil Shaban has played Hamlet, among many other roles. But such casting might seem aesthetically innovative, and it could well foreground the conventions that are used to understand and analyse the play. Something new would be presented to the audience, and this would change the conventions by which the play was watched.

One example that suggests the extent to which these conventions can be explored in performance comes from Philip Auslander's essay 'Humanoid Boogie: Reflections on Robotic Performance' (2006). Auslander develops a discussion about whether robots can be said to perform. He describes a piece of work from 2001 called *Abacus* (Venice Biennial International Exposition of Art), which consisted of 'over forty crouching figures draped in black, which face an open door and pray in numerous languages representing a multitude of faiths while making reverential movements appropriate to prayer' (p. 87).

Auslander's essay draws from this and other examples a series of the sorts of idea that form the interpretive framework of spectatorship. Spectators bring with them a set of expectations that may change if they realise the performers are not human and are programmed to move in the specific sequence of the art work. Auslander deconstructs the ideas of intention, artistry, originality, self-expression and liveness. He suggests that these analyses are all valuable approaches to the enjoyment of performance but that they could be found in different parts of the process – the creativity of the programmer or the originality of the artist, for example. The fact that these experiences do not cohere and that they cannot be concentrated on a single spectatorial experience does not necessarily mean that the audience sees a moving sculpture rather than a piece of live performance.

Auslander suggests that the pleasures of watching the performance are multiple and complex, moving beyond mimesis. Mimesis is the process of representing something or someone in an imitative way through action. Although it sounds as if the word refers to the act of copying or 'mimicking', in theatre mimesis is a form of corporeal analysis. It uses the body to represent on stage and in fiction what happens in reality according to a form of analysis and simplification. The performance is then presented on stage as a text – as a body of material that is there to be analysed.

Acting bodies

Mimesis in theatre is not at all like photographic documentation. Acting exhibits aesthetic and analytical processes. The act of analysing acting might benefit from a little analysis itself. Acting is a form of mimetic performance, and it is a terribly complex phenomenon. Theatre offers composite stage pictures, multiple authors, diverse vantage points and a whole series of variable connections to the world outside. When we discuss the work of an actor on stage it is easy to get confused about what exactly it is that we are watching.

Generally we know whether the acting is good or bad, whether the performance had any impact on us, whether it made us think hard, or laugh, or cry. It is not so easy to explain what it was that the actor was doing or to talk precisely about how he or she contributed to the performance. There is a general tendency to fall back on qualitative statements such as 'She was terrible – she overacted horribly' or 'He was brilliant – I was completely gripped'.

In the 1930s, a group of structuralist analysts and theatre-makers, sometimes known as the Prague School structuralists, offered a series of ways to analyse the act of performing. Structuralism is an approach to complex texts that enables us to understand them in relation to the social and communicational structures that underlie society. Writing from this perspective in an essay titled 'Dramatic Text as a Component of Theater' (1941), Jiri Veltrusky said:

> In theater, the sign created by the actor tends, because of its overwhelming reality, to monopolise the attention of the audience at the expense of the immaterial meanings conveyed by the linguistic sign; it tends to divert attention from the text to the voice performance, from speeches to physical actions and even to the physical appearance of the stage figure, and so on. (p. 115)

Bodies are distractions. In performance we are likely to become engrossed in the means of performing the play and not the abstract referent that lies beyond the play. This sounds rather similar to Bernhardt's rationale for banning unusual bodies from the stage, but the argument is taken a little further. It is not simply that *unusual* bodies distract the spectator: *all* bodies threaten to distract the spectator from the art of performing. Theatre is founded upon a tension between being engrossed in the physical world of the room where the performance takes place and being engrossed in the fictional world of the play. The physical conditions are so important that if we start to doubt that a specific act is intentional, the coherence of the artistic structure is threatened. Freeing the expressivity of the body is, for this reason, an important part of actor training. If we see that theatre perpetually threatens the spectator with the distraction of the real, it would seem that theatre relies on a process of simultaneously acknowledging the body on stage and learning not to focus exclusively on the specific body. The 'overwhelming reality' of the body appears to be an important part of the spectator's experience.

One might argue that an exception to this example can be found in documentary theatre and other forms where people use their own words to represent their own experience. Forms such as verbatim theatre claim to be repetitions of real words that were spoken by real people because recorded testimony is spoken word for word by the performers. Indeed, in The Tricycle Theatre's tribunal play *The Colour of Justice* (London, 1999) it is the claim of truthfulness that validates the performance. The black London teenager Stephen Lawrence was murdered in 1993 by a gang of racist white youths, and no one was ever convicted of the murder because of flaws in the police investigation. The play presents edited transcripts of the public inquiry into that investigation. The audience could, without too much trouble, have acquired the full transcripts of the tribunal. The fact that the audience chose instead to sit in a room full of other people and to watch actors speaking the words of the people involved is significant.

Even in the play's bland, realistic depiction of the tribunal, the act of acting and the context of theatre promised the audience something it wanted. The audience did not want *truth*, if truth is thought to be a full understanding of all the available facts. Or, if they did want truth, they were in some way deluded into thinking that a heavily edited piece of theatre could teach them something about the bungled police investigation that they could not have understood better by reading the transcripts. The explanation lies not in the notion of truthful representation but in the other corporeal experiences that are available to audience members in a live performance. In other words, the bodies, and the embodiment of the testimony, are *the point* of this piece of theatre, irrespective of its relationship to some separate truth.

Both tremendous virtuosity and terrible acting can cause me to look exclusively at the actor's performance as something distinct from the play and can be objects of contemplation in their own right. A failure of convention within the production can also mean that the actor's body is not *allowed* to stand for the character. Actresses on the Restoration stage were said to lack skill, simply to *appear* in the way that the cat in Martin McDonagh's *The Lieutenant of*

Inishmore or the ponies in *Cinderella* appear – not as a guarantee of realism but as a clever trick that exists apart from the fiction. In Beckett's *Not I*, the expectations of character and representation are confounded. The audience do not see the body, but they are aware of the actor's body as the means of performing. At the same time the uncanniness of the disembodied mouth disturbs the perception of a living, speaking human being.

The gap between actor and role or performer and performance offers a particular form of spectatorial pleasure, and to understand this it is important to recognise that actors are not *copying* behaviour but are performing in a way that involves a formal and aesthetic relationship to the play, the conventions of theatre and the world outside the theatre. This is an integral part of the pleasure of the art work. We have looked at the possible shifting of the relationship between character and performance, but the notion of representation and the conditions for representation are still in dispute.

Even if a work of art represents an external reality, it must necessarily do so selectively and analytically. In Samuel Beckett's play *Endgame* (Royal Court, London, 1957, Hamm is blind and uses a wheelchair. The relationship between Hamm and Clov, a master and servant trapped together in a post-apocalypse world, is seen as complete mutual dependence. The fictional world in which this relationship exists has no apparent equivalent in lived reality. It makes no sense to refer to *Endgame* as a searingly insightful depiction of real lives, but it does make sense to attempt to understand the fictional relationships, the mutual dependence and the despair of the characters, and the relationships between the play and the world.

Hamm and Clov open up a series of possible metaphorical readings. These are based on ideas of impairment, entrapment and dependence that the audience bring with them. If we remember that bodies are cultural texts, we have the opportunity in theatre to read these texts within a controlled and intentional context, to read them as an act of communication, so our thoughts are not unmotivated flashes of lone brilliance but a considered and social response to a shared cultural text.

Although mimesis is without doubt an important notion, it would be a mistake to concentrate exclusively on this way of analysing the relationship between theatre, the body and the world. Just as the conventions of theatre change in relation to audience experience and aesthetic innovation, so do the connections between the public contemplation of bodies in theatre and the arts and the conceptualization of human bodies in science and philosophy.

Bodies and minds

I have already alluded to the often difficult relationship between art and knowledge. Some fascinating research has been carried out into the science of art and the relationship between art and consciousness. Unfortunately, I do not have space in this book to do justice to these ideas, but I would like to return to the perpetually vexing question of the relationship between mind and body. The methodology of theatre studies places spectators at the centre of their own perceptual universe, engaged in working out their own responses to the entire performance event with reference only to the event itself and their own knowledge and perception. Is spectatorship a form of experience, or is it a process of investigation?

René Descartes

The seventeenth-century philosopher René Descartes (1596–1650) struggled with the implications of the development of mechanical sciences. Following Galileo (1564–1642), the new mechanical sciences found that all objects in the world are subject to physical laws of force and motion. As physical objects in the world, human bodies must therefore be subject to the same laws that govern the movement of inanimate objects, such as clockwork and planetary motions. This was difficult for Descartes to reconcile with his Christian belief system, according to which humans are more than physical objects – they must be, because they have immortal souls that are not subject to such mechanical laws. Descartes wondered where the will comes from that enables humans to act upon the world by free choice as self-determining beings made in God's image.

Descartes' attempt to resolve the philosophical problem was brilliant and innovative, and it had a huge impact. He tried to construct a logical sequence of ideas about the world, and about what could be known. Although Descartes is frequently caricatured as a man who tried to prove that he existed, and that he was awake, it is important to see his work as trying to escape the perpetual discursive circularity of pre-modern philosophy. Living at a time when science and religion clashed furiously, Descartes set himself the task of working from first principles to resolve their apparently irreconcilable differences. To do this he had to establish these principles for himself. In the introduction to his *Meditations on the First Philosophy* (1641), Descartes claimed that he wanted to 'set myself seriously and freely to the general destruction of all my former opinions' (p. 95). He taught himself to doubt everything that had previously seemed obvious, and this included the information yielded by the senses:

> Everything I have learned up to now as being absolutely true and assured I have learned from the senses. But I have sometimes found that these senses played me false, and it is prudent never to trust entirely those who have once deceived us. (p. 96)

He tried to doubt everything, but found that he was still left within the meditation with the act of doubting. To doubt is to think, and if thinking is taking place then a thinker must exist. I think therefore I exist.

Descartes insists on the reader becoming a thinker in his or her own right, working through concepts, connecting concepts logically and developing theses from them. He also moves bodies in and out of different imagined states. I admire the boldness of Descartes' imaginative suspension of himself, devoid of sensory perception, for the sake of philosophical inquiry. The performer David Blaine, who in 2003 suspended himself above the River Thames in a transparent box without food for 44 days, offers a bodily version of the same experiment. Blaine's performance was created for an audience, and it assumed a form of corporeal empathy, a notion that Descartes did not develop at all.

Descartes' method is to make all certainties into contingencies by shifting the entire context surrounding the human subject. He places himself in an imaginary context in order to examine possible reactions, and so he works through the principles that allow him to think and to exist. This seems to me to be extravagantly theatrical, but, as Descartes admits, it doesn't get us very far, because none of us seriously doubts our existence or the existence of the world. At this point in the meditations Descartes has developed a way of offering a first principle of experience and of separating cognition from the senses. Having found evidence for the existence of the self, Descartes attempts to find evidence for the existence of the physical world.

Sensing as a mode of thinking

> Because the ideas I received through the senses were much more vivid and distinct than those I could form for myself by meditation, or which I found imprinted in my memory, it seemed that they could not proceed from my mind, but that they had been caused in me by some other objects. The external objects must have the properties I

perceive because those properties are not already in my memory. (p. 152)

Descartes talks about optical illusions and phantom limbs, which demonstrate for him that there is a possibility for error in the senses. Dreams also pose a problem because they present images to the mind which have no existence in the world, which shows that the mind can generate images without the help of the senses. This idea connects with a method that we will later understand as phenomenology.

> I know with certainty that I exist. ... I am a thinking thing, or a substance whose whole essence consists in thinking. And although perhaps I have a body to which I am very closely united [and which doesn't think], it is certain that I, that is to say my mind, is entirely and truly distinct from my body, and may exist without it. (p. 156)

There seems to be a contradiction between this absolute distinction of mind and body and the problem, which Descartes recognises, of how the body communicates with the mind:

> Nature teaches me by feelings of pain, hunger, thirst, etc., that I am not only lodged in my body like a pilot in his ship, but, besides, that I am joined to it very closely and indeed so compounded and intermingled with my body, that I form a single whole with it. (p. 159)

At points, Descartes sounds as though he is articulating a tension between monism (a doctrine that holds that all being is part of a single entity) and dualism. While playwrights and performers would rarely say that they are informed by Cartesian dualism, it is an important pattern of thought, and dualism informs much idiom and expression of our experiences. Cultural artefacts such as poems, plays and sculpture show not just how the world appeared in pictorial or representational terms but also how it was thought about. For the audience of *A Day in the Death of Joe Egg* there is a tension between the appearance of the human child and the knowledge that although her body looks entirely normal she cannot, and never will, participate in human culture through language or voluntary movement. The play examines the emotional appeal of the human form, our wish to empathise with others who are humans like us and the difficulty that arises when we think that the other is in some way different from us.

The ghost in the machine

In 1949, the philosopher Gilbert Ryle (1900–76) produced a critique of the dualism of mind and body. He coined the phrase 'the ghost in the machine' to describe Descartes' conception of the relationship between mind, or the immaterial ghost, and body, or the mechanical machine. Ryle rejects Descartes and mind/body dualism wholly and completely, and in a very persuasive way.

His objections are these: mind and matter are not entities that are different in essence. Ryle sees the ghost in the machine as a fallacy based on a confusion of categories. To say that the mind and the body are different entities, that the body is entirely physical and subject to mechanical laws and that the mind is entirely and truly distinct from the body, opens up some serious problems. First, there is the question of how a non-physical entity can have an impact on the body. How does a thought or an intention become a bodily action? How can the immaterial act upon the material? Descartes has us thinking about thoughts or intentions as being separate from actions, but there is no satisfactory explanation of how a thought can become an action.

Second, there is a question about how knowable our own minds are, and how ideas can affect the physical world. Descartes characterises a knowable mind, a mind that is transcendent and permanent and that is lodged temporarily in the body. The self is accessible through moments of self-awareness and is knowable in moments of introspection. But Ryle suggests that this account allows no space for the development of the ability to reflect on the self. Does the self grow in response to its environment? Does one think in words? Are words and language a part of the physical external world, or are they part of the transcendent immaterial world of the self? The connection between the exterior physical world and the inner world remains unexplained.

Third, in Descartes theory, there is the problem of other people. How do we know what other people are thinking, and how do we say that we know or understand them?

Ryle suggests that Cartesian dualism is mistaken, not in its details or in some aspects, but wholly and entirely mistaken from its very basis. The error is a category mistake. In separating thought and action, mind and matter, we are talking about the same idea in different terms. To talk about the eye's perception of light as something entirely separate from the mind's reflection on that light is nonsense — perception can be talked about as an activity of the mind and an activity of the body. To try to hold the two discursively separate is an impossible task. For Ryle, Cartesian dualism is like an attempt to say 'She had a left glove and a right glove and a pair of gloves'. It makes sense to talk about a left glove and a right glove or to talk about a pair of gloves. But to try to schematise the connections between the two gloves and the pair of gloves is to misunderstand the categories that each belongs to. For Ryle, a philosopher who was grounded in phenomenology, it was simply wrong to think about the body hammering a nail into a wall while the mind went through a parallel but unrelated series of thoughts about the action. For Ryle, there is one action, the hammering of the nail.

If I accept that Gilbert Ryle's argument convinces me, then why have I wasted so much time in discussing Descartes? This is a short book, so is there any need to discuss discredited ideas?

The status of those ideas is crucial because they are actively used and contested in culture and discourse. When we contemplate or discuss or otherwise engage in arts and culture we play perpetually with ideas. It is one thing to know that we are made up of particles of matter, for example, but quite another to *live as though* we are made up of particles of matter. Indeed, I have no idea how one might do this. It is not possible to play through or to use *all* our knowledge about the world at all times. We can live and work so as to know something intellectually and yet act in quite another way. I might go through a whole day with a sense of foreboding because I had a disturbing dream. I talk to the dog. Yet I know that dreams are not prophetic and that the dog doesn't have so much as the potential to acquire language. In other words, I can, without straying into particularly eccentric behaviour, know things (or believe things) without that knowledge (or those beliefs) having any kind of impact on my actions. What is more, I suspect that most people experience this conflict between their conceptualisation of the world and their action in the world.

This is not because we are hypocritical, or even because we are stupid. It is because the status of knowledge, experience and belief is a constant and absorbing preoccupation for all of us, and also because it is somehow difficult to live the implications of ideas. To use Ryle's example out of his context, it might be said that in watching any performance, one simultaneously watches the performance and the character and attends to the other possible cultural meanings of the performance.

The relationship between scientific discourses and other cultural discourses is confused and confusing. Thinking and doing, acting and reflecting seem to be entirely different from each other. The development of technology has had a profound effect on the ways in which we think about the body and the mind. Sigmund Freud was delighted by the invention of a wax notepad which seemed, to him, to offer an image for the form of the relationship between the conscious, the preconscious and the unconscious. I might talk un-self-consciously about using a piece of music to 'reboot' my brain. This doesn't mean that I think my brain operates like my computer, any more than Freud thought that the unconscious was made of wax. The image provides a way of understanding and representing an idea, and this image has an effect on my thoughts, actions and decisions.

The act of talking about a bodily process such as thinking, sleeping, remembering and feeling involves the adoption of images and conventions that schematise the process, making the idea at the centre of the process comprehensible. When I talk about 'rebooting' my brain, I adopt the computer as a way of representing the mind/body distinction. My understanding of mind and body is metaphorical, but the raw material of metaphor is culture and technology.

Descartes' earnest, engrossing journey through his meditations is hugely important because it shifts philosophy from theological doctrine to a process of reasoning about the experience of embodiment.

Case study: Orlan

Orlan is a performance artist who engaged in a project of self-portraiture. Her experiences of cosmetic surgery are an experiment in the composition of self-hood and an assertion of the independence and importance of the thinking and speaking 'I'. Orlan developed a computer-generated image that was a hybrid of representations of mythological Greek goddesses. These images were mixed with an image of her own face to create a 'self-portrait' which she then attempted to realise in her own face through a series of cosmetic surgical procedures, each of which was performed live for an audience, with costumes, choreography and text.

Orlan speaks of herself giving her body to art, and she attacks the notion that the body should not be altered. In his essay 'The Surgical Self' (1997), Auslander explores the problem that Orlan poses. On the one hand, she seems to tap into the dualistic idea that body is radically different from self. This perspective is exhibited in arguments in favour of elective plastic surgery, in which the self-determining individual is free to choose to surgically alter her body so that it conforms to her idea of the 'real' or 'inner' self. However, Orlan explicitly chooses images from 'the outside', from cultural representations of mythological goddesses.

The feminist writer Susan Bordo suggests that cultural representations are incorporated into the image of the self. In *Unbearable Weight* (1993), she claims that the body is a medium of culture – a text to be read and also written through action, clothing, dress – but also a direct locus of social control (p. 165). Orlan offers this social control as a performance, proffering her body as a medium of the art work. The performances and the resulting 'art' are difficult to look at, and this offers an opportunity for the spectator to analyse the relationship between body, subject and culture. The mind/body problem, instituted by Descartes, exists as a spectatorial and an authorial question in Orlan's work.

Ideas about what we can say of our experiences and those of others are extremely important, as is the way that individual experiences can be extrapolated into general principles. But Descartes' brilliant journey is flawed because of his inability really to shift the grounds of his own presumptions. Descartes' sincere attempts to resolve the apparent conflicts between the new mechanical sciences and the premodern belief in God show a pattern of questioning, reasoning and doubting. For me, Descartes opens up an area that is theoretically liminal, a place where we explore and ponder the connections between the private thought and the public action. The patterns that Descartes and Ryle inscribe in thought are hugely important, and are worth investigating and reading for the indelible mark they have left on theatre as a form of cultural inquiry.

Phenomenology

The contingent and dramatic interdependence between body and role is a key image. It helps us to develop an understanding of acting and performance and to find a way to use mind/body problems in theatre. Many of Beckett's late plays explore this relationship. The physical experience of watching the performer struggle with the restrictions of role and staging is absolutely crucial. The idea of the body as social text is metaphorically engaged here, but there is also a form of *experience* that occurs only in the moment of performance, only in the interaction of dramatic text, actor and audience.

I want to find a tool to analyse experience, and the phenomenological work of Maurice Merleau-Ponty (1908–61) seems particularly useful for this purpose. In *Volatile Bodies*, Grosz explains Merleau-Ponty's importance in this context:

> Merleau-Ponty renders experience of immediate and direct relevance to philosophy and the production of knowledge. ... He locates experience midway between mind and body. Not only does he link experience to the privileged locus of consciousness; he also demonstrates that experience is always necessarily embodied, corporeally constituted, located in and as the subject's incarnation. Experience can only be understood between mind and body – or across them – in their lived conjunction. (p. 95)

Merleau-Ponty's work is merely one branch of phenomenology, but it is a popular branch by virtue of its attempts to understand perception through experience. The connections with the methods of Descartes' *Meditations* are striking because there is a process of applying reasoned analysis to experience. Indeed, Descartes must rarely have been far from Merleau-Ponty's mind when he was writing *Phenomenology of Perception* (1945): a huge segment of this work is a response to the ideas explored by Descartes in the *Meditations*.

Merleau-Ponty's phenomenology aimed to deconstruct dualism by finding the ways in which body and mind, sensation and matter were connected. Just as Descartes discussed the 'mingling' of the two faculties, Merleau-Ponty attempted to look at the ways in which the subject and the object of perception were connected in a moment of experience. Much of his inquiry was related to how anomalous brains worked. People who had brain damage, people who were amputees and people who were blind were all useful in the process of understanding the structures of perception. Here specific, anomalous *bodies* and their reported experiences became the focus of the investigation.

Merleau-Ponty saw huge problems with the act of *analysing* experience. To analyse something is to break it down into its components to see how they fit together, and it is very difficult to do this without recourse to preconceptions. It is also true to say that actions do not usually need analysis. If you want to pick something up or touch something, you simply perform the action. There is no need to break the action down into processes. The intention and the action are one moment. In *Phenomenology of Perception*, Merleau-Ponty offers a useful image for the relationship between the body and the world: 'Our own body is in the world as the heart is in the organism: it keeps the visible spectacle constantly alive, it breathes life into it and sustains it inwardly, and with it forms a system' (p. 235). According to Merleau-Ponty the body acts as a perspective. You can know in theory that a cube has six equal faces, but you cannot know this in any way other than in abstract or theoretical terms because you can't see all the sides at once. The perception of the cube is interpreted, and the cube is understood in abstract terms.

If the body is one's vantage point and point of contact with the world, then it is obvious that, just as the cube is both an abstraction and a sensation, there can be no vantage point from which I can see the whole body. The processes by which I acquire a sense that I am a subject and that I have a body are analogous to the process of seeing the cube. The fact that amputees may experience pain or movement in a limb that has been removed demonstrates that body image is not simply a reflection of an objective body. The perception of the body must be based in part on an inner perception of the body. Body image is dynamic and based on a relationship to the world.

Phenomenology gives a precise and important role to theatre. Theatre is a place where bodies can be experienced and reflected on in ways that present the experiences as complete, as stimulating and as direct. This area of theory runs counter to, and is incompatible with, the structural analyses that I introduced earlier. It also makes drama as fiction broadly irrelevant, because the direct experience of bodies in the world is the pleasurable point of theatre.

Phenomenology is an important reference point for many scholars and practitioners of disability theatre. There is a huge difference between talking about 'the body' and its experience of a theatre performance and talking about 'bodies' and their experiences. *The body* supposes that there is an ideal or assumed body and that all people gain access to the pleasures of performance in broadly the same way. When we think about *bodies* as entities that see, feel and move in radically different ways, as in disability theatre, the idealized *body* becomes disparate *bodies*. We can't suppose that the play offers one overriding 'meaning' or a single coherent performance.

In the play *peeling* by Kaite O'Reilly (The Door, Birmingham, 2002), the lines spoken by the actors are projected onto a screen as surtitles. In part, this is a practical way of making dialogue accessible to deaf audience members. But it is also an important aesthetic device, setting up a relationship between the written word and the actor's voice in a series of experiences that are different according to whether you are an audience member who sees or hears the dialogue. The audio and visual worlds of the play are changed by the expectation that the audience will access the play through different sorts of bodies. The play is an example of access aesthetics: the play and its meanings are marked and mediated by the expectation that the audience will have different sensory experiences. Graeae Theatre Company's production of Sarah Kane's *Blasted* (UK Tour, 2006) involved the actors vocalizing brief descriptions of their actions as they performed. Graeae's *Static* by Dan Rebellato (The Tron, Glasgow, 2008) was a play about music written and performed to open the experience to deaf audiences through the use of British Sign Language and Sign-Song.

The predominant world of experience for phenomenology is the visual field. In the example of the cube, it is perfectly possible to understand the shape fully through directly experiencing all six equal faces simultaneously – by touching it. You could hold it, or you could put it in your mouth. Phenomenology supposes that we can reflect on perception to find the underlying truth of all systems of perception, but it suggests that bodies have the same sorts of relationships with the world – a view that disability studies scholars would dispute.

Feminists have also questioned this perspective, suggesting that in a world in which men and women are represented and treated very differently, their experiences of embodiment may also be different from the abstract notion of 'the body'. In 'Performative Acts and Gender Constitution' (1988), Judith Butler suggests that within phenomenology:

> The body is understood to be an active process of embodying certain cultural and historical possibilities, a complicated process of appropriation which any phenomenological theory of constitution needs to describe. (p. 403)

Butler suggests that the body is more than the individual's perceptual centre of the world. We embody and perform cultural ideals such as gender, living as actions a whole history of bodily action, interaction and interpretation.

Bodies and culture

Theatre frequently creates tension from incongruity. The gap between the body that one has (or is) and the actions that are expected from it appears to be part of the structure of theatre. For example, much of Henrik Ibsen's dramatic work is structured around the process of gradually and inexorably revealing character traits and exposing the unconventional or shocking past of the upstanding member of society. Another example of the dynamic of concealment/revelation is in the comic tension upon which the entire genre of farce relies. The secret truth is revealed to the audience so that they can enjoy the desperate and ludicrous measures taken to keep it hidden from the other characters. The notion of the 'real' character, or the development of a notion of truth, can be used in discussion and analysis, but always as a contingent part of the fiction. It is tempting to wonder whether – or hope that – the body is the basis of all this playful contingency.

The real bodies of real actors are the materials with which we play. There are fictions, but there is also a reality. However, some writers suggest that perhaps even physical bodies are part of this contingent fiction. To take a made-up example: a theatre-maker claims that it is self-evident that a male actor cannot play a female role because, let's say, he cannot understand the experience of childbirth. The theatre-maker is asserting that there are specific conceptual and experiential boundaries to the apparently flexible conventions through which meaning is communicated and understood in performance. And this claim has implications beyond the theatre. The theatre-maker is also making a claim about the ability that humans have to understand and empathise with other people, as well as choosing the basis upon which difference is to be understood in her theatre.

Performativity

Judith Butler's book *Gender Trouble* (1990) examines the idea of bodies as ways of regulating subjects. It looks particularly at the idea that gender is a regulatory fiction – a fiction that enforces certain behaviour – and that this is inscribed in language. For Butler, gender is inscribed upon bodies through the process of teaching and learning a *stylised repetition of acts* that give the appearance of substance or nature. When you find that learned actions seem to express something that is central or integral to the person who acts, then you have a system that regulates behaviour through the effect of depth or substance in the appearance of the individual's self.

Butler suggests that when we take any action we *cite* gender. By this she means that gender is present in the social world as a pre-existing series of actions, gestures, words, feelings and appearances. When we are born we are placed into this system by the relatively arbitrary means of looking at our genitals. One is placed into a pre-existing social role in the exclamation 'It's a girl', moving in that moment from 'it' to 'she'. From that moment we are a part of a system of compulsory heterosexuality, with its rigid and restrictive determination of the emotional, sexual and physical life of the child. From the moment of emplacement (also called *interpellation*), the child must strive to be that gender and must also understand itself through ideas attached to that gender.

The laws of subjectivity and the laws for participation in society are not written down anywhere, but one's

gendered behaviour is harshly regulated through preju-
dice, carelessness and outright violence. Claire Dowie's
theatre monologue *Why Is John Lennon Wearing a Skirt?*
(Traverse Theatre, Edinburgh, 1990) explores the ways
in which an individual encounters gender as a regulatory
regime. Dowie recounts the process of a child growing
up to realise that femininity is an inadequate framework
for her interests and her sense of self. 'Female' seems to
describe an individual, but Dowie's play shows what happens when the individual subject feels that the category is
not a good description. She is reluctant to play the role that
society demands she play, and refuses to become a girl.
The exploration of the discrepancy between the interpel-
lated role and her sense of self reveals that gender is not
a description but something more like a set of rigorously
enforced instructions.

Butler claims that gender is *performative*. Some people
assume this means that Butler thinks we are all acting.
She doesn't think this, she has never thought this, and
it would make no sense in the terms of her argument.
'Performativity' is a philosophical term with a precise
usage, and it should never be confused with 'performance'. A performative utterance is a form of speech that
is *canonical* (it is recognised as part of our language and
culture) and that does what it says it does *simply by saying
it*. It is language that acts. Examples of performative utter-
ances are 'I promise ... ', 'I apologise ... ', 'I love you'. They
are formal words that are in some way conventional. The
performative utterance needs the correct context to work.

For example, although a declaration of war is a performative act, it doesn't work if I say 'I declare war' because I do not have the means to conduct a war.

The notion of performative gender is important because it posits the idea that bodies and their actions appear within a regulative frame. Bodies are rarely encountered as objects in themselves and always form a part of politicised discursive structures. For Butler, the way to challenge the compulsory gender system is to try to find ways to make it seem *incredible*. All ways of straining the boundaries that produce gender as binary and compulsory might help to disturb the impression of naturalness, depth and inevitability. Makers of drag, queer and gay performance and people who have transsexual identities have found in Butler's writing a strong sense that somehow their work might contribute to the process of showing the cracks and inconsistencies in binary gender. Performance can explore alternative cultural forms of expression for people who do not fit easily into compulsory heterosexuality but who nevertheless wish for liveable (and that means culturally legible) lives.

Science is a difficult issue for all the writers that I have surveyed in this book. Science claims a degree of independence, a certain amount of impartiality. It is one way of studying the body as a living organism, of interpreting bodies and of deciding what bodies and bodily differences mean. But there are many ways of studying bodies. The notion of 'pure' science is problematic. Many late twentieth-century philosophers explored the connection between science and culture, and Butler's approach to this distinction is particularly important. In *Bodies That Matter* (1993), she asks whether there is really anything that we can call the body itself, without recourse to language or discourse. Of course, it seems that we can imagine such a thing. We can imagine bodies as inert matter, as masses of cells or bones or flesh. However, for Butler there is no thinking about, or talking about, or conceptualising of bodies or aspects of bodies outside discourse.

The notion of a raw, non-cultural body is an absolute impossibility, so long as it is a notion. Butler sees bodies as always already figured in language. Bodies are not inert lumps of matter that are there to be studied or interpreted but analytical tools to help us articulate and to investigate elements of human behaviour and action. One doesn't need to accept this radical perspective to recognise that theatre uses bodies in a way that mirrors or replicates the performative. Regardless of whether the actions that take place in theatre buildings have any kind of consequences outside those buildings, theatre still models and explores complex relationships between humans. Theatre shows words that seem to work, imagined actions and their immediately imagined consequences.

At the start of this book, I mentioned that the body was a place where science, critical theory and performance clashed. My final section is an attempt to explore the meeting places of all these ideas in an area that has been regarded as terrible hoax, miraculous medicine and cutting-edge science.

Psychoanalysis

Psychoanalysis was born at the moment when transgressive, unruly female hysterics were persuaded to turn their symptoms into words. Hysteria is an important and a highly theatrical starting-point. 'Hysteria' is a term no longer used in medicine. Although it has a long history, it seems to have changed in its manifestation throughout that history. It had a whole series of different symptoms, and these were played out in different ways by different sufferers. The manifestations of the disease all concern inexplicable, uncontrollable bodily or behavioural symptoms that seem to have no organic cause or logic. Fainting, fits, depression, paralysis, headaches and other unexplained pains, hypersensitivity and asthma might all have seemed to be hysterical symptoms in women before the end of the nineteenth century. The disease was constituted by its diagnosis, and the diagnosis was one that supposed that female bodies were susceptible to the disease. It was sometimes said that all women were in some way hysterical.

Psychoanalysis originated in Vienna at the start of the twentieth century when Freud stopped trying to use hypnotic methods on his hysterical patients and began to encourage them to free associate. His treatment of Dora, his first psychoanalytic patient, is recorded as a case study that reads as a literary work. The process of analysing and interpreting the images within Dora's words and fitting them into patterns that you can examine in detail in Freud's work *The Interpretation of Dreams* (1900) forms the basis of psychoanalysis, a discipline which aims to convert 'hysterical misery into common unhappiness' ('Studies on Hysteria', p. 305).

In 1885, as a young researcher with an interest in hysteria, Freud spent a few months at the Salpêtrière hospital in Paris, studying under the pioneering doctor and flamboyant showman Jean Martin Charcot. Charcot claimed that hysteria was caused by a neurological disorder. Freud had on his study wall an image of one of Charcot's 'Leçons du Mardi', a sort of medical performance in which Charcot hypnotised one of his young female patients as part of a lecture–demonstration of the symptoms of hysteria. Issues of power are important. The picture depicts two types of performance – the active, knowledgeable exhibitor and the passive exhibition, the body under medical investigation. Charcot is talking directly to his male audience, and the female patient is swooning helplessly, presented as object of knowledge.

The medical display is set up as a mind/body exhibition, with the knowledge offered by the doctor and the uncontrolled body supplied by the patient. Structurally, it holds much in common with the freak show, but without its mass appeal. In the book *In Dora's Case* (1985), Charles Bernheimer talks about the Leçons as 'immensely successful spectacles' at which professional men crowded into the lecture theatre to take scoptophilic pleasure (a sexual pleasure gained in the act of looking) from the 'coached performances' of the specimen hysterics (p. 7).

During this time Freud also watched Sarah Bernhardt in *Theodora*. Of the famously histrionic actor's performance he wrote to his fiancée on 8 November 1885, 'I have never seen an actress who surprised me so little; I at once believed everything about her.' He described her performance in this way: 'Every inch of this little figure was alive and bewitching. As for her caressing and pleading and embracing, the postures she assumes, the way she wraps herself round a man, the way she acts with every limb, every joint … .' He concludes his report rather sadly: 'I had to pay for this pleasure with an attack of migraine.'

Freud was a spectator of theatre and of medical performances, and he was impressed by both. In *Freud, Dora, and Vienna 1900* (1991), Hannah S. Decker points out that when it came to choosing a pseudonym for his own hysterical patient Ida Bauer, he chose the name 'Dora', unconsciously echoing his immersion in the performance of Bernhardt, the transgressive and independent actor whose performance sounded like an attack of hysteria.

Freud's work *Fragment of an Analysis of a Case of Hysteria* (1901) is a famous case study that has been written and rewritten. Dora's narrative is contested by Freud and is reinterpreted to fit into Freud's pattern of thinking about female sexuality. One of the remarkable aspects of this piece of writing is that Freud manages to make clear the points where he thinks he is talking about Dora but is obviously talking about himself. In the process of analysis, Freud and Dora between them develop an understanding of how the events of the past, traumas that have been repressed by Dora, have been inscribed on her body in the form of hysterical symptoms.

This discussion of mimetic strategies has had a profound effect on the reading of bodies and their relationship to the unconscious and to the world. Freud started by treating neuroses through hypnosis, but he quickly abandoned the technique in favour of the 'talking cure', the process of finding connections between symptoms and infantile experiences. The psychoanalytic solution is to put the subject in control of the returned material in such a way that it is resolved into a narrative and stops being such a disruption.

Theatre and theatre criticism are not therapeutic; they don't aim to 'cure' the individual of neuroses. The connection between theatre and psychoanalysis is complex, and it rests upon techniques of reading and interpreting. *The Interpretation of Dreams* finds connections between images, and Freud uses techniques that one might use to analyse a poem or a painting:

1. Condensation. Two or more ideas become condensed into the same image through a relationship of association. For example a door comes to stand for one's family members. This is similar to the literary analytical technique of the metonym.

2. Displacement. One idea or image is substituted for another in a symbolic system of meaning – a purse comes to symbolise a vagina, for example. This is similar to the concept of the metaphor.

Feminist readings of hysteria have examined the ways in which hysteria was an expression of the impossibility of being female in a patriarchal society. The female hysteric offers a performance of the conflict between the female psyche and the body. In 'Some General Remarks on Hysterical Attacks' (1909), Freud himself offered to bring hysteria and performance together in this way:

> When one carries out the psycho-analysis of a hysterical woman patient whose complaint is manifested in attacks, one soon becomes convinced that these attacks are nothing else but phantasies translated into the motor sphere, projected onto motility and portrayed in pantomime. (p. 229).

French feminist Hélène Cixous claims an affinity with the hysterics and sees their action as a form of corporeal protest. For her, in hysterical symptoms and in the narrative that Freud wrote in 1901, the *body* of Dora speaks directly in a way that culture prohibited.

Case study: *The Rise and Fall of Little Voice*

In this analysis of *The Rise and Fall of Little Voice* (Cottlesloe, London, 1992) by Jim Cartwright, I want to show how one might use psychoanalytic theory to examine the relationship between the mother, Mari, the daughter, Little Voice, and the dead husband/father. In the analysis I explore the different realisations of femininity presented with each character and the relationship between these realisations.

The character Little Voice has an uncanny ability to impersonate singers from Lulu to Marilyn Monroe. Her father died, exhausted by his loud and disorderly wife, leaving only his collection of records. Little Voice (abbreviated

to LV throughout the play) is probably agoraphobic and possibly anorexic. She hardly speaks, and the ringing telephone terrifies her. Her only activity is playing the records her father left, listening to them so intently that she absorbs them and can sing them, correct to every detail of pitch, intonation and phrasing, and is recognisably the singer whose rendition she sings.

Although Mari finds LV's singing repulsive, LV is inadvertently 'discovered' by Mari's boyfriend, Ray Say, and is coerced into performing in the local working men's clubs. She agrees to perform once only, as a tribute to her dead father's love of music. Ray and Mari make her perform several times, and LV withdraws her co-operation, rendering herself unable to perform by stopping eating, drinking, moving or talking.

Just before a scheduled performance, Ray Say breaks off his relationship with Mari and attempts to persuade LV out of her room. He slaps her and 'voices begin to rush out of her uncontrollably, some sung, some spoken' (p. 248). The voices are those from the records – Judy Garland, Edith Piaf, Marilyn Monroe, Shirley Bassey, Billie Holiday. Ray realises that LV is not going to appear at the club, that his use of her is at an end, and he rushes out of the house. As he does so, the iron falls off the ironing board and starts a fire. The house burns down. LV is rescued by her friend, Billy, the shy telephone engineer, on a hydraulic crane or cherry picker.

The female characters in the play are subject to the bodily constraints of their social roles. LV is melancholic.

Melancholia is an incorporation of a representation of a lost love into the unconscious as a way of preserving that person inside the self. Unable to let go of the lost father, she retains him as a presence in her unconscious by incorporating those elements of her father that live most strongly in her memory. She is unable to sing with her own voice until the end of the play, when the records are broken and the house has burnt down and Billy has taken her away from the house. Agoraphobia and anorexia are both hysterical symptoms, brought about by the melancholia she experiences.

Mari is unwilling to play her role – of age or sex or relationship. She would not be the quiet and orderly wife that her husband needed. LV charges her with 'Your nights of neglect. Things forgotten everywhere. No soap in the dish, no roll in the toilet, no clean blouse for school' (p. 259). Mari skives off work, buys things she can't afford, doesn't clean and doesn't cook.

Whereas LV is almost completely silent, Mari enters into paroxysms of outpouring language – punning, laughing, swearing. She feels emotions and presentiments in her body, 'that twat bone feeling', and she celebrates by dancing to the Jackson Five. She is verbose and energetic and chaotic. Even at her most despondent she still makes jokes. When she returns to her burnt-down house, she finds LV looking for her records. Mari has given up.

> I've been jumping the coals for years, now I've finally fallen in. Nobody wants the burnt bits,

have you noticed. They love a blazing bint but
when the flames have gone who wants the char?
(p. 257)

The 'blazing bint' is too fleshy, too human. Real female
bodies are problematic. Mari drinks and talks, and ages.
She is unlike the other 'blazing bints' whose voices are
recorded and fetishised on the vinyl records. LV and her
father are both passionately attached to these objects and
to the disembodied voices that are recorded on them.
When her father died, LV embodied the voices, and the
sounds of the records are articulated through LV. She can
embody her father's perfect diva because she is otherwise
voiceless, whereas Mari talks continuously; she never goes
out, unlike Mari, who doesn't even eat at home; unlike
Mari, she is as close as possible to absent and bodiless, eating almost nothing and so meeting the anorexic desire to
kill off the appetite.

Susan Bordo's essay 'Anorexia Nervosa: Psychopathology
as the Crystallisation of Culture' in *Unbearable Weight*
(1993) explains that the notion of the body as a weak, fleshy
envelope that inhibits freedom and causes sin is central to
dualistic Western philosophy. The idea of controlling this
body, of overcoming its flaws through discipline of one sort
or another, is a cultural obsession. Some young women
experience horror and revulsion at the prospect of acquir-
ing secondary sexual characteristics such as a higher pro-
portion of body fat and the development of breasts and cause
this process to halt by stopping eating. The development of

adult female bodies is seen as evidence of corruption, weakness and defeat. Although 15 per cent of anorexics die from the condition, Bordo says:

> Some authors interpret these symptoms as a species of unconscious feminist protest, involving anger at the limitations of the traditional female role, rejection of values associated with it, and fierce rebellion against allowing their futures to develop in the same direction as their mothers' lives. (p. 156)

The relationship between the quiet husband with his 'parlour lips' and the quiet daughter playing board games and listening to records seems to signify, to Mari, a sense of stasis, a stability that is resigned to inadequacy, a sense of being satisfied with very little. LV blames Mari for the death of her father: 'You drove him as fast as you could to an early grave,' she says (p. 258). Mari actively threatens LV's search for the order and stillness that her father gave her. The loss of the father, then, is a sort of theft, for which LV blames her mother. When Mari accuses LV of taking everything away from her by destroying the relationship with Ray Say and burning down the house, LV responds immediately with the charge that Mari stopped her from speaking, killed her father and never allowed any kind of care or order in her childhood. Mari finds herself reduced to ashes, burnt out and defeated. The only remnants of the energy and drive she once had are the ashes of her possessions that cover her house.

In *Mourning Sex* (1997), feminist performance theorist Peggy Phelan reminds us that hysteria can be melancholic. Anna O., a patient of Freud's collaborator Josef Breuer (1842–1925), is stuck in time after the death of her father and, like LV, she resorts to paralysis: 'The first symptoms Anna O. and Elizabeth von R. [another patient] developed were sympathetically reproduced somatizations of their fathers' pain. These symptoms were the result of a kind of stilling kinaesthetic empathy: each woman became partially paralysed' (p. 56). Agoraphobia and mental distress are brought about through the loss of the father. LV is singing with her father's voices. Ray attempts to dramatise the melancholia by presenting the ventriloquism as real and constituting a body for the voice. But the voice is just LV's hysterical mourning of her father – melancholia speaking through her. When Mari breaks all the records and when Billy rescues her, LV sings, for the first time, in her own voice.

Phelan explains that Anna O.'s hysteria is an attempt to play out the trauma of loss and that it is this performance that resists interpretation as mere symptom of illness.

> For many feminists, this excess is femininity itself – that part of Anna O's body that remains outside the discursive frame of the always already 'masculine' discursive case history. This excess marks the place of the trauma at the heart of Freud's theory of sexual difference. As Freud developed psychoanalysis, he constructed a theory of anxiety about sexual difference in which

penis envy and the castration complex are said to
be psychic responses to the fear of somatic [bod-
ily] absence. (p. 64)

LV's own voice emerges when the physical relic of her
father's memory is destroyed. Mari drops the records out
of the window and they smash. Mari's disordered realm is
destroyed in the fire, releasing LV from the house she has
been unable to leave. LV finds her voice in defence of her
father in her confrontation with Mari, and in singing for
Billy. The troublesome Mari, who was at the centre of this
entire confusion, is left on a pile of wrecked records as Billy
and LV ascend in the cherry picker.

Conclusion: saying and doing

The Bernhardt story with which I opened offers a useful perspective from which to survey the argument of this book. For
Bernhardt, the body exists as a tool to be overcome, a skilled
instrument of a genius performer. For Stanislavski, the body
is a limiting factor, and for Beckett it is a metaphor for the
restrictive experiences of the human psyche and its failure to
escape from its own painful restrictions. Descartes has the
body as a perspective, and Orlan has it as a politically useful
material for sculpting. In each case there is a contestation, a
struggle for meaning and a struggle for control of the way
that the body is placed into its context and the way that it is
read. Although I am interested in the question, prompted by
Foucault and Butler, 'Do bodies really exist?', I must con-
cede, for the moment, that this is the wrong question.

In theatre bodies have to both exist and not exist. They need to be used and manipulated and foregrounded to make any kind of theatre at all. They must have so many different possibilities to have the semiotic flexibility to enable us to develop an understanding of the different sorts of causal and poetic connections that theatre can possibly pose. It might be easier, or more productive, to ask whether bodies are *theatrical*.

It is striking to see the extent to which thinkers have used the example of theatre to *think*. The performance of medical knowledge in Charcot's Salpêtrière was not an oddity: surgical procedures still take place in operating *theatres*, even if the audience is no longer so extensive. Freud was following medical tradition as well as theatrical tradition when he started to see the tension between what is performed and what is spoken. The development of his 'talking cure' has theatrical origins. The processes of speculating about human life and knowledge, of offering imaginative contexts for the body, and of developing and positing the basis for the perception or understanding of difference are all central to theatre and the world in which it is used.

Although the notion of 'the body' or 'bodies' is a profound simplification of a complex set of cultural and philosophical beliefs, theatre exists as a place where we might animate and experiment with these simplified schema. Bodies bring these perspectives/positions/entities together, and theatre uses this meeting point in very varied ways. The questions that are asked about theatre and the body, or theatre and bodies, then, become a central and absorbing guide to theatre-goers who intend to analyse the connections between the theatrical matter and the real lived cultural matter of their lives.

How can it matter that a particular actor is playing a particular character? How can it matter that you have seen seventeen different productions of *Hamlet*? It does matter – insofar as this is precisely the nature and the structure of theatre. It is integral to theatre that one is able to hold multiple characterisations and contexts in one's mind simultaneously. The ability to read dynamics of concealment and revelation, identity and disguise into human behaviour is a basic human social skill. The pleasures of exercising this skill and the analysis of bodies and their actions are among the important pleasures of theatre spectatorship.

further reading

Theatre and the body is a vast and complex area, and I have certainly glossed over some important ideas in the process of trying to communicate others. The books listed here are the ingredients of my book, and you will be able to trace the ideas that I cite in the text back to their source by referring to this list. However, I hope very much that you will not let my argument and my approach act as anything other than a starting-point for your own investigation. I shall use this section to highlight some important works that take you beyond the scope of this book.

If you are interested in engaging further in notions of gender, body and performance, you should certainly look next at Elizabeth Grosz's magisterial work *Volatile Bodies*, which deals with notions of embodiment, politics and the meaning of bodies, chiefly using phenomenological and psychoanalytic perspectives. Its counterpart in the discipline of theatre and performance studies is Geraldine Harris' book

Staging Femininities. Harris takes as her central topic the implications that theory and practice have for each other when they meet as bodies in performance.

I warned you in my introduction that the area of body art and extreme forms of body-centred performance would not be closely investigated in this short book, but if you want to develop your reading about this area of performance you might start with Rebecca Schneider's book *The Explicit Body in Performance*, which explores contexts and practices of feminist performance art. Works by the art historian Amelia Jones are frequently cited in this field, and I would suggest that you read her *Body Art/Performing the Subject*, which looks at live and performance art from the 1950s and 1960s onwards. An approachable and broad-ranging collection of essays about recent important live and performance art is *Live*, edited by Adrian Heathfield.

I hope that you have been persuaded to read some of Freud's writing, which cannot really be appreciated second-hand. Start with 'The Uncanny' and with 'Psychopathic Characters on the Stage'. Work that is concerned with the mind–body problem is abundant, but the work of Daniel Meyer-Dinkgrafe in *Theatre and Consciousness* offers a perspective from consciousness studies, an area that I have sadly been unable to write about in this book.

I have argued that the concepts of *bodies* and *the body* mean and do different things when we consider them. Petra Kuppers' *Disability and Contemporary Performance* is a fascinating investigation of the difference that disabled bodies make to the way we watch and understand performance. Finally, the multi-disciplinary collection of essays *Writing on the Body*, edited by Katie Conboy, Nada Medina and Sarah Stanbury, is a valuable resource for students across a number of disciplines. It contains a useful range of primary sources and is accompanied by some helpful introductions to the works.

Arendt, Hannah. *The Human Condition*. [1958]. 2nd ed. Chicago: U of Chicago P, 1998.

Auslander, Philip. 'Humanoid Boogie: Reflections on Robotic Performance'. *Staging Philosophy*. Ed. David Krasner and David Z. Saltz. Ann Arbor: U of Michigan P, 2006. 87–103.

———. 'The Surgical Self: Body Alteration and Identity'. *From Acting to Performance: Essays in Modernism and Postmodernism*. London: Routledge, 1997. 126–40.

Austin, J. L. *How to Do Things with Words*. [1962]. Oxford: Oxford UP, 1975.

Beckett, Samuel. *The Complete Dramatic Works*. London: Faber & Faber, 1986.

Bernhardt, Sarah. *The Art of the Theatre*. London: Geoffrey Bles, [1924?].

Bernheimer, Charles, and Claire Kahane, eds. *In Dora's Case: Freud – Hysteria – Feminism*. New York: Columbia UP, 1985.

Bersani, Leo. *The Freudian Body: Psychoanalysis and Art*. New York: Columbia UP, 1986.

Bordo, Susan. *Unbearable Weight: Feminism, Western Culture and the Body*. Berkeley: U of California P, 1993.

Butler, Judith. *Gender Trouble: Feminism and the Subversion of Identity*. London: Routledge, 1990.

———. *Bodies That Matter: On the Discursive Limits of Sex*. London: Routledge, 1993.

———. 'Performative Acts and Gender Constitution: An Essay in Phenomenology and Feminist Theory'. [1988]. *Writing on the Body: Female Embodiment and Feminist Theory*. Ed. Katie Conboy, Nada Medina, and Sarah Stanbury. New York: Columbia UP, 1997. 401–17.

Calbi, Maurizio. *Approximate Bodies: Gender and Power in Early Modern Drama and Anatomy*. London: Routledge, 2005.

Cartwright, Jim. 'The Rise and Fall of Little Voice'. *Plays 1*. London: Methuen, 1996.

Conboy, Katie, Nada Medina, and Sarah Stanbury, eds. *Writing on the Body: Female Embodiment and Feminist Theory*. New York: Columbia UP, 1997.

Decker, Hannah S. *Freud, Dora, and Vienna 1900*. New York: Free Press, 1991.

Descartes, René. *Discourse on the Methods and the Meditations*. [1637]. London: Penguin, 1968.

Diamond, Elin. *Unmaking Mimesis*. London: Routledge, 1997.

Dowie, Claire. *Why Is John Lennon Wearing a Skirt? And Other Stand-Up Theatre Plays*. London, Methuen, 2000.

Edelman, Gerald M., and Giulio Tononi. *Consciousness: How Matter Becomes Imagination*. London: Penguin, 2000.

Elam, Keir. *The Semiotics of Theatre and Drama*. [1980]. London: Routledge, 1988.

Foucault, Michel. *The History of Sexuality*. Vol. 1. [1978]. Trans. Robert Hurley. London: Penguin, 1990.

Freud, Sigmund. 'The Interpretation of Dreams'. [1900]. *The Standard Edition of the Complete Psychological Works of Sigmund Freud*. Vols. IV–V. Trans. and Ed. James Strachey. London: Vintage, 2001. 1–627.

———. 'Fragment of an Analysis of a Case of Hysteria'. [1901]. *The Standard Edition of the Complete Psychological Works of Sigmund Freud*. Vol. VII. Trans. and Ed. James Strachey. London: Vintage, 2001. 3–122.

———. 'Psychopathic Characters on the Stage'. [1905]. *The Standard Edition of the Complete Psychological Works of Sigmund Freud*. Vol. VII. Trans. and Ed. James Strachey. London: Vintage, 2001. 303–10.

———. 'Some General Remarks on Hysterical Attacks'. [1909]. *The Standard Edition of the Complete Psychological Works of Sigmund Freud*. Vol. IX. Trans. and Ed. James Strachey. London: Vintage, 2001. 227–34.

———. 'The Uncanny'. [1919]. *The Standard Edition of the Complete Psychological Works of Sigmund Freud*. Vol. XVII. Trans. and Ed. James Strachey. London: Vintage, 2001. 219–56.

Freud, Sigmund. 'The Ego and the Id'. [1923]. *The Standard Edition of the Complete Psychological Works of Sigmund Freud*. Vol. XIX. Trans. and Ed. James Strachey. London: Vintage, 2001. 3–66.

———. 'Some Psychical Consequences of the Anatomical Distinction between the Sexes'. [1925]. *The Standard Edition of the Complete Psychological Works of Sigmund Freud*. Vol. XIX. Trans. and Ed. James Strachey. London: Vintage, 2001. 241–58.

Freud, Sigmund, and Joseph Breuer. 'Studies on Hysteria'. [1895]. *The Standard Edition of the Complete Psychological Works of Sigmund Freud*. Vol. I. Trans. and Ed. James Strachey. London: Vintage, 2001. 1–335.

Grosz, Elizabeth. *Jacques Lacan: A Feminist Introduction*. London: Routledge, 1990.

———. *Volatile Bodies: Towards a Corporeal Feminism*. Bloomington: Indiana UP, 1994.

Harris, Geraldine. *Staging Femininities*. Manchester: Manchester UP, 1999.

Heathfield, Adrian, ed. *Live: Art and Performance*. London: Routledge, 2004.

Jones, Amelia. *Body Art/Performing the Subject*. Minnesota: U of Minnesota P, 1998.

———. *Self/Image: Technology, Representation and the Contemporary Subject*. London: Routledge, 2006.

Kuppers, Petra. *Disability and Contemporary Performance: Bodies on Edge*. London: Routledge, 2004.

Marlowe, Christopher. *Dr Faustus*. Ed. Roma Gill. 2nd ed. London: A & C Black, 1989.

Matejka, Ladislav, and Irwin R. Titunic, eds. *Semiotics and Art: Prague School Contributions*. Cambridge, MA: MIT Press, 1976.

McMullan, Anna. *Theatre on Trial: Samuel Beckett's Later Drama*. London: Routledge, 1993.

McTeague, James H. *Before Stanislavski: American Professional Acting Schools and Acting Theory 1875–1925*. London: Scarecrow, 1993.

Merleau-Ponty, Maurice. *Phenomenology of Perception*. [1945]. Abingdon, UK: Routledge, 2002.

Meyer-Dinkgrafe, Daniel. *Theatre and Consciousness*. Bristol, UK: Intellect, 2005.

Miglietti, Francesca Alfano. *Extreme Bodies: The Use and Abuse of the Body in Art*. Milan: Skira, 2003.

Mitchell, David T., and Sharon Snyder, eds. *The Body and Physical Difference: Discourses of Disability in the Humanities*. Ann Arbor: U of Michigan P, 1997.

Mitchell, Juliet. *Psychoanalysis and Feminism*. New York: Vintage, 1975.

Moi, Toril. *Sexual/Textual Politics*. London: Routledge, 1985.

Nichols, Peter. *A Day in the Death of Joe Egg*. London: Faber & Faber, 1967.

Norton-Taylor, Richard. *The Colour of Justice*. London: Oberon, 1999.

O'Dell, Kathy. *Contract with the Skin: Masochism, Performance Art and the 1970s*. Minnesota: U of Minnesota P, 1998.

O'Reilly, Kaite. *peeling*. London: Methuen, 2002.

Padel, Ruth. *In and Out of the Mind: Greek Images of the Tragic Self*. Princeton, NJ: Princeton UP, 1992.

Phelan, Peggy. *Mourning Sex: Performing Public Memories*. London: Routledge, 1997.

Ramachandran, V. S., and Sandra Blakeslee. *Phantoms in the Brain*. [1998]. London: Fourth Estate, 1999.

Ryle, Gilbert. *The Concept of Mind*. [1949]. London: Penguin, 1990.

Schneider, Rebecca. *The Explicit Body in Performance*. London: Routledge, 1997.

Sedgwick, Eve Kosofsky. *Epistemology of the Closet*. [1990]. London: Penguin, 1994.

Shepherd, Simon. *Theatre, Body and Pleasure*. London: Routledge, 2006.

Shiac, Morag. *Hélène Cixous: A Politics of Writing*. London: Routledge, 1991.

Showalter, Elaine. *Hystories: Hysterical Epidemics and Modern Culture*. Basingstoke, UK: Picador, 1997.

Stanislavski, Konstantin. *An Actor's Work*. Ed. and Trans. Jean Benedetti. London: Routledge, 2008.

————. *My Life in Art*. Ed. and Trans. Jean Benedetti. London: Routledge, 2008.

Tait, Peta. *Circus Bodies: Cultural Identity in Aerial Performance*. London: Routledge, 2005.

Tajiri, Yoshiki. *Samuel Beckett and the Prosthetic Body: The Organs and Senses in Modernism*. Basingstoke, UK: Palgrave, 2007.

Veltrusky, Jiri. 'Dramatic Text as a Component of Theater'. [1941]. *Semiotics of Art: Prague School Contributions*. Ed. Ladislav Matejka and Irwin R. Titunic. Cambridge, MA: MIT Press, 1976. 94–117.

Vergine, Lea. *Body Art and Performance: The Body as Language*. Milan: Skira, 2000.

Wald, Christina. *Hysteria, Trauma and Melancholia: Performative Maladies in Contemporary Anglophone Drama*. Basingstoke, UK: Palgrave Macmillan, 2007.

Warner, Richard, and Tadeusz Szubka, eds. *The Mind-Body Problem: A Guide to the Current Debate*. Oxford: Blackwell, 1994.

Warr, Tracy, and Amelia Jones, eds. *The Artist's Body: Themes and Movements*. London: Phaidon, 2000.

Wendell, Susan. *The Rejected Body: Feminist Philosophical Reflections on Disability*. London: Routledge, 1996.

Wertenbaker, Timberlake. *Our Country's Good*. London: Methuen, 1988.

Whitelaw, Billie. *Billie Whitelaw ... Who He?* London: Hodder & Stoughton, 1995.

Whitford, Margaret. *Luce Irigaray*. London: Routledge, 1991.

Wittgenstein, Ludwig. *Philosophical Investigations*. [1953]. Trans. G. E. M. Anscombe. 3rd ed. Oxford: Blackwell, 1967.

Woods, Leigh. '2-A-Day Redemptions and Truncated Camilles: The Vaudeville Repertoire of Sarah Bernhardt'. *New Theatre Quarterly* 10.37 (1994): 11–23.

Worthen, William B. 'Beckett's Actor'. *Modern Drama* 26 (1983): 415–24.

index

acknowledgements

I am grateful to Dan Rebellato and to Kate Haines for their thoughtful editorial comments.

This book is for Lucy, with thanks for her help at all stages of writing.

INTRODUCTION

This Spanish grammar has been written to meet the demands of language teaching in schools and colleges and is particularly suited for study at GCSE level. The essential rules of the Spanish language have been explained in terms that are as accessible as possible to all users. Where technical terms have been used then full explanations of these terms have also been supplied. There is also a full glossary of grammatical terminology on pages 9-16. While literary aspects of the Spanish language have not been ignored, the emphasis has been placed squarely on modern spoken Spanish. This grammar, with its wealth of lively and typical illustrations of usage taken from the present-day language, is the ideal study tool for all levels — from the beginner who is starting to come to grips with the Spanish language through to the advanced user who requires a comprehensive and readily accessible work of reference.

In this new edition we have revised the text throughout, improved the layout of the page and checked that the examples and translations are fully up-to-date.

PREFACE

This grammar is divided into two main sections:

Part I, THE FUNCTIONS OF SPANISH, explains how to use Spanish to refer to things and actions, to express conditions, emotions and the like. This list of functions does not claim to be exhaustive, but it does contain those most likely to cause difficulties for the English-speaking learner.

Part II, THE FORMS OF SPANISH, explains the formation of all the principal elements of the language. Here you can check the formation of tenses etc, or any unknown form you may come across in your reading.

A considerable effort has been made to explain not only *how* Spanish operates in different contexts, but, more importantly, to explain *why* it operates the way it does. This is an essential aspect of the book, because experience shows that what the learner of a foreign language *really* requires is not so much rules as understanding.

Experience also shows that the pattern of errors among learners of Spanish is by and large predictable. Most make essentially the same mistakes in the same proportions. To help you to avoid these pitfalls, any aspect of Spanish which is traditionally a cause of frequent errors has been highlighted in the Grammar by the symbol ⚠. These are areas where special attention is required.

Hugh O'Donnell

CONTENTS

CONTENTS

CONTENTS

CONTENTS

GLOSSARY OF GRAMMATICAL TERMS

ABSTRACT NOUN

An abstract noun is one which refers not to a concrete physical object or a person or animal but to a quality or a concept. Examples of abstract nouns are *happiness, life, length*.

ACTIVE

The active form of a verb is the basic form as in *I remember her*. It contrasts with the passive form of the verb as in *she will be remembered*.

ADJECTIVAL NOUN

An adjectival noun is an adjective used as a noun. For example, the adjective *young* is used as a noun in *the young at heart*.

ADJECTIVE

An adjective is a describing word telling us what something or someone is like (eg *a small house, the Royal Family, an interesting pastime*).

ADVERB

Adverbs are normally used with a verb to add extra information by indicating **how** the action is done (adverbs of manner), or **when, where** and **to what extent** the action is done (adverbs of time, place and degree). Adverbs may also be used with an adjective or another adverb (eg *a very attractive girl, surprisingly well*).

AGREEMENT

In Spanish, words such as adjectives, articles and pronouns are said to agree in number and gender with the noun or pronoun they refer to. This means that their form changes according to the **number** of the noun (singular or plural) and its **gender** (masculine or feminine).

APPOSITION

A word or a phrase is said to be in apposition to another when it is placed directly after it without any joining word (eg *Mr Jones, our bank manager, rang today*).

GLOSSARY

ARTICLE

See DEFINITE ARTICLE and INDEFINITE ARTICLE.

AUGMENTATIVE

An augmentative is an ending added to a noun to indicate largeness or awkwardness, eg *un hombrón, una mujerona*.

AUXILIARY

Auxiliary verbs are used to form compound tenses of other verbs, eg **have** in *I **have** seen* or **will** in *she **will** go*. The main auxiliary verbs in Spanish are **haber, estar** and **ser**.

CARDINAL

Cardinal numbers are numbers such as *one, two, ten, fourteen*, as opposed to **ordinal** numbers (eg *first, second*).

CLAUSE

A clause is a group of words which contains at least a **subject** and a **verb**: *he said* is a clause. A clause often contains more than this basic information, eg *he said this to her yesterday*. Sentences can be made up of several clauses, eg *he said / he'd call me / if he were free*. See SENTENCE.

COLLECTIVE

A collective noun is one which refers to a group of people or things but which is singular in form. Examples of collective nouns are *flock* and *fleet*.

COLLOQUIAL

Colloquial language is the sort of language that can be used in everyday informal conversation but is avoided in formal writing such as legal contracts etc.

COMPARATIVE

The comparative forms of adjectives and adverbs are used to compare two or more things, persons or actions. In English, *more ... than, -er than, less ... than* and *as ... as* are used for comparison.

COMPOUND

Compound tenses are verb tenses consisting of more than one element. In Spanish, the compound tenses of a verb are formed by using the

auxiliary verb with the **present** or **past participle** : *estoy hablando, han llegado.*

COMPOUND NOUNS

Compound nouns are nouns made up of two or more separate words. English examples are *goalkeeper* or *dinner party*. Spanish compound nouns are normally linked by *de*, eg *un muro **de** piedra.*

CONDITIONAL

The conditional **mood** is used to describe what someone would do, or to say what would happen if a condition were fulfilled (eg *I **would come** if I was well; the chair **would have broken** if he had sat on it*). It is also used to express "future in the past", eg *he said he **would come***.

CONJUGATION

The conjugation of a verb is the set of different forms taken in the particular **tenses** and **moods** of that verb.

CONJUNCTION

Conjunctions are linking words (eg *and, but, or*). They may be coordinating or subordinating. Coordinating conjunctions are words like *y, o, pero* ; subordinating conjunctions are words like *que, si, aunque.*

DEFINITE ARTICLE

The definite article is *the* in English and *el, la, los, las* in Spanish.

DEMONSTRATIVE

Demonstrative adjectives (eg *this, that, these*) and pronouns (eg *this one, that one*) are used to point out a particular person or thing.

DIMINUTIVE

A diminutive is an ending added to a noun (or occasionally to an adjective) to indicate smallness or a favourable attitude on the part of the speaker, eg *mes**ita**, hij**ito**.*

DIRECT OBJECT

A direct object is a noun or a pronoun which in English follows a verb without any linking preposition, eg *I met **a friend***. Note that in English the preposition before an **indirect object** is often omitted, eg *I sent him a present – him* is equivalent to *to him – a present* is the direct object.

GLOSSARY

ENDING

The ending of a verb is determined by the **person** (1st/2nd/3rd) and **number** (singular/plural) of its subject.

EXCLAMATION

Exclamations are words or phrases used to express surprise, annoyance etc (eg *what!*, *wow!*, *how lucky!*, *what a nice day!*). Exclamations in Spanish begin with an upside-down exclamation mark, eg *¡caramba!*

FEMININE

See GENDER.

GENDER

The gender of a noun indicates whether the noun is **masculine** or **feminine**. In Spanish, the gender of a noun is not always determined by the sex of what it refers to, eg *la víctima* (*the victim*) is a feminine noun, even when it refers to a man.

IDIOMATIC

Idiomatic expressions (or idioms) are expressions which cannot normally be translated word for word. For example, *it's raining cats and dogs* is translated by *está lloviendo a cántaros*.

IMPERATIVE

The imperative **mood** is used for giving orders (eg *stop!*, *don't go!*) or for making suggestions (eg *let's go*).

INDEFINITE

Indefinite pronouns are words that do not refer to a definite person or thing (eg *each*, *someone*).

INDEFINITE ARTICLE

The indefinite article is *a* in English and *un*, *una* in Spanish.

INDICATIVE

The indicative **mood** is normally used in making statements or asking questions, as in *I like*, *he came*, *we are trying*. It contrasts with the **subjunctive**, **conditional** and **imperative**.

INDIRECT OBJECT

An indirect object is a pronoun or noun which follows a verb sometimes with a linking preposition (usually *to*), eg *I spoke to **my friend/him**, she gave **him** a kiss.*

INFINITIVE

The infinitive is the form of the verb as found in dictionaries. Thus *to eat, to finish, to take* are infinitives. In Spanish, all infinitives end in **-r**: *tomar, beber, vivir.*

INTERROGATIVE

Interrogative words are used to ask a question. They may be used in a direct question (***when** will you arrive?*) or an indirect question (*I don't know **when** he'll arrive*). See QUESTION.

MASCULINE

See GENDER.

MOOD

Mood is the name given to each of the four main areas within which a verb is conjugated. See INDICATIVE, SUBJUNCTIVE, CONDITIONAL, IMPERATIVE.

NEUTER

There are no neuter nouns in Spanish. Only the definite article *lo*, the pronoun *ello* and the demonstrative pronouns *esto, eso* and *aquello* have a neuter form. The article *lo* is used with adjectives, eg *lo bueno* (that which is good, the good thing), and the demonstratives are used to refer to an entire situation, eg *no acepto **eso*** (I don't accept that).

NOUN

A noun is a word which refers to living creatures, things, places or abstract ideas, eg *postman, cat, shop, passport, life.*

NUMBER

The number of a noun indicates whether the noun is **singular** or **plural**. A singular noun refers to one single thing or person (eg *boy, train*) and a plural noun to several (eg *boys, trains*).

GLOSSARY

OBJECT

See DIRECT OBJECT, INDIRECT OBJECT.

ORDINAL

Ordinal numbers are numbers such as *first, second, third, fourth* etc, as opposed to **cardinal** numbers (eg *one, three*).

PASSIVE

A verb is used in the passive when the subject of the verb does not perform the action but is subjected to it. In English, the passive is formed by using a part of the verb *to be* and the past participle of the verb, eg *he **was rewarded***.

PAST PARTICIPLE

The past participle of a verb is the form which is used after *to have* in English to form the perfect tense, eg *I have **eaten**, I have **said**, you have **tried***.

PERSON

In any tense, there are three persons in the singular (1st: *I ...*, 2nd: *you ...*, 3rd: *he/she/it ...*), and three in the plural (1st: *we ...*, 2nd: *you ...*, 3rd: *they ...*). See also ENDING.

PERSONAL PRONOUNS

Personal pronouns are used to stand for a noun. In English they are words like *I, you, he/she/it, we, they* or *me, you, him/her/it, us, them*.

PLURAL

See NUMBER.

POSSESSIVE

Possessives are used to indicate possession or ownership. They are words like *my/mine, your/yours, our/ours*.

PREPOSITION

Prepositions are words which indicate relationships in space and time, such as *with, in, to, at*. They are normally followed by a noun or a pronoun.

PRESENT PARTICIPLE

The present participle is the verb form which ends in **-ing** in English (**-ndo** in Spanish).

PROGRESSIVE

The progressive tenses are formed in English by the verb *to be* and the **present participle**, eg *I **am speaking**, he **was writing***. In Spanish it is formed by *estar* and the **present participle**, eg *estoy hablando, estaba escribiendo*.

PRONOUN

A pronoun is a word which stands for a noun. The main categories of pronouns are:

- **Personal pronouns** (eg *you, him, us*)
- **Possessive pronouns** (eg *mine, yours, his*)
- **Reflexive pronouns** (eg *myself, himself*)
- **Interrogative pronouns** (eg *who?, what?, which?*)
- **Relative pronouns** (eg *who, which, that*)
- **Demonstrative pronouns** (eg *this, that, these*)
- **Indefinite pronouns** (eg *something, none*)

QUESTION

There are two question forms: **direct** questions stand on their own and require a question mark at the end (eg *when will he come?*); **indirect** questions are introduced by a clause and require no question mark (eg *I wonder **when he will come***). Direct questions begin in Spanish with an upside-down question mark, eg *¿qué haces?*

REFLEXIVE

Reflexive verbs 'reflect' the action back onto the subject (eg *I dressed myself*). They are always found with a reflexive pronoun and are more common in Spanish than in English. Verbs are often used reflexively in Spanish where English would use the **passive**.

SENTENCE

A sentence is a group of words made up of one or more clauses (see CLAUSE). The end of a sentence is indicated by a punctuation mark (usually a full stop, a question mark or an exclamation mark).

GLOSSARY

SINGULAR

See NUMBER.

STEM

See VERB STEM.

SUBJECT

The subject of a verb is the **noun** or **pronoun** which performs the action. In the sentences *the train left early* and *she bought a record*, *the train* and *she* are the subjects.

SUBJUNCTIVE

The subjunctive is a verb form which is rarely used in English (eg *if I **were** you*, *God **save** the Queen*). It is very much more common in Spanish.

SUPERLATIVE

The superlative is the form of an **adjective** or an **adverb** which, in English, is marked by *the most ...*, *the -est* or *the least ...*

TENSE

Verbs are used in tenses, which indicate when an action takes place, eg in the present, the past, the future.

VERB

A verb is a 'doing' word, which usually describes an action (eg *to sing*, *to work*, *to watch*). Some verbs describe a state (eg *to be*, *to have*, *to hope*).

VERB STEM

The stem of a verb is its 'basic unit' to which the various **endings** are added. To find the stem of a Spanish verb remove **-ar, -er** or **-ir** from the infinitive. The stem of *hablar* is **habl**, of *beber*, **beb**, of *vivir*, **viv**.

VOICE

The two voices of a verb are its **active** and **passive** forms.

Part I
FUNCTIONS

1. REFERRING TO THINGS: THE NOUN

The word 'thing' is used here not just to refer to objects – books, houses, cars etc, also known as *inanimate* nouns – but also to people and animals – *animate* nouns – and to what are known as *abstract* nouns. Abstract nouns refer not to things which you can touch or see, but only to ideas which you can think about – justice, peace, democracy and so on.

A. USES OF THE DEFINITE AND INDEFINITE ARTICLES

For the formation of the definite and indefinite articles, see pages 155-7.

There is a considerable degree of agreement between Spanish and English as to when a noun is used with a definite or an indefinite article. However, some important differences also occur.

The traditional terms 'definite article' ('the' in English) and 'indefinite article' ('a', 'an' in English) are to some extent misleading, since it is not necessarily the case that the definite article refers to a specific object (or idea) and the indefinite article does not. For example, in the sentences:

la casa es vieja
the house is old

and:

hemos comprado una casa en el campo
we have bought a house in the country

both nouns refer to a specific house.

Moreover, there are in fact *three* different cases to consider:

    cases where the noun is used with a definite article
    cases where the noun is used with an indefinite article
    cases where the noun is used with no article at all

As you will see later, *truly* indefinite nouns are in fact used without any article in Spanish.

a) Nouns which are used to represent *all* of the thing or things they are referring to – *all* butter, *all* wine, *all* Spaniards and the like – are preceded by the definite article in Spanish:

> **me gusta la cerveza, pero no me gusta el vino**
> I like beer (all beer, beer in general), but I don't like wine (wine in general)

> **los españoles beben mucho vino**
> Spaniards (all Spaniards) drink a lot of wine

If the noun is used with an adjective or an adjectival phrase, it will still take the definite article if it refers to all of the thing or things indicated by the noun plus the adjective or phrase:

> **no me gusta el vino tinto**
> I don't like red wine

Here **el vino tinto** does not represent all wine, but it does stand for all red wine.

> **los granjeros del sur de España cultivan muchas frutas**
> farmers in the south of Spain grow a lot of fruit

This refers to all farmers in the south of Spain.

b) Abstract nouns take the definite article in Spanish, since they also refer to the idea as a whole:

> **la justicia es necesaria si la democracia va a sobrevivir**
> justice is necessary if democracy is to survive

> **la inflación está subiendo**
> inflation is going up

If the abstract noun is used with an adjective, then in some cases it can take the indefinite article:

> **me miró con una curiosidad creciente**
> he looked at me with growing curiosity

c) Names of languages take the definite article:

> **el español es muy interesante, pero no me gusta el francés**
> Spanish is very interesting, but I don't like French

However, no article is used after **en, de** and the verbs **hablar** and **estudiar**:

> **¿hablas español?**
> do you speak Spanish?

> **el libro está escrito en español**
> the book is written in Spanish

Again, if a particular example of the language is being referred to rather than the language as a whole, the indefinite article is used:

> **John habla un español excelente**
> John speaks excellent Spanish (ie the particular Spanish that he speaks is excellent)

d) Names of academic subjects follow the same pattern as in 3:

> **no me gustan las matemáticas, prefiero la física**
> I don't like maths, I prefer physics

but no article is necessary in the following cases:

> **he comprado un libro de química**
> I've bought a chemistry book

> **estudia matemáticas**
> he is studying mathematics

> **es licenciado en física**
> he has a degree in physics

e) Names of illnesses and diseases usually take the definite article, unless the idea of 'a case of' is clearly meant, in which case no article is used:

> **¿tiene algo contra la laringitis?**
> do you have anything for laryngitis?

but:

> **tengo laringitis**
> I have laryngitis

f) In general physical descriptions names of parts of the body take the definite article:

> **tiene el pelo castaño y los ojos verdes**
> she has brown hair and green eyes

However, if the description highlights how one person's eyes etc are different from everyone else's, the indefinite article is used:

tiene unos ojos azules que nadie puede resistir
she has blue eyes which no-one can resist

When the part of the body is the subject of the verb the possessive adjective is normally used:

sus ojos son azules como el mar
her eyes are blue like the sea

g) **Where English uses the possessive adjective, Spanish uses the definite article (sometimes together with the indirect object pronouns for greater precision) to indicate possession in relation to parts of the body and items of clothing:**

levantó la cabeza
he lifted his head

me duele la cabeza
my head is sore

su madre le lavó la cara
his mother washed his face

se puso la chaqueta y salió
he put on his jacket and went out

h) For reasons of style the definite article is frequently omitted in lists of words, even where you might expect it to appear:

necesitarás entusiasmo e interés
you will need enthusiasm and interest

B. CASES IN WHICH NO ARTICLE IS USED

a) In general, no article is used with the noun if:

the noun does not refer either to the thing as a whole or to a specific example of the thing in question:

me llamó ladrón
he called me a thief

the noun refers to an indefinite amount or number of the thing(s) in question:

no bebo cerveza
I don't drink beer

b) No article is used with general statements of profession or occupation, political or religious conviction, and the like:

> **mi padre es médico y mi tía es enfermera**
> my father is a doctor and my aunt is a nurse

> **ella es católica; él es comunista**
> she is a Catholic; he is a communist

However, if the noun is made more precise by being used with an adjective, then the indefinite article is used:

> **su padre es un cirujano conocido**
> his father is a well known surgeon

Not all surgeons are famous.

c) Frequently (though not always) when a noun is dependent on a negative or a question no article is used:

> **¿tienes coche? – no, no tengo coche**
> have you got a car? – no, I don't have a car

Again, this is not a reference to any particular car. If you did wish to refer to a particular car, you would use the indefinite article:

> **¿tienes un coche rojo?**
> do you have a red car?

d) When the noun is used with one of a small number of adjectives the article is omitted. These are **otro** (other), and **tal, semejante** and **parecido** (all meaning 'such'), and **cierto** (certain, some):

> **¿me das otro libro, por favor?**
> would you give me another book, please? (ie any other *undefined* book)

> **semejante situación nunca se había producido antes**
> such a situation had never arisen before (a situation of this general kind)

> **estoy de acuerdo contigo hasta cierto punto**
> I agree with you up to a point (an *undefined* point)

e) No article is used after **qué** and **vaya** in exclamations:

> **¡qué lástima!**
> what a shame!

> **¡vaya sorpresa!**
> what a surprise!

> **¡vaya paliza!**
> what a bore!

Note that any adjective used in such an exclamation is usually preceded by **tan** or **más**:

> **¡qué día más magnífico!**
> what a magnificent day!

This **más** is not considered comparative (see page 44), and does not become **mejor** or **peor** when used with **bueno** or **malo**:

> **¡qué idea más buena!**
> what a good idea!

f) No article is used after **como** in expressions such as the following:

> **te hablo como amigo**
> I'm speaking to you as a friend

I am speaking to you not as a particular friend, but as any friend would.

> **mándenos diez cajas como pedido de prueba**
> send us ten boxes as a trial order

Compare this with the following:

> **ya hemos recibido un pedido de prueba de esa empresa**
> we have already received a trial order from this firm

This is a reference to a specific trial order.

g) The article is not used when expressing indefinite quantities:

> **¿tienes mantequilla?**
> do you have (any) butter?

> **no quiero vino, siempre bebo cerveza**
> I don't want (any) wine, I always drink beer

Compare this with **la cerveza** in A.I. above, which meant 'all beer, beer in general'.

buen número de personas no querían aceptar eso
a good number of people did not want to accept this

parte/buena parte/gran parte del dinero se invirtió en el proyecto
part/a good part/a large part of the money was invested in the project

tengo cantidad/infinidad de preguntas que hacerte
I've got loads/masses of questions to ask you

h) The article is omitted with nouns in apposition:

vive en Madrid, capital de España
he lives in Madrid, the capital of Spain

C. NAMES OF PERSONS, COUNTRIES ETC

A proper noun is invariably the name of a person, country, continent, organisation or the like. Most proper nouns, including virtually all feminine names of countries, are used without any article in Spanish (see page 156 for a list of names of countries which do take the article):

Alemania es un país mucho más rico que España
Germany is a much richer country than Spain

However, the article is used in the following cases:

a) When a person's name is preceded by a title of some kind:

el señor Carballo no estaba
señor Carballo wasn't in

el general Olmeda ya se había marchado
General Olmeda had already left

The exceptions to this are:

– the titles **don** and **doña**

– when the title is used in direct address

– foreign titles

¿qué piensa de esto, señor Carballo?
what do you think of this, señor Carballo?

Lord Byron era un poeta inglés muy conocido
Lord Byron was a very famous English poet

b) When the noun is used with an adjective:

el pobre Juan no sabía qué hacer
poor Juan didn't know what to do

esto ha ocurrido muchas veces en la historia de la Europa occidental
this has happened many times in the history of Western Europe

However, **Gran Bretaña** and **Estados Unidos** have come to be regarded as proper nouns in their own right, so that the definite articles are no longer used in these cases:

Gran Bretaña votó en contra de la propuesta
Great Britain voted against the proposal

c) Acronyms

An acronym is a name consisting of the initial letters of a series of words. Known as **siglas**, these are very widely used in Spanish. With the exception of certain names of political parties, **siglas** always take the definite article, and their gender is determined by the gender of the first noun in their expanded form.

A few common acronyms:

la UE	la Unión Europea	the EU
la OTAN	la Organización del Tratado del Atlántico Norte	NATO
el INI	el Instituto Nacional de Industria	Government Department in charge of nationalised industries
el INEM	el Instituto Nacional de Empleo	Department of Employment
el PSOE	el Partido Socialista Obrero Español	Socialist party
IU	Izquierda Unida	Communist-led coalition

España es miembro de la UE
Spain is a member of the EU

España sigue siendo miembro de la OTAN
Spain is still a member of NATO

Even those acronyms which are not names of organizations take the definite article:

la EEB	la Encefalopatía Espongiforme Bovina	BSE
el IVA	el Impuesto sobre el Valor Añadido	VAT
el PVP	el Precio de Venta al Público	retail price

el comercio de productos cárnicos se ha visto gravemente afectado por la EEB
the trade in meat products has been hard hit by BSE

D. THE NEUTER ARTICLE *lo*

1. Abstract nouns

The neuter article **lo** is used almost exclusively with adjectives and adverbs. When used with an adjective, **lo** transforms the adjective into the corresponding abstract noun. For example **lo bueno** means 'that which is good'. The translation of such 'nouns' varies according to their context:

lo esencial es que todos estemos de acuerdo
the essential thing is for all of us to agree

lo verdaderamente importante es que todos lo acepten
what's really important is for everyone to accept it

los más absurdo es que él no sabía nada
the most absurd part of it is that he knew nothing

2. Meaning 'how'

lo + adjective expresses the idea of 'how' in constructions such as the following. Note that in these constructions the adjective agrees with the noun it describes:

no me había dado cuenta de lo caros que son
I hadn't realised how expensive they are

If there is no noun, the uninflected form of the adjective is used:

¿no ves lo práctico que es?
can't you see how practical it is?

E. USING A VERB AS A NOUN

A verbal noun is a verb used as the subject or object of another verb. In Spanish the *infinitive* is used to express the verbal noun, whereas in English we use the present participle. When used as the subject of a verb, the infinitive is sometimes preceded by the definite article **el**, though it is more common without:

> **fumar es peligroso para la salud**
> smoking is dangerous for your health

> **detesto tener que hacer esto**
> I hate having to do this

⚠ Under *no* circumstances can a present participle be used as a verbal noun in Spanish as it is in English. Note in particular that the infinitive is the *only* form of the verb which can come after a preposition in Spanish:

> **tomó un café antes de salir**
> he had a coffee before leaving

> **se sintió mejor después de dormir un rato**
> he felt better after sleeping a while

F. SITUATING SOMETHING IN PLACE OR TIME: DEMONSTRATIVES

This function is carried out in Spanish by the demonstrative adjectives and pronouns (see page 158). The difference between the three demonstrative adjectives in Spanish is as follows:

1. Used to denote place

este	refers to something which is close to the speaker
ese	refers to something which is close to the listener
aquel	refers to something which is remote from both speaker and listener

> **¿me das ese libro?**
> will you give me that book? (ie the one near you)

> **tomo esta caja**
> I'll take this box (ie this one I'm holding, pointing to etc)

> **aquellas flores son muy hermosas**
> those flowers are very beautiful (ie those over there)

2. Used to denote time

este is used, as in English, if the *noun* refers to present time:

> **esta semana fuimos a la playa**
> we went to the beach this week

Both **ese** and **aquel** can be used to refer to past time with little difference in meaning, though **aquel** may suggest that the action is more remote:

> **en esa época no se permitían los partidos políticos**
> at that time political parties were not allowed

> **en aquella época la población de Madrid era de sólo un millón de personas**
> at that time the population of Madrid was only one million

3. 'those who', 'those of'

Note that 'those who' is expressed in Spanish as **los que** or **las que**. The actual demonstratives are not used:

> **los que piensan eso se equivocan**
> those who think that are wrong

Likewise, 'that of', 'those of' are expressed as **el de, la de, los de, las de**. **el** takes the same contractions as it does when it is used as a definite article – ie **a + el** becomes **al** and **de + el** becomes **del** (see page 155):

> **preferimos las mercancías de Vds. a las de sus competidores**
> we prefer your goods to those of your competitors

> **prefiero el coche de Luis al de Paco**
> I prefer Luis's car to Paco's (to that of Paco)

4. The demonstrative pronouns

For the formation of the demonstrative pronouns, see page 158.

The demonstrative pronouns denote time and place in the same way as the demonstrative adjectives. Note, however, the use of **aquél** and **éste** to express the idea of 'the former' and 'the latter':

> **éste es más difícil que aquél**
> the latter is more difficult than the former

The neuter demonstrative pronouns **esto, eso** and **aquello** are used to represent an unknown object, a general situation, an entire idea.

They can *never* be used to represent a specific noun whose identity is known to the speaker:

> **¿qué es esto?**
> what's this? (unknown object)

> **no puedo aceptar esto**
> I can't accept this (this situation)

Compare this with:

> **no puedo aceptar esta situación**
> I can't accept this situation

G. LINKING NOUNS

For a list of coordinating conjunctions, see page 244.

1. *y* and *o*

The simplest way of linking nouns is by using the conjunctions **y** (and) and **o** (or). Note that **y** is replaced by **e** if the pronunciation of the next word begins with the vowel **i**. It is the pronunciation that is important, not the way the noun is spelled:

> **padres e hijos**
> parents and children

Likewise, **o** is replaced by **u** if the next word begins with the sound **o**:

> **siete u ocho**
> seven or eight

In the Spanish press, **o** is frequently written **ó** between numbers to avoid confusion with the number **0**:

> **60 ó 70**
> 60 or 70

2. Expressing 'both'

a) 'both' + plural noun

When 'both' is followed by a *single* plural noun, **los dos** or **las dos** is used, depending on the gender of the noun. In more formal Spanish, the adjective **ambos** may be used:

los dos hermanos vinieron/ambos hermanos vinieron
both brothers came

comí las dos tartas/comí ambas tartas
I ate both cakes

⚠ Neither *los/las dos* nor *ambos* may be used to express the idea of 'both ... and ...' in Spanish.

b) 'both' + two adjectives

'both' used to link two adjectives referring to the same noun is **a la vez**:

encuentro este libro a la vez divertido e interesante
I find this book both entertaining and interesting

c) 'both' + two nouns or pronouns

By far the commonest way of expressing 'both ... and ...' linking two dissimilar things in Spanish is **tanto ... como ....** Since **tanto** is used as an adverb in this construction, it never changes, no matter what the number or gender of the nouns involved:

tanto tú como yo queremos resolver este problema
both you and I want to solve this problem

2. RELATIONSHIPS BETWEEN THINGS

A. PREPOSITIONS

The commonest way of expressing relationships between nouns is by the use of prepositions. For a detailed list of both simple and compound prepositions and their uses, see pages 169-179. However, the following deserve special mention:

1. *por* and *para*

As well as having a variety of other meanings, both **por** and **para** can be used to express the ideas of 'for' and 'by' in Spanish. Their uses in these meanings can be summarized as follows:

a) Meaning 'for'

(i) In a general sense, it can be said that **por** refers to *causes*, whereas **para** refers to *aims* or *objectives*.

The following short examples, both of which mean 'I am doing it for my brother', may clarify the difference:

> **lo hago por mi hermano**

Here the emphasis is on what *caused* the speaker to decide to do what he is doing. He is doing it because his brother asked for it to be done, or because his brother needed help in some way.

> **lo hago para mi hermano**

para here indicates that the action is being done in order to secure some advantage for the brother in the future.

Likewise, the question **¿por qué hiciste esto?** asks for an explanation of what caused the action to be done, whereas the question **¿para qué hiciste esto?** asks for an explanation of the future objectives.

Here are some other examples showing the distinction between **por** and **para** (note that, although the basic ideas remain unchanged, 'for' is not always the best translation in English):

lo hizo por necesidad
he did it out of necessity

cometió el error por cansancio
he made the mistake through tiredness

lo dejaron para otro día
they left it for another day

estamos estudiando para un examen
we're studying for an exam

(ii) If there is any idea of an exchange, **por** is always used:

pagué diez mil euros por este coche
I paid ten thousand euros for this car

voy a cambiar mi viejo coche por otro más moderno
I am going to exchange my old car for a more modern one

(iii) To express the idea of 'as regards', 'as far as it concerns', use **para**:

este libro es demasiado difícil para mí
this book is too difficult for me

tal situación sería inaceptable para España
such a situation would be unacceptable for Spain

b) Meaning 'by'

(i) When introducing the person or thing by whom an action was carried out (when using the passive mood), **por** is always used:

el edificio fue inaugurado por el rey Juan Carlos
the building was inaugurated by King Juan Carlos

(ii) When 'by' refers to a future deadline, **para** is used:

necesitamos las mercancías para finales de octubre
we need the goods by the end of October

2. *a* and *en*

Basically **a** indicates motion *towards* a thing or place, whereas **en** indicates position *in* or *on* a thing or place. The difference is usually clear in English, but problems can arise when translating the preposition 'at'. If 'at' indicates position *in* or *on*, **en** must be used:

Juan está en casa
Juan is at home

vi este ordenador en la feria de muestras
I saw this computer at the exhibition

3. *antes de, delante de, ante*

a) **antes de** usually refers to time:

llegamos antes de medianoche
we arrived before midnight

Colloquially, it may also refer to place, though the idea of 'before you arrive at ...' is usually involved:

la iglesia está antes del cruce
the church is before the junction

b) **delante de** refers to physical position:

el buzón está delante de Correos
the post box is in front of the Post Office

c) **ante** refers to mental position, and is usually used with abstract nouns. It expresses roughly the same idea as the English expressions 'in the presence of', '(when) faced with' and the like:

el gobierno no sabía como reaccionar ante este problema
the government did not know how to react when faced with this problem

There are a few set expressions where **ante** may refer to physical position, but these are very limited and often refer to legal contexts:

compareció ante el juez
he appeared before the judge

B. POSSESSION

For the formation of the possessive adjectives and pronouns, see pages 159-160.

The weak forms of the possessive adjectives, which are *by far* the commonest, are placed before the noun. The strong forms go after the noun.

1. The weak possessive adjectives

⚠️ It is important to note that, like any other adjective, the possessive adjective agrees in gender and number with the noun it describes. The 'owner' of the things described is irrelevant from this point of view:

¿dónde están nuestras maletas?
where are our suitcases?

nuestras is in the feminine plural form because **maletas** is feminine plural. The owners ('we') could be either male or female.

los chicos hablaban con su abuelo
the boys were speaking with their grandfather

las chicas ayudaban a su madre
the girls were helping their mother

su is singular because both **abuelo** and **madre** are singular. The fact that there were a number of boys or girls does not alter this in any way.

2. The strong possessive adjectives

In contemporary Spanish, the strong forms of the possessive adjectives are for all practical purposes restricted to forms of direct address, or to expressing the idea 'of mine', 'of yours' etc:

esto no es posible, amigo mío
this is not possible, my friend

unos amigos míos vinieron a verme
some friends of mine came to see me

3. The possessive pronouns

The possessive pronouns take the definite article unless they are used with the verb **ser**:

¿quieres el mío?
do you want mine?

esta radio no es tuya, es nuestra
this radio isn't yours, it's ours

su casa es mucho más grande que la mía
his house is much bigger than mine

4. Cases where confusion might arise

On occasions, confusion may arise with the use of the adjective **su** and the pronoun **suyo**. These forms can mean 'his', 'her(s)', 'your(s)' (singular), 'their(s)', 'your(s)' (plural). In most cases the context will make it clear which meaning is involved. However, if confusion is likely to arise, the following forms can be used instead:

his	de él
her(s)	de ella
your(s) (singular)	de Vd.
their(s)	de ellos, de ellas
your(s) (plural)	de Vds.

María no ha perdido su propia maleta , ha perdido la de ellos
María has not lost her own suitcase, she has lost *theirs*

¿es de ella este coche?
is this car hers?

5. Possession in general

There is no equivalent of the English 'apostrophe s' in Spanish. Possession is expressed in various ways, the most common being the use of the preposition **de**. The order in which the nouns are expressed is the exact opposite of English:

el amigo de mi padre
my father's friend

Note that **de** + **el** becomes **del**:

el primo del amigo del profesor
the teacher's friend's cousin

6. Expressing 'whose'

'whose' in a question is **¿de quién?**

¿de quién es este lápiz?
whose is this pencil?

In an adjectival clause, 'whose' is expressed by the adjective **cuyo**, which agrees with the thing owned:

el hombre cuya ventana rompieron está furioso
the man whose window they broke is furious

la mujer cuyos hijos se fueron
the woman whose children went away

7. The verb *pertenecer*

Possession of objects can sometimes be expressed by the use of the verb **pertenecer** (to belong). However, this is rather formal and is much less common than the use of **de**:

¿a quién pertenece esto? – pertenece al profesor
whose is this? – it's the teacher's

The more common meaning of **pertenecer** is 'belong' in the sense of 'be a member of':

pertenece al partido socialista
he belongs to the socialist party

8. With parts of the body and items of clothing

⚠ When used as the object of a verb, parts of the body and items of clothing take the definite article, not the possessive adjective as in English. The 'owner' is often indicated by means of the indirect object pronoun:

su madre le lavó la cara
his mother washed his face

se quemó la mano
he burned his hand (ie his own hand)

C. **COMPOUND NOUNS**

A compound noun consists of a group of nouns which go together to express a more complex idea, eg kitchen table, bedroom carpet.

a) Using *de*

In Spanish, the elements of a compound noun are usually joined by a preposition, which will in most cases be **de**:

una pared de piedra
a stone wall

un portavoz del ministerio de energía
an energy department spokesman

Note that the order in which the nouns are expressed is again the opposite of English, and that the gender of the compound noun in Spanish is based on the gender of the first noun:

un sombrero de paja viejo
an old straw hat (**viejo** agrees with **sombrero** and not with **paja**)

b) Other compounds

In recent years a number of compound nouns have appeared in Spanish which do not have a preposition of any kind. The two nouns simply appear side by side, or are joined by a hyphen. Such nouns take the gender of the first noun, and are also made plural by making the first noun plural:

un coche-bomba	**coches-bomba**
a car bomb	car bombs
la fecha límite	**fechas límite**
the closing date	closing dates
un retrato robot	**retratos robot**
an identikit portrait	identikit portraits

You should beware of inventing your own compound nouns of this type. Use only those you know for certain to exist. Otherwise always use the construction with **de** as described above.

3. DESCRIBING THINGS

A. AUGMENTATIVES AND DIMINUTIVES

For the formation of augmentatives and diminutives, see pages 161-162.

A particular characteristic of Spanish is to suggest a different view of something by adding either an augmentative or a diminutive to the end of the noun. Both augmentatives and diminutives can have a merely physical meaning, or they can introduce more subjective elements into the way in which the noun is presented.

Both augmentatives and diminutives require a certain amount of care in Spanish, and the learner should beware of inventing his own at random. Use only those of whose connotations you are sure.

Diminutives

Diminutives are widely used in spoken Spanish, though they are much less common in formal written Spanish, and would frequently be out of place there. They may simply express size, but they more often suggest a favourable/unfavourable attitude of the speaker towards what he is describing. There is often no simple translation for a diminutive used in this way.

a) Size

> **un momentito, por favor**
> just a moment, please

> **había una mesita en el rincón**
> there was a small table in the corner

b) Favourable attitude

This is expressed primarily by the diminutive **-ito**, which is the commonest of all the diminutives:

> **me miraba con la carita cubierta de lágrimas**
> he looked at me with his face covered in tears

> **'hola', me dijo con su vocecita encantadora**
> 'hello', she said in her charming little voice

c) Unfavourable attitude

This is expressed by the diminutive **-uelo** which is comparatively rare:

> **pasamos por dos o tres aldehuelas sin interés**
> we passed through two or three uninteresting little villages

Augmentatives

Augmentatives indicate mostly size, though sometimes the idea of clumsiness or even ugliness may also be implied:

> **llegó un hombrón y se puso a trabajar**
> a big fellow arrived and started to work

> **un hombrote, un hombrazo, un hombracho**
> a big brute of a fellow

> **una mujerona**
> a big strong woman

Some augmentatives and diminutives have now become words in their own right and no longer have any of the connotations mentioned above:

el sillón	armchair
la tesina	dissertation
el gatillo	trigger

B. THE ADJECTIVE

I. Agreement

For the formation of the feminine and plural of adjectives, see pages 164-165.

All adjectives in Spanish must agree both in gender and number with the noun they are describing:

> **las paredes eran blancas, y el suelo era blanco también**
> the walls were white, and the floor was white as well

If a single adjective refers to a mixture of masculine and feminine nouns, it takes the masculine form:

> **las paredes y el suelo eran blancos**
> the walls and the floor were white

If a plural noun is followed by two or more adjectives and each adjective refers to only one of the things mentioned in the noun, each adjective may take the singular form:

> **los partidos socialista y comunista votaron en contra de la ley**
> the socialist and communist parties voted against the bill (there is only one socialist party and one communist party)

2. Lists of adjectives

A number of adjectives may be used to describe the same noun, as in English. Those adjectives considered most important should be placed closest to the noun. This will usually result in an order of adjectives in Spanish which is the exact opposite of English:

> **un diputado socialista español conocido**
> a well known Spanish socialist MP

> **la política agraria común europea**
> the European common agricultural policy

3. Choice of position

Although most adjectives usually follow the noun (see page 163), they can be placed in front of the noun for emphasis. This option is widely used in contemporary written Spanish, though it is less common in spoken Spanish:

> **este equipo da una fiel reproducción del sonido original**
> this equipment gives a faithful reproduction of the original sound

This is very much a question of style, and should be used with caution unless you have seen or heard the particular example you wish to use.

C. THE INDEFINITE ADJECTIVES

For the forms of **alguno** and **cualquiera** see pages 163-164.

1. 'some'

In the singular, the adjective **alguno** means 'some' in the sense of 'some ... or other':

> **compró el libro en alguna librería**
> he bought the book in some bookshop (or other)

In the plural it simply means 'some'. In this case it can be replaced without change of meaning by the appropriate form of **unos/unas**:

vinieron algunos/unos hombres y se pusieron a trabajar
some men turned up and started to work

2. 'any'

Both the adjective **alguno** and the adjective **cualquiera** can be translated into English as 'any', and the difference between the two is often difficult for the English-speaking learner to grasp.

alguno in this sense appears mostly in questions, and is used to find out whether a specific thing or group of things actually exists. **cualquiera**, on the other hand, refers in a completely indefinite way to things which are known to exist. It expresses much the same idea as the English phrases 'any at all', 'any whatsoever'.

Compare the following:

¿hay alguna librería por aquí?
are there any bookshops around here?

This question is asked to see if any bookshops exist: ie are there any actual bookshops? (Note that *in a question* **alguno** is almost always used in the *singular* in Spanish, even when a plural would normally be used in English).

puedes encontrar este libro en cualquier librería
you can find this book in any bookshop

ie you can buy it in any bookshop whatsoever. This statement assumes that there are indeed bookshops.

In other cases, the logic of the statement will require one adjective to be used rather than the other:

cualquier mecánico podría hacer eso
any mechanic could do that

ie any mechanic at all. **algún** would not make any sense in this context.

Note that very often English 'any' is not translated into Spanish:

¿tiene mantequilla?
do you have any butter?

no tenemos plátanos
we don't have any bananas

The order of 'indefiniteness' in Spanish is as follows:

alguna librería	some bookshop (or other)
algunas/unas librerías	some bookshops
cualquier librería	any bookshop whatsoever
librerías	bookshops

D. VARYING THE FORCE OF AN ADJECTIVE

1. Diminutives and augmentatives

It is possible to add diminutives, and in a small number of cases augmentatives, to certain adjectives. The connotations involved are as for nouns. This feature requires extra special care. Use only those you know to exist and about which you feel confident:

el agua está calentita hoy
the water is nice and warm today

¡qué tontita eres!
how silly you are!

el niño está muy grandón
the child is very big (for his age)

2. Adverbs

A whole range of adverbs can be used to vary the force of an adjective. For the formation of adverbs, see page 186. A list of adverbs of degree can be found on page 190.

Any adjective modified by an adverb in this way *must* go after the noun, even if the simple form normally precedes the noun:

me dió un libro sumamente interesante
he gave me an extremely interesting book

⚠ It is essential to remember that adverbs are invariable, in other words, they *never* change their form, no matter what the gender or number of the adjective they modify.

3. Increasing the force of the adjective

encuentro todo esto muy aburrido
I find all of this very boring

muy cannot be used on its own. If there is no adjective to follow it, it is replaced by **mucho**. In this case **mucho** is used as an adverb and never changes its form:

> **¿encontraste interesante la revista? – sí, mucho**
> did you find the magazine interesting? – yes, very

> **este libro es sumamente (or extremamente or extremadamente) interesante**
> this book is extremely interesting

4. Decreasing the force of the adjective

The adverb **poco** is used to lessen or even *negate* the force of an adjective:

> **me parece poco probable que venga**
> it seems unlikely to me that he will come

⚠️ *poco* must not be confused with *un poco*, which means 'a little'. *la sopa está poco caliente* (the soup is not very hot) is clearly not the same as *la sopa está un poco caliente* (the soup is a little hot).

E. COMPARING THINGS: THE COMPARATIVE AND THE SUPERLATIVE

THE COMPARATIVE

For the formation of comparatives, see pages 166-167.

Simple comparison

a) The comparison of equality (one thing is as good, as interesting etc as another)

If the comparison is based on an adjective, it is expressed by **tan** + adjective + **como**:

> **Juan es tan alto como su hermana**
> Juan is as tall as his sister

> **Luisa no es tan trabajadora como su hermana**
> Luisa isn't as hard-working as her sister

If the comparison is based on a noun (ie it is one of quantity – 'as much as', 'as many as'), it is expressed by **tanto** + noun + **como**.

tanto is used as an adjective here and therefore agrees with the noun:

> **yo tengo tantos discos como tú**
> I have as many records as you

b) The comparison of superiority (one thing is better, longer etc than another)

When the comparison is based on an adjective, the construction **más** + adjective + **que** is used (see page 166 for irregular comparatives):

> **María es más inteligente que su hermano**
> María is cleverer than her brother

If the comparison is one of quantity, the construction **más** + noun + **que** is used:

> **ellos tienen más dinero que nosotros**
> they have more money than us

If the comparison is made with a specific number or amount, **de** is used instead of **que**:

> **vinieron más de cien personas**
> more than one hundred people came

> **esperamos más de media hora**
> we waited for over half an hour

c) The comparison of inferiority (one thing is less good, less interesting than another)

The comparison of inferiority is expressed by **menos**. It follows the same patterns as the comparison of superiority:

> **esta revista es menos interesante que aquélla**
> this magazine is less interesting than that one

> **tú haces menos errores que yo**
> you make fewer mistakes than me

> **pagué menos de mil pesetas**
> I paid less than a thousand pesetas

d) Note that, whereas English uses the terms 'ever' and 'anyone' in a comparison, Spanish uses the corresponding *negative* terms:

la situación es más grave que nunca
the situation is more serious than ever

él sabe más que nadie
he knows more than anyone

Other indefinite comparisons are usually expressed by using the adjective **cualquiera** (see page 163):

Isabel es más inteligente que cualquier otro estudiante
Isabel is more intelligent than any other student

Comparison with a clause

When the comparison is being made not with a noun but with a clause, **que** is replaced by more complex forms.

a) Comparison based on an adjective

When the comparison is based on an adjective, the clause is introduced by **de lo que**:

la situación es más compleja de lo que piensas
the situation is more complex than you think

el problema era más difícil de lo que habían dicho
the problem was more difficult than they had said

b) Comparison based on a noun (ie comparison of quantity)

In this case, the appropriate form of **del que, de la que, de los que, de las que** is used. The form chosen must agree in gender and number with the noun:

vinieron más personas de las que esperábamos
more people came than we expected

surgieron más problemas de los que habíamos previsto
more problems arose than we had foreseen

The **los** in **de los que** agrees with **problemas**, which is masculine.

gasté más dinero del que ahorré
I spent more money than I saved

The **el** in **del que** agrees with **dinero**.

Other phrases of comparison

a) 'more and more' is expressed in Spanish by the phrase **cada vez más**:

> **encuentro su comportamiento cada vez más extraño**
> I find his behaviour more and more odd

vez may be replaced by another word indicating time without the idea of 'more and more' being lost:

> **la situación se pone cada día más grave**
> the situation is becoming more and more serious every day

'less and less' is **cada vez menos**:

> **encuentro sus explicaciones cada vez menos verosímiles**
> I find his explanations less and less plausible

b) 'the more/less … the more/less …' is expressed by **cuanto** + comparative … **tanto** + comparative … If used with an adjective or adverb **cuanto** is invariable, but agrees in comparisons of quantity (ie with nouns).

In all cases the **tanto** can be omitted, and it is in fact more common to omit it:

> **cuanto más fáciles son los ejercicios, más le gustan**
> the easier the exercises are, the more he likes them

> **cuanto más dinero tiene, más quiere**
> the more money he has, the more he wants

> **cuantos menos problemas tengamos, más contento estaré**
> the fewer problems we have, the happier I'll be

c) 'all the more' + adjective + 'because' is expressed in Spanish as **tanto** + comparative + **cuanto que**. This construction is limited to very formal Spanish:

> **esto es tanto más importante cuanto que nos queda poco tiempo**
> this is all the more important because we don't have much time

THE SUPERLATIVE

For the formation of superlatives, see page 168.

The relative superlative

a) The relative superlative is used to express one thing's superiority over all others of its kind:

> **el español es là asignatura más interesante de las que estudio**
> Spanish is the most interesting subject I study

> **Luisa se puso su mejor traje**
> Luisa put on her best suit

b) The scope of the superlative

The preposition **de** is used to introduce the scope of the superlative, whereas in English we use 'in':

> **es el hombre más rico de la ciudad**
> he's the richest man in town

> **Estados Unidos es el país más poderoso del mundo**
> The United States is the most powerful country in the world

c) Order of superlatives

A descending order of superlatives ('the second oldest man', 'the third richest woman') is expressed as follows:

> **el segundo hombre más viejo**
> the second oldest man

> **la tercera mujer más rica**
> the third richest woman

The absolute superlative

It is important to distinguish clearly in Spanish between the relative superlative used to compare one thing with others, and the absolute superlative which refers only to one thing without reference to others (for the formation of the absolute superlative see page 168):

> **eso es rarísimo**
> that's most unusual

No comparison is involved here – the statement is simply that something is *very* unusual.

The absolute superlative can also be expressed by one of the adverbs of intensity:

> **encuentro esto sumamente interesante**
> I find this most interesting

F. ADJECTIVAL PHRASES

Spanish, like English, can use a wide range of adjectival phrases to describe a noun. Such phrases are often the only way to translate certain compound adjectives into Spanish. They consist mostly of nouns introduced by the preposition **de** though other prepositions do occur:

> **un hombre de dos metros de altura**
> a man two metres tall

> **una mujer de pelo rubio y ojos azules**
> a fair-haired, blue-eyed woman

> **refugiados sin casa ni dinero**
> homeless, penniless refugees

G. ADJECTIVAL CLAUSES

Adjectival clauses are used to describe things. The thing being described is referred to as the 'antecedent'. Like all clauses, an adjectival clause *must* contain a verb.

The relative pronoun

For the formation of the relative pronouns, see page 180.

⚠ Unlike English, *all* adjectival clauses in Spanish must be introduced by a relative pronoun. Failure to use a relative pronoun will result in a failure to communicate successfully with your listener or reader.

1. The relative pronoun *que*

In most cases, the simple relative pronoun **que** can be used:

> **los hombres que están charlando son españoles**
> the men who are chatting are Spanish

> **¿viste la película que pusieron ayer?**
> did you see the film (that/which) they put on yesterday?

2. Adjectival clauses with prepositions

⚠️ Note that a preposition can *never* appear at the end of an adjectival clause in Spanish. Such a construction is meaningless to a Spaniard. Any preposition *must* be placed before the relative pronoun:

los muchachos con quienes jugaba se han marchado
the boys he was playing with (with whom he was playing) have gone away

la carta en que leí esto por primera vez está en la mesa
the letter I read this in for the first time (the letter in which I read this ...) is on the table

If the antecedent is a *person*, **que** may not be used. It is usually replaced by **quien** (or plural **quienes**), though the appropriate forms of **el que** or **el cual** are also sometimes used:

el hombre con quien hablaba es mi tío
the man I was speaking with is my uncle

los turistas a quienes vendí mi coche
the tourists I sold my car to

If the antecedent is a *thing*, the following rules apply:

a) If the relative pronoun is preceded by a compound preposition (ie one consisting of more than one word, eg **detrás de**), one of the compound forms of the relative pronoun must be used. You must choose the form of **el que** or **el cual** which agrees in number and gender with the antecedent:

la casa detrás de la cual se encuentra el lago
the house behind which the lake is to be found

el árbol debajo del cual nos besamos por primera vez
the tree under which we first kissed

Since the **el que** and **el cual** forms are in fact forms of the definite article followed by **que** or **cual**, the usual contractions occur (see page 155):

el edificio delante del cual esperábamos
the building we were waiting in front of

preferimos tu nuevo coche al que tenías antes
we prefer your new car to the one you had before

b) After the simple prepositions **de, en, con** etc, **que** may be used, though in more formal Spanish the compound forms are often preferred in such cases:

> **la casa en que vivimos es muy vieja**
> the house we live in is very old

3. *lo que, lo cual*

If the antecedent is not an identifiable thing or things, but refers instead to an entire situation or an idea, then the neuter forms **lo que** or **lo cual** *must* be used. They are interchangeable:

> **Juan insistió en acompañarnos, lo que no me gustó nada**
> Juan insisted on coming with us, which did not please me at all

What displeased you was not Juan, but the fact that he insisted on coming along.

> **María se negó a hacerlo, lo que no entiendo**
> María refused to do it, which I don't understand

Again, it is not María that you do not understand, but the fact that she refused to do it.

Adjectival clauses with an indefinite or negative antecedent

An adjectival clause has an indefinite antecedent if the noun being described refers to something (object/person/idea) which may or may not exist.

The antecedent is negative if the noun being described refers to something which does not exist.

 In both these cases, the verb in the adjectival clause *must* be put into the subjunctive.

For the formation of the subjunctive see pages 205-209. Use the present or the imperfect subjunctive, depending on which is more logical in the context.

1. Indefinite antecedents

> **busco a alguien que hable español**
> I am looking for someone who can speak Spanish

This person may not exist – you may not find him or her.
Compare this with **busco a un hombre que habla español**, where the use of the indicative **habla** indicates that you know a specific gentleman who in fact speaks Spanish, but you just cannot find him at the moment.

> **los que no quieran participar pueden irse ahora**
> those who don't wish to take part can leave now

There is no way of telling how many people will not want to take part. In fact everyone might want to take part.

This construction is frequently used with adjectival clauses which refer to the future:

> **los que no lleguen a tiempo no podrán entrar**
> those who don't arrive on time will not be allowed in

Obviously, everyone might arrive on time.

In formal Spanish, **quien** is used on its own as an indefinite relative pronoun meaning 'someone (who)', 'anyone (who)'. It can be either the subject or the object of the adjectival clause:

> **busco quien me ayude**
> I am looking for someone to help me (who can help me)

> **quien diga eso no entiende nada**
> anyone who says that understands nothing

2. Negative antecedents

> **no hay nadie que sepa hacerlo**
> there is no-one who knows how to do it

> **no tengo libro que te valga**
> I haven't got any books which would be any use to you

> **no conozco ningún país donde permitan eso**
> I don't know any country where they allow that

4. REFERRING TO ACTIONS: THE VERB

The word 'actions' is used here not just to refer to actions as they are normally understood. It also includes mental activities such as 'thinking', 'considering' and the like, as well as states such as 'being', 'seeming', 'appearing' and so on.

A. WHO IS PERFORMING THE ACTION?: THE SUBJECT

1. The subject pronoun

For the subject pronouns, see page 181.

a) Cases where the subject pronoun is not stated

In English, the subject of the verb is either explicitly stated – 'my friend went back to Spain yesterday' – or it is replaced by a pronoun – 'he went back to Spain yesterday'.

However, the ending of the verb in Spanish usually makes it clear who the subject is – for example **hablo** can only mean 'I speak', **hablamos** can only mean 'we speak'. Consequently, it is also possible in Spanish to use the verb on its own without a subject pronoun:

¿qué piensas de todo esto?
what do you think of all this?

iremos a la playa mañana
we'll go to the beach tomorrow

This is in fact more common than using the subject pronoun with the verb. However, **Vd.** and **Vds.** are used more frequently than other pronouns. This is to avoid confusion with, for example, **él, ella** and **ellos, ellas** since the verb endings are the same.

¿por qué estudia Vd. español?
why are you studying Spanish?

Note that the subject pronoun is also not used in constructions such as the following:

los escoceses preferimos la cerveza
we Scots prefer beer

los españoles bebéis mucho vino
you Spaniards drink a lot of wine

b) Use of the subject pronouns

However, the subject pronouns *are* expressed (1) for emphasis or (2) where obvious confusions would arise:

¿qué piensas tú de todo esto?
what do *you* think of all this?

él salió al cine, pero ella se quedó en casa
he went out to the cinema, but she stayed at home

If the pronouns were not expressed here, it would not be clear who did what.

Remember that **nosotros, vosotros** and **ellos** have feminine forms which must be used if only girls or women are involved:

María y Carmen, ¿qué pensáis vosotras de esto?
María and Carmen, what do you think of this?

Note also the difference between Spanish and English in constructions such as the following:

¿quién es? – soy yo/somos nosotros
who is it? – it's me/it's us

soy yo quien quiere hacerlo
it's me who wants to do it

As can be seen, the verb **ser** agrees here with its expressed subject.

c) *ello*

ello is a *neuter* pronoun in Spanish and can *never* be used to refer to a specific object. It is used to refer to an entire idea or situation. Its use as a genuine subject is rare and is by and large restricted to a few constructions in formal Spanish:

todo ello me parece extraño
all of that seems very strange to me

ello here refers to a situation which has just been described.

por ello decidió no continuar
he therefore decided not to continue

d) Emphasising the subject pronoun

The subject pronouns are emphasised by using the appropriate form of the adjective **mismo**:

lo hice yo mismo
I did it myself

A woman saying this would obviously say **lo hice yo misma**.

me lo dijeron ellos mismos
they told me so themselves

e) *tú* and *usted*

Traditionally, **tú** has been reserved for close friends and relatives, and children, **usted** being used in any more formal situation. However, there is little doubt that the use of **tú** has increased dramatically in Spain in recent years, and any young person going to Spain can confidently expect to be automatically addressed as **tú** by people of his or her own age, and should also respond using **tú**.

Even the not-so-young will find themselves addressed as **tú** by people they have never spoken to before. However, a certain amount of caution is still required. When addressing an older person, or someone in authority, for the first time, **usted** is certainly to be recommended. In general, you should take your lead from the Spaniards you are talking to. If everyone is using **tú**, it would be silly (and unfriendly) to persist with **usted**.

2. The indefinite subject

In colloquial English, the indefinite subject is expressed as 'you' and less frequently as 'they'. In more formal spoken and written English, it is expressed as 'one'. In Spanish it can be expressed in the following ways:

a) Use of *tú*

In colloquial Spanish the **tú** forms of the verb can also be used to express an indefinite subject:

bajas por esta calle y tomas la primera a la izquierda
you go down this street and you take the first on the left

Like its English equivalent, this is not a reference to the person addressed, but is a truly indefinite subject.

In formal spoken and in written Spanish, however, this construction would be out of place. Two alternative constructions are available, as follows.

b) Reflexive use of the verb

> **se dice que los precios en España son muy bajos**
> they say that prices are low in Spain

> **se cree que habrá menos turistas este año**
> they think there will be fewer tourists this year

c) The use of *uno* or *la gente*

> **uno no puede por menos de reírse**
> one cannot help laughing

> **la gente no cree todo lo que dice el gobierno**
> people don't believe everything the government says

Either **uno** or **la gente** is obligatory if the verb itself is used reflexively:

> **a la larga uno se acostumbra a todo**
> you can get used to anything in the long run

3. Agreement of subject and verb

The verb in Spanish *must* agree in number and person with the subject.

⚠ Remember in particular that nouns such as *la gente, el gobierno* and phrases such as *todo el mundo* are grammatically *singular*. They may be logical plurals (ie they refer to a number of people), but they are singular nouns and *must* take a singular verb:

> **la gente no quiere que el gobierno haga eso**
> people don't want the government to do that

> **todo el mundo lo sabe**
> everyone knows it

la mayoría and **la mayor parte** (both meaning 'the majority', 'most') take a singular verb. However, if they are followed by a second plural noun, the verb is usually plural:

> **la mayoría votó en contra de la propuesta**
> the majority voted against the proposal

> **la mayoría de los diputados votaron en contra de la propuesta**
> most of the MPs voted against the proposal

On the other hand, there are a small number of plural nouns which are perceived as referring to a singular object, and which are regularly followed by a singular verb:

> **Estados Unidos ha expresado su desacuerdo con esta decisión**
> the United States has expressed its disagreement with this decision

Estados Unidos is treated here simply as the name of a country. This also occurs with the name of the trade union **Comisiones Obreras**:

> **Comisiones Obreras se opuso a la política del gobierno**
> Comisiones Obreras opposed the government's policy

However, if the article were used, the verb would indeed be plural:

> **los Estados Unidos no están de acuerdo**
> the United States are not in agreement

Note also that if the verb **ser** is followed by a plural noun, it is itself plural, even if its apparent subject is singular:

> **el problema son los elevados precios del petróleo**
> the problem is the high prices of petrol

B. TO WHOM IS THE ACTION BEING DONE?: THE OBJECT

1. Direct and indirect objects

If the action of a verb applies *directly* to a person or thing, that person or thing is the *direct object* of the verb.

If the action does not apply directly, but the idea of 'to someone or something' or 'for someone or something' is involved (even if this idea is not explicitly expressed) then the person or thing is the *indirect object* of the verb.

A verb can have both a direct and an indirect object at the same time:

> **le escribí una carta a mi hermano**
> I wrote a letter to my brother

In this sentence **carta** is the direct object since it is the letter which is written, and **hermano** is the indirect object since it is the brother that the letter is written *to*.

a) 'to' or 'for'

This can sometimes be confusing for an English-speaking learner of Spanish because the difference between direct and indirect objects is not always clear in English, whereas it must *always* be clearly signalled in Spanish. Take the following examples:

I gave the dog to my brother
I gave the dog a bone

In the first sentence, 'the dog' is the direct object of the verb 'give', since the dog is what you actually gave, and 'brother' is the indirect object, since you gave the dog *to* your brother.

In the second sentence, 'the dog' is no longer the direct object, since here you are not giving the dog at all. What you are giving is 'a bone', and 'bone' is now the direct object. You gave the bone *to* the dog, so 'the dog' is now the *indirect* object. Although 'the dog' has changed from being the direct to the indirect object, there is nothing in the words used in English to indicate this change.

This is not the case in Spanish. An indirect object is *always* clearly marked in Spanish by being preceded by the preposition **a**. Consequently the Spanish translation of the sentences given above is:

le di el perro a mi hermano
le di un hueso al perro

(For the use of the pronoun **le** here, see page 59.) As can be seen, if both nouns are expressly stated in Spanish (as opposed to being replaced by pronouns), the direct object precedes the indirect object.

b) 'from'

Unlike English, Spanish uses an indirect object to indicate the person 'from' whom something is taken, stolen, bought or hidden:

le compré el coche a mi padre
I bought the car from my father

le robó el dinero a su madre
he stole the money from his mother

trataron de ocultar la verdad al profesor
they tried to hide the truth from the teacher

2. The personal *a*

 If the direct object of a verb is a particular person or a particular group of people, it is *essential* to precede it in Spanish by the preposition *a*.

It must be clearly understood that this *a* does not transform the direct object into an indirect object. This *a* is not translated in English:

> **veo a mi hermano**
> I can see my brother

> **encontré a mi padre**
> I met my father

If the direct object is a person but is not a *particular* person, the **a** is not used:

> **buscamos un médico**
> we are looking for a doctor

Not a particular doctor, but any doctor at all.

The personal **a** is also used with certain pronouns referring to people, even though these may not always refer to specific people:

> **conozco a alguien que puede ayudarte**
> I know someone who can help you

> **no veo a nadie**
> I can't see anyone

The personal **a** is also used with animals if it is a specific animal which is being referred to:

> **llevé a mi perro a dar un paseo**
> I took my dog for a walk

3. The object pronouns

The function of a pronoun is to stand for a noun. For example, in the sentence 'John wanted the book, so I gave it to him', 'it' stands for 'the book', and 'him' stands for 'John'. For the forms of the object pronouns, see page 181.

a) Direct and indirect object pronouns

⚠️ The direct object pronoun can only stand for the direct object of a verb as explained above. If there is *any* idea of 'to' or 'for', the indirect object pronoun *must* be used in Spanish, even though the words 'to' or 'for' may not actually be used in the equivalent English expression.

This does not apply with verbs of motion – for example *ir a* – or where the idea of 'to' or 'for' is contained in the verb – for example *buscar*, meaning 'to look for' (for a list of such verbs, see page 233):

> **le dí el dinero**
> I gave him/her the money (I gave the money to him/her)

> **les ofreció diez mil euros**
> he offered them ten thousand euros (he offered ten thousand euros to them)

> **le mandé una carta ayer**
> I sent her a letter yesterday (I sent a letter to her)

In both spoken and written Spanish, the third person indirect object pronoun is almost always used even when the indirect object is explicitly stated:

> **le dí el libro a mi amigo**
> I gave the book to my friend

> **él *se* lo dio a su hermano**
> he gave it to his brother

b) *le* and *lo* as direct object pronouns

Strictly speaking, **le** is used as the direct object referring to a man or boy (a masculine *person*), whereas **lo** is used as the direct object referring to a masculine *thing*:

> **¿ves a mi hermano? – sí, sí, le veo**
> can you see my brother? – yes, yes, I can see him

> **¿ves el libro? – sí, sí, lo veo**
> can you see the book? – yes, yes, I can see it

However, in spoken Spanish, and occasionally also in written Spanish, these forms are often mixed up, giving rise to what is known as **loísmo** (the use of **lo** for **le**):

¿ves a mi hermano? – sí, sí, lo veo
can you see my brother? – yes, yes, I can see him

leísmo – the use of **les** for **los** in the plural – also occurs:

¿tienes los libros? – sí, les tengo
have you got the books? – yes, I've got them

You will almost certainly come across these at some point, though it is probably best not to imitate them.

4. The neuter pronoun *lo*

The neuter pronoun **lo** can never refer to an identifiable person or thing. It refers only to a whole idea or situation:

¿sabes que ha llegado Juan? – sí, ya lo sé
do you know that Juan has arrived? – yes, I do (I know it)

What you know is that 'Juan has arrived'. **lo** in this sense often translates 'so' in English:

tú mismo me lo dijiste
you told me so yourself

lo can also be used after either of the verbs 'to be' (**ser** and **estar**). In this case it usually refers back to the last adjective, though in the case of **ser** it can also refer back to a noun.

Remember that **lo** *never* changes its form, no matter what the gender or number of the adjective or noun to which it refers:

ellos están cansados, y nosotros lo estamos también
they are tired, and so are we

lo here refers back to **cansados**.

su padre es médico, y el mío lo es también
his father is a doctor, and so is mine

lo here refers back to the noun **médico**.

5. The strong object pronouns

For the forms of the strong object pronouns, see page 182. The strong pronouns are used after prepositions:

¿este dinero es para mí? – no, es para ellos
is this money for me? – no, it's for them

The strong pronouns are also used with the preposition **a** to lend emphasis to direct or indirect pronouns which are stated in the same sentence:

me dio el libro a mí, no a ti
he gave the book to *me*, not to you

te veo a ti, pero no la veo a ella
I can see *you*, but I can't see *her*

This emphasis can be further heightened by placing the strong pronoun before the verb:

a mí no me gusta nada
I don't like it at all

C. EMPHASISING THE ACTION

In English all verb tenses have two forms – the standard form ('I read') and the progressive form ('I am reading'). As well as this, the present and past tenses have an emphatic form ('I do read', 'I did read'), which is used to give special emphasis to the verb, or to ask questions. In Spanish, only the standard and progressive forms of the verb are available.

If you wish to emphasise the verb, other constructions must be used, for example:

sí que te creo; te aseguro que te creo
I *do* believe you

ella sí que no vendrá; seguro que ella no vendrá
she *definitely* won't come

Occasionally an action is emphasised by using first the infinitive and then the appropriate part of the verb:

¿tú bebes? – beber no bebo, pero fumo mucho
do you drink? – I don't drink, but I smoke a lot

D. NEGATING THE ACTION

1. Simple negation

In simple negation, **no** is placed in front of the verb:

no leo muchas revistas, no me gustan
I don't read many magazines, I don't like them

no le vi porque no vino
I didn't see him because he didn't come

2. Compound negation

With compound negatives, two possibilities are usually available:

a) **no** is placed in front of the verb and the other negative is placed after the verb. In most cases this construction is preferred:

no conozco a nadie aquí
I don't know anyone here

no sabe nada
he doesn't know anything

Note that this does *not* constitute a 'double negative' as in English. This applies even when the second negative is in a different clause:

no quiero que hables con nadie
I don't want you to speak to anyone

no es necesario que hagas nada
it isn't necessary for you to do anything

b) **no** is omitted and the negative is placed before the verb on its own. By and large this construction is usually confined to uses of **nadie** as subject of the verb, and to **tampoco, nunca** and **jamás**:

nadie sabe adonde ha ido
no-one knows where he has gone

Luisa nunca llega a tiempo
Luisa never arrives on time

a mí tampoco me gusta
I don't like it either

 Note that *también no* is not used in Spanish.

3. Other negatives

The phrases **estar sin** + infinitive and **estar por** + infinitive negate the action in a way which can suggest that it has *not yet* been done:

la puerta está todavía sin reparar
the door hasn't been repaired yet

este problema está todavía por resolver
this problem has still to be solved

estar can be replaced by **quedar**:

queda mucho trabajo por hacer
there's still a lot of work to do

4. Negatives after prepositions

Note that the prepositions **sin** and **antes de** are followed by negatives whereas in English they are followed by the corresponding positive term:

salió sin hablar con nadie
he went out without speaking to anyone

decidió comer algo antes de hacer nada más
he decided to eat something before doing anything else

5. More than one negative

A number of negatives may be used together in Spanish as in English. In English, however, only the first term is negative. In Spanish, *all* terms are negative:

nadie sabe nunca nada
no-one ever knows anything

no hablo nunca con nadie
I never speak to anyone

6. Emphasising the negative *(nouns)*

With nouns, the negative can be emphasised by using the negative adjective **ninguno** (see page 163). **ninguno** is seldom used in the plural:

no me queda ningún dinero
I have no money left

For added emphasis, the appropriate form of **alguno** may be placed *after* the noun:

no tiene miedo alguno
he's not the least bit afraid

In colloquial Spanish, **nada de** can also be used before the noun:

no me queda nada de dinero
I have no money left at all

The order of 'negativeness' in Spanish is:

no tengo miedo	I'm not afraid
no tengo ningún miedo	I'm not at all afraid

no tengo miedo alguno/	I'm not the slightest bit afraid
no tengo nada de miedo	

Note also the following:

no tengo ni idea/	I haven't the slightest idea
no tengo ni la menor idea/	
no tengo la más mínima idea	

7. Emphasising the negative *(adjectives)*

In the case of an adjective, the negative can be emphasised by placing **nada** before the adjective. **nada** is invariable:

no encuentro sus libros nada interesantes
I don't find his/her books at all interesting

8. Emphasising the negative *(verbs)*

nada can also be used as an emphatic negative rather than meaning 'nothing', though this construction is seldom used if the verb takes a direct object:

la película no me gustó nada
I didn't like the film at all

no he dormido nada
I haven't slept at all

If the verb has an object, a phrase such as **en absoluto** may be used:

no entiendo esto en absoluto
I don't understand this at all

Note that, on its own, **en absoluto** means 'not at all':

¿me crees? – en absoluto
do you believe me? – not at all

E. ASKING QUESTIONS

As was the case with negations, questions are formed using the standard or progressive forms of the verb, as appropriate.

1. Simple questions

Simple questions do not begin with an interrogative word. They can have the subject after the verb as in English:

¿está aquí tu hermano?
is your brother here?

However, they can sometimes be identical in form to statements, though this tends to suggest that the speaker expects the answer **sí**. In this case, the fact that they are questions is conveyed to the listener by the speaker's tone of voice:

> **¿el agua está fría?**
> is the water cold?

The idea of 'isn't it?' etc is expressed in Spanish by **¿no es verdad?**, **¿verdad?**, or more colloquially, simply **¿no?**. These expressions are all invariable:

> **tú le diste el dinero, ¿verdad?**
> you gave him the money, didn't you?

> **te gusta hablar español, ¿no?**
> you like speaking Spanish, don't you?

> **éste está mejor, ¿no es verdad?**
> this one's better, isn't it?

2. Interrogative pronouns and adjectives

⚠ A preposition can *never* be placed at the end of a question in Spanish. Any preposition present must be placed in front of the interrogative pronoun or adjective. A Spanish speaker will not connect a preposition placed anywhere else in the question with the interrogative word, and will consequently not understand the question:

> **¿a quién le diste el dinero?**
> who did you give the money to? (to whom did you give the money?)

> **¿con quién fuiste al cine?**
> who did you go to the cinema with?

Note that **cuál** is an interrogative pronoun. If the noun is expressed, **cuál** must be followed by **de**:

> **¿cuál de los coches prefieres?**
> which of the cars do you prefer?

> **¿cuál te gustó más?**
> which did you like best?

qué is used (l) as an indefinite interrogative pronoun or (2) as an interrogative adjective immediately in front of a noun:

¿qué quieres?
what do you want?

¿qué libro te gustó más?
which book did you like most?

Note that **qué** is invariable.

3. Indirect questions

Indirect questions are introduced either by the conjunction **si** (whether), or by an interrogative pronoun or adjective. The tenses used are identical to those used in English:

me preguntó si había visto la película
he asked me if I had seen the film

no sé cuál de los coches prefiero
I don't know which of the cars I prefer

Again, any preposition *must* precede the pronoun or adjective:

se negó a decirme con quién había salido
he refused to tell me who he had gone out with

F. REFLEXIVE USES OF THE VERB

1. The reflexive pronouns

A verb is used reflexively if the subject of the verb performs the action on himself/herself/itself. The verb is made reflexive in Spanish by using it with the appropriate form of the reflexive pronoun (see page 182).

In English, a number of verbs can be used either with or without the reflexive pronoun without changing their meaning. For example, there is no real difference between 'I wash' and 'I wash myself', between 'he shaves' and 'he shaves himself'. This freedom to choose is not available in Spanish. If a particular action is perceived as reflexive, the reflexive forms of the verb *must* be used.

The number of actions which are perceived as reflexive is much greater in Spanish than in English:

se levantó, se lavó, se vistió y salió
he got up, got washed, got dressed and went out

The indirect reflexive pronouns express the idea of 'for oneself':

se compró un disco
he bought himself an album

⚠ The reflexive pronouns are also essential with actions done to parts of one's own body or one's own clothes. Where English would use the possessive adjective, the noun is preceded by the *definite article* in Spanish:

se rompió la pierna
he broke his leg

se puso la chaqueta
he put on his jacket

2. The prefix *auto-*

In contemporary Spanish a number of reflexive verbs also have the prefix **auto-** (meaning 'self') joined to them to emphasise the reflexive nature of the action. However, such verbs should be used with care. Use only those you have seen and know to exist:

se autoexcluyeron
they opted out (they excluded themselves)

estos grupos se autoubican en la izquierda
these groups claim to be (place themselves) on the left

This prefix is also found in a large number of nouns: **autodominio** (self-control), **autocrítica** (self-criticism) etc.

3. Reciprocal action

A verb can be used reflexively not only to express the idea of doing an action to oneself, but also to express the idea of doing the action 'to each other'. In such cases the verb is invariably plural:

nos encontramos en la calle
we met each other in the street

nos vemos mañana
see you tomorrow (we'll see each other tomorrow)

If the verb is itself reflexive, the reciprocal action may be indicated by the use of **uno a otro**, though this also may be omitted if the context makes it clear that reciprocal action is involved.

se felicitaron uno a otro
they congratulated each other

If the verb takes a preposition before its object, this preposition will replace the **a** of **uno a otro**:

se despidieron uno de otro
they said goodbye to each other

se despidieron would simply mean 'they said goodbye'.

In very formal language, **uno a otro** can be replaced by the adverbs **mútuamente** or **recíprocamente**:

se ayudan mútuamente
they help each other

4. Other meanings

A number of verbs can be used reflexively in Spanish with little or no true reflexive meaning, and with very little difference in meaning from the non-reflexive forms. The commonest of these are:

caer, caerse	to fall
morir, morirse	to die

Others change their meanings in largely unpredictable ways:

comer	to eat	**comerse**	to eat up
dormir	to sleep	**dormirse**	to go to sleep
ir	to go	**irse**	to go away
llevar	to carry	**llevarse**	to take away
quedar	to remain, to be left	**quedarse**	to stay

G. GIVING COMMANDS

For the formation of the imperative, see pages 208-9. For the position of pronouns with imperatives, see page 183.

It is important to remember that the imperative proper is used only for positive commands addressed either to **tú** or **vosotros/vosotras**. In *all* other cases (positive commands addressed to **Vd.** and **Vds.**, and *all* negative commands) the appropriate form of the subjunctive is used:

no leas esa revista, lee ésta
don't read that magazine, read this one

tenéis que escribir la carta en español, no la escribáis en inglés
you have to write the letter in Spanish, don't write it in English

vengan mañana, no vengan hoy
come tomorrow, don't come today

The subjunctive is also used for third person imperatives, which are usually preceded by **que**:

¡qué lo hagan ellos mismos!
let them do it themselves!

First person imperatives (ie 'we') may be formed either by the subjunctive, or by **vamos a** followed by the infinitive of the verb. The use of the subjunctive implies a more committed attitude to the action in question:

vamos a ver
let's see

vamos a empezar
let's start

hagamos eso ahora mismo
let's do it right now

H. THE PASSIVE

1. *ser* plus the past participle

The passive is formed in Spanish by **ser** plus the past participle. It must be borne clearly in mind that the passive is used exclusively to express an *action*. If you are not referring to an action but are describing a state, then **estar** will be used.

In this construction the past participle *always* agrees with the subject, ie with the thing or person to whom the action was done:

el palacio fue construido en el siglo XV
the palace was built in the 15th century

This is a reference to the castle actually being built. Compare also the following:

la ventana fue rota por la explosión
the window was shattered by the explosion

cuando entré en la sala vi que la ventana estaba rota
when I went into the room I saw that the window was broken

The first of these sentences refers to an action which occurred at a precise moment in time. The second describes a state. The corresponding action took place some time before you entered the room – you are now describing the *state* the window was in when you entered the room.

 ser + past participle cannot be used to express the idea of 'to' or 'for' as the equivalent construction can in English – there is no direct Spanish equivalent of 'I was given a book' (a book was given *to* me). If you have to express such an idea in

Spanish, a different construction must be used (see below).

2. Use of the reflexive

An alternative method of expressing the passive in Spanish is to put the verb into the reflexive form. This is not a way of 'avoiding' the passive. On the contrary, this construction is interpreted as a genuine passive by Spaniards. On hearing the sentence:

el palacio se construyó en 1495
the palace was built in 1495

no Spaniard believes, even for the merest fraction of a second, that the palace actually built itself.

se dice con frecuencia que España es un país atrasado
it is often said that Spain is an underdeveloped country

las mercancías pueden mandarse por vía aérea
the goods can be sent by air freight

This construction can be used to express the idea of 'to' or 'for' by combining it with the appropriate form of the indirect object pronoun. However, this is very formal, and the construction using the third person plural of the active form would normally be preferred:

se me concedió un libro como premio/me concedieron un libro como premio
I was given a book as a prize

3. Use of the active forms of the verb

Although by no means rare, the passive forms are rather less used in Spanish than in English. It is always possible to use the active forms of the verb instead, and indeed this construction is necessary in certain circumstances. For example, 'I was given a book by the teacher' must be expressed in Spanish as **el profesor me dio un libro**.

el vendedor me ofreció un descuento del diez por ciento
I was offered a ten per cent discount by the salesman

If no agent is expressed, the third person plural form of the verb is used:

construyeron la central hace dos años
the power station was built two years ago

suprimirán todos los derechos de aduana
all customs duties will be abolished

5. SITUATING ACTIONS IN TIME

A. EXPRESSING TIME THROUGH VERBAL PHRASES

Verbal phrases of time are extremely useful in that they can be applied to any time, present, past or future, without any change in their form.

1. Preposition + infinitive

a) Prepositions of time + infinitive

Most verbal phrases of time are formed by a preposition of time followed by a verb in the infinitive. This construction is most often used when the subject of the infinitive is the same as the subject of the main verb of the sentence:

> **tomé un café antes de salir**
> I had a coffee before leaving

> **después de terminar mis deberes, escucharé la radio**
> after finishing my homework, I'll listen to the radio

In rather literary style, it is possible for the infinitive to have a different subject from the main verb, but this subject must be placed *after* the infinitive:

> **me cambié de ropa antes de llegar mis amigos**
> I changed before my friends arrived

b) *al* + infinitive

This is a very useful construction in Spanish, though it is more common in the written than in the spoken language. The closest English equivalent is 'on' + present participle. It expresses simultaneous actions in present, future or past time. It may even take its own subject which can be different from that of the main verb in the sentence:

> **al entrar vieron los otros salir**
> when they came in (on coming in) they saw the others leaving

> **al aparecer el cantante, el público aplaudió**
> when the singer appeared, the audience applauded

This construction can also have a causal meaning:

> **al tratarse de una emergencia, llamamos a un médico**
> since it was an emergency, we called a doctor

2. Preposition + past participle

In literary Spanish, both **después de** and **una vez** can be used with the past participle to form a phrase of time, though this construction is never used in the spoken language. The past participle agrees with the subject of the phrase:

> **después de terminadas las clases, volvimos a casa**
> after classes had finished we returned home

> **pagaremos la factura una vez entregadas las mercancías**
> we shall pay the invoice once the goods have been delivered

B. EXPRESSING PRESENT TIME

1. The use of the progressive forms of the present tense

The progressive forms consist of the appropriate form of **estar** (see pages 95, 224) followed by the present participle of the verb (verbs other than **estar** may also be used, as explained below). The use of the progressive forms in Spanish is by and large similar to their use in English, though they are less common in Spanish.

a) *estar* + present participle

The progressive forms present any action essentially as an *activity*. If something cannot be viewed as an activity, the progressive forms are not used in Spanish, for example:

> **me siento bien**
> I feel fine/I'm feeling fine

The progressive forms are used for an action which is seen as actually taking place:

> **no hagas tanto ruido, estoy escuchando la radio**
> don't make so much noise, I'm listening to the radio (I'm listening to it right now)

They are also used when an activity was begun in the past and the speaker still feels involved in it, even though it may not actually be happening right now:

estoy escribiendo una tesis sobre la política española
I'm writing a thesis on Spanish politics

I may not be writing it at this very minute (in fact, I may not have worked on it for several weeks), but I've already started and it's one of my current activities.

Compare

no me interrumpas, estoy pensando
don't interrupt me, I'm thinking

and

pienso que tienes razón
I think you're right

In the first sentence, 'thinking' is seen as an activity, in the second it is not.

Unlike English, the progressive forms in Spanish cannot be used to express intentions or to refer to future time. In such cases the standard present must be used:

vamos a España la semana que viene
we are going to Spain next week

They are also rather less widely used in questions and negative statements than their English counterparts:

¿por qué me miras así?
why are you looking at me like that?

no estudio griego
I'm not studying Greek

However, they can be used in such constructions if the idea of activity is to be emphasised:

no está cantando, está gritando
he isn't singing, he's shouting

b) *ir* + present participle

ir emphasises the gradual nature of an action, and also suggests its continuation into the future:

poco a poco nos vamos acostumbrando
we are slowly getting used to it (and will continue to do so)

la tasa de inflación va aumentando
the rate of inflation is rising (and will continue to rise)

c) *venir* + present participle

venir indicates that the action has continued from the past to the present. In fact, it points so clearly towards the past that it is often translated into English not by a present tense, but by a perfect tense:

las medidas que vienen adoptando son inútiles
the measures they have been adopting are pointless

los ejercicios que venimos haciendo no son interesantes
the exercises we've been doing aren't interesting

2. The general present

All other aspects of present time (repeated actions, general truths, and the like) are expressed by the standard forms of the present tense:

vamos a España todos los años
we go to Spain every year

la vida es dura
life is difficult

C. FUTURE TIME IN A MAIN CLAUSE

I. The committed and uncommitted future

Spanish differentiates between a committed future and an uncommitted future, and can also express a completed future. All of these variations on future time can also be expressed as futures in the past.

The committed future is expressed in Spanish by the *present* tense of the verb. The uncommitted future is expressed by the standard future tense. Note however that the present tense can only be used to refer to the future if there is some other word in the sentence which points clearly to future time or if the context clearly relates to the future.

The present tense can also be used to express a committed future in English (eg 'I'm leaving tomorrow', 'the ship sails next Tuesday'), but its use is less widespread than it is in Spanish.

a) present and future tenses

It must be stressed that the difference between these two futures is in no way related to the action being referred to, or to its distance from the speaker in time. It is quite possible to use both futures in relation to the same action. What determines the speaker's choice is his level of commitment to the action to which he is referring.

Compare the following:

lo hago mañana
lo haré mañana

Both of these mean 'I will do it tomorrow'. However, the first expresses a much more solid intention on the part of the speaker to actually do it.

The committed future is rather more common in the first person singular and plural ('I' and 'we'). However, it is also used with the third persons if the speaker is referring to an event about which he is absolutely certain:

los Reyes visitan Alemania la semana que viene
the King and Queen are visiting (will visit) Germany next week

el primer centenario de la democracia se celebra en 2077
the first centenary of democracy will take place in 2077

Both of these sentences could have been written using the future tense (**visitarán** and **celebrará**), but the speaker would in this way have indicated a certain remoteness from the event.

The present tense is also widely used in direct requests for immediate action:

¿me prestas veinte euros?
will you lend me twenty euros?

A less direct alternative is to use the verbs **poder** or **querer** followed by the infinitive:

¿puedes darme esas tijeras?
will you give me that pair of scissors?

¿quieras pasarme ese bolígrafo?
will you pass me that pen?

The use of the future tense in a request indicates that an immediate response is not being asked for:

¿me terminarás eso?
will you finish that for me? (at some point in the future)

b) *ir a* + infinitive

As in the English construction 'I am going to do that later', a committed future can also be expressed in Spanish using **ir a** followed by the infinitive, though it is rather less common than its English equivalent:

voy a estudiar medicina en la universidad
I am going to study medicine at university

van a ver esa película mañana
they're going to see that film tomorrow

c) points to note

⚠ An apparent future in English is sometimes not an expression of future time, but of willingness or refusal. Such ideas are expressed by the verbs *querer, negarse* or similar in Spanish.

For example:

se niega a tomar el desayuno por la mañana
he won't eat his breakfast in the morning

no quiere aceptar las reglas
he won't accept the rules

2. The completed future

The completed future is used to relate one action in the future to another action. It indicates that the action in question will have been completed by the time the second action applies. In a main clause, the completed future is expressed by the future perfect tense (for formation see page 203):

ya lo habré hecho cuando vuelvas
I'll already have done it when you come back

si llegamos tarde, ya se habrá marchado
if we arrive late he'll already have gone

It can also be used to indicate that the action will have been completed before a particular moment in time:

lo habré terminado para sábado
I will have finished it by Saturday

ya habrá venido
he will already have arrived

3. Future in the past

The following sentence gives an example of future in the past:

me dijo que iba a España la semana siguiente
he told me he was going to Spain the following week

He said **voy a España**, referring to the future. However, he said this in the past, so this is a case of future in the past.

In a main clause, future in the past is expressed either by the imperfect (committed future) or by the conditional (uncommitted future). However, the conditional is considerably more common in this construction than the imperfect:

me explicó que lo haría después de volver de sus vacaciones
he told me he would do it when he came back from his holidays

The conditional perfect expresses completed future in the past:

me aseguró que habría terminado el trabajo antes de medianoche
he assured me that he would have finished the work by midnight

77

D. THE FUTURE IN SUBORDINATE CLAUSES OF TIME

A subordinate clause of time is a clause which is introduced by a word or phrase of time such as **cuando, así que, antes de que** and the like.

⚠️ In a subordinate clause of time, future time is expressed by the appropriate tense of the subjunctive of the verb.

1. The future

The future is expressed by the present subjunctive. There is no distinction between a committed and an uncommitted future:

en cuanto llegue, se lo diré
as soon as he arrives, I will tell him

¿qué harás cuando termine tu contrato?
what will you do when your contract runs out?

Note that after the conjunctions **mientras** and **hasta que**, both meaning 'until', the word **no** is sometimes placed before the verb in the subordinate clause. It must be kept in mind that this does *not* make the verb negative. It is simply a quirk of style and does not affect the verb in any way:

no podemos hacerlo mientras no nos autoricen
we can't do it until they authorise us

no podemos mandar las mercancías hasta que no nos manden el pedido
we can't send the goods until they send us the order

2. The completed future

In a subordinate clause of time, the completed future is expressed by the perfect subjunctive:

podrás salir cuando hayas terminado tus deberes
you will be able to go out when you've finished your homework

insisto en que te quedes hasta que lo hayas hecho
I insist that you stay until you have done it

3. Future in the past

In a subordinate clause of time, future in the past is expressed by the imperfect subjunctive:

me aseguró que lo haría en cuanto llegara
he assured me that he would do it as soon as he arrived

nos informaron que los mandarían tan pronto como fuese posible
they informed us they would send them as soon as possible

E. PAST TIME

Spanish distinguishes between four levels of past time. These are:

past related to the present	expressed by	the perfect tense
the past in progress	expressed by	the imperfect tense
the completed past	expressed by	the preterite tense
the more distant past	expressed by	the pluperfect tense

It must be emphasised that the tense you choose is not dependent in any sense on the action to which you are referring. It is not dependent on the nature of the action (ie whether it is a single action or a repeated action), nor on the duration of the action (whether it lasted one second or a century), nor on its position in time (whether it happened a minute ago or a thousand years ago).

The tense you choose is determined *entirely* by your subjective perception of the action, particularly as regards its relation to present time and its relation to other actions to which you also refer.

1. Past related to the present

The perfect tense is used to refer to a past action which, though completed, the speaker sees as somehow related to the present. The relationship seen between the past action and present time is often indicated by the presence of related verbs or adverbs referring to present time. There is no limit to how long ago the action or series of actions may have taken place.

By and large, the uses of the perfect tense in Spanish and English coincide (but see 'SPECIAL CASES', page 83):

he visitado a muchos países europeos últimamente
I have visited many European countries recently

en los últimos diez años he aprendido diez idiomas extran-
jeros
in the last ten years I have learned ten foreign languages

2. The past in progress

The past in progress is expressed by the imperfect tense. An action
will be expressed in the imperfect tense if what is uppermost in the
speaker's mind is the fact that the action was in progress as opposed
to having been completed. There is no limit to how short or long the
action can be.

As a rule, the imperfect is used in Spanish where English would use
the imperfect progressive forms ('I was talking', 'he was writing' etc),
or forms such as 'I used to talk', and the like:

cuando era pequeño, iba todos los días a la piscina
when I was little, I went (used to go) to the swiming pool every
day

mientras Pepe veía la televisión, Juan hacía sus deberes
while Pepe was watching TV, Juan was doing his homework

⚠ In particular, if one action is presented as occurring while another is already in progress, the action 'occurring' will be expressed by the preterite, and the action in progress by the
imperfect:

mientras Juan llamaba a la puerta, el teléfono sonó
while Juan was knocking on the door, the telephone rang

Like the present tense, the imperfect also has a progressive form,
formed by the imperfect of **estar** plus the present participle of the
verb. This again presents the action primarily as an activity:

estábamos escuchando la radio cuando María entró
we were listening to the radio when María came in

⚠ Note that an apparent conditional in English is not always a
genuine conditional. In a sentence such as 'he would always
read his paper on the train', the 'would' is used to highlight
the fact that the action is seen extending over time. This is
translated by the *imperfect* in Spanish:

siempre leía su periódico en el tren
he would always read his paper on the train

3. The completed past

The completed past indicates that the aspect of the action (or series of actions) which is most important for the speaker is the fact that it has been completed. Whether the action was a repeated one, or whether it lasted a great length of time is unimportant. If completion is being stressed, the preterite will be used:

hizo esto cada día durante casi diez años
he did this every day for almost ten years

viví en España durante más de veinte años
I lived in Spain for over twenty years

It should be possible from these examples to see that it is perfectly feasible in Spanish to use either the imperfect or the preterite to refer to the same action, depending on how your subjective perception of the action changes. The following small narrative should illustrate the point:

Juan llamó a la puerta. Mientras llamaba a la puerta, el teléfono sonó. Mientras el teléfono sonaba, el bebé empezó a llorar.
Juan knocked at the door. While he was knocking at the door, the telephone rang. While the telephone was ringing, the baby started to cry.

4. Stylistic expressions of past time

a) Present for preterite

For reasons of style, past time is often expressed, particularly in written Spanish, by the present tense of the verb (the so-called historic present). This is used to lend a dramatic quality to a narrative. The historic present is also used in English, though to a lesser extent than in Spanish:

en el siglo quince sale Colón para América
in the fifteenth century Columbus set sail for America

It would also have been possible to use the present tense in English here.

b) Imperfect for preterite

Again in written Spanish, and once more for reasons of style and dramatic effect, an action is sometimes expressed in the imperfect where a preterite would have been the everyday choice:

> **en 1975 moría Franco y comenzaba la transición a la democracia**
> in 1975 Franco died and the transition to democracy began

5. The more distant past

a) Pluperfect

The more distant past is expressed by the pluperfect. An action belongs to the more distant past if the speaker wishes to indicate that it was completed *before* another action in the past:

> **llegué a las tres, pero Juan ya se había marchado**
> I got there at three, but Juan had already gone

> **no podía salir porque había perdido su llave**
> he couldn't go out because he had lost his key

b) Past anterior

In very literary Spanish, the more distant past in a subordinate clause of time is sometimes expressed by the past anterior:

> **cuando hubimos terminado, nos marchamos**
> when we had finished, we left

The past anterior is not used in spoken Spanish, and would give a distinctly literary flavour in contemporary written Spanish. The pluperfect or the simple preterite are usually used instead.

F. SPECIAL CASES

1. Actions on the limits of present and past time

a) The future limit

Actions which are about to take place are expressed in Spanish by the present tense of **estar a punto de** or less commonly **estar para** followed by the infinitive:

> **estoy a punto de empezar**
> I'm just about to start

el tren está para salir
the train is just about to leave

The imperfect is used when this idea is expressed in the past:

estaba a punto de salir cuando Juan llegó
I was just about to go out when Juan arrived

b) The past limit

Actions which have just taken place are expressed by the present tense of **acabar de** followed by the infinitive:

acabamos de ver el programa
we have just seen the programme

acaban de volver del cine
they've just come back from the cinema

Again, the imperfect is used if this idea is expressed in the past:

acabábamos de poner la tele cuando entraron
we had just switched on the telly when they came in

2. Actions continuing from one time to another

An action which starts in the past and continues right up to the present (and may well continue into the future) is considered in Spanish to belong to present time, and is therefore expressed by the present tense.

a) Present tense + *desde (hace)*

The length of time involved is introduced by **desde** if a starting point is indicated, or by **desde hace** if a length of time is stated. This is in complete contrast with English which uses the perfect tense with 'for':

¿desde cuándo esperas aquí?
how long have you been waiting here for?

espero aquí desde hace casi media hora
I've been waiting here for almost half an hour

estudio español desde 1986
I've been studying Spanish since 1986

estudio español desde hace dos años
I've been studying Spanish for two years

b) *hace* + present tense + *que*

Alternatively, the time span can be introduced by **hace** followed by a subordinate clause introduced by **que**:

> **hace media hora que espero aquí**
> I've been waiting here for half an hour

c) *llevar* + present participle

A further possibility is to use the present tense of the verb **llevar** followed by the present participle of the verb:

> **llevamos tres meses aprendiendo el ruso**
> we've been learning Russian for three months

d) Continuing actions in the past

When these actions are expressed in the past, all the constructions given above are used in the imperfect (as opposed to the pluperfect in English):

> **trabajaba desde hacía diez años como profesor**
> he had been working as a teacher for ten years

> **hacía veinte años que vivían en España**
> they'd been living in Spain for twenty years

> **llevaba quince minutos esperando**
> I had been waiting for fifteen minutes

6. DESCRIBING AN ACTION

A. THE ADVERB

For the formation of adverbs, see page 186.

⚠ It is essential to remember that adverbs are invariable – they never change their form whatever the circumstances in which they are used:

entraron lenta y silenciosamente
they came in slowly and quietly

tú trabajas mucho más rápidamente que yo
you work much more quickly than I do

1. Adverbial phrases

Rather than a simple adverb, Spanish very often uses adverbial phrases formed mostly with the nouns **manera** or **modo**:

esto nos afecta de una manera indirecta
this affects us indirectly

Noun/adjective combinations may also be used:

hablar en alta voz/en voz baja
to speak loudly/quietly

2. The use of adjectives

An attractive feature of Spanish is its ability to use adjectives with almost adverbial force. In this case the adjectives must agree with the *subject* of the verb:

vivieron felices durante muchos años
they lived happily for many years

le miramos atónitos
we looked at him in astonishment

B. VARYING THE FORCE OF AN ADVERB

1. Another adverb

As in English, one adverb may be used to vary the force of another:

lo hizo increíblemente bien
he did it unbelievably well

Adverbs of time and place can be emphasised by adding **mismo** after them. **mismo** is invariable in this usage:

aquí mismo, ahora mismo
right here, right now

2. Comparative and superlative

The comparative and superlative of adverbs are formed in exactly the same way as those of adjectives (see pages 166-168).

tú trabajas más rápidamente que yo
you work more quickly than I do

However, when a phrase of possibility is placed after a superlative, **lo** is always placed before **más** (this construction is rarely translated by a superlative in English):

lo hicimos lo más rápidamente posible
we did it as quickly as possible

7. RELATIONSHIPS BETWEEN ACTIONS

A. THE PRESENT PARTICIPLE

For the formation of the present participle, see page 201.

a) Expressing means

Only the present participle can be used in Spanish to express the idea of 'by doing', 'by going' and the like. No other construction is available:

> **gané este dinero trabajando durante las vacaciones**
> I earned this money by working during the holidays

> **conseguí hacerlo dejando otras cosas para más tarde**
> I managed to do it by leaving other things till later

⚠️ *por* followed by a present participle is not possible in Spanish. *por* followed by an infinitive does not express means, but *cause*, eg: *le sirvieron primero por ser cliente regular* (they served him first because he was a regular customer).

b) Expressing simultaneous action

The present participle is widely used to express an action taking place simultaneously with another:

> **entró corriendo**
> he rushed in (he came in running)

> **'está bien', dijo sonriendo**
> 'OK', he said smiling

This construction is often the only way of expressing certain phrasal verbs of motion in English (see 'he rushed in' above):

> **pasó corriendo**
> he ran past

⚠️ The present participle is invariable in Spanish, in other words it *never* changes its form, irrespective of the gender or number of the subject of the verb:

> **las chicas salieron corriendo**
> the girls rushed out

After a verb of perception (seeing, hearing etc), the present participle may be replaced by an infinitive. In fact this construction is, if anything, more common than the use of the present participle:

> **vi a mi hermano atravesando/atravesar la calle**
> I saw my brother crossing the street

c) Cause

A present participle can also express cause:

> **estando en Madrid, decidí visitar a mi amigo**
> since I was in Madrid, I decided to call on my friend

> **no sabiendo como continuar, decidió pedir ayuda**
> not knowing how to proceed, he decided to ask for help

d) Continuation

The present participle is used with the verbs **seguir** and (less frequently) **continuar** to express the continuation of an action:

> **siguió trabajando a pesar de todo**
> he went on working in spite of everything

> **continuaron repitiendo la misma cosa**
> they kept on repeating the same thing

B. INFINITIVE OR SUBORDINATE CLAUSE?

When two verbs are linked in Spanish, you must choose whether to put the second verb into the infinitive form (preceded or not by a preposition) or whether to put it into a subordinate clause introduced by **que**.

If the subject of both verbs is the same, in most cases you can use the simple infinitive. If the subjects are different, you must, with very few exceptions, put the second verb into a subordinate clause (and frequently also into the subjunctive). Compare:

1. Same subject

> **quiero hacerlo**
> I want to do it

I am not only the person 'wanting', I am also the person who wants 'to do' it. No-one else is involved.

> **entré sin verle**
> I came in without seeing him
>
> *I* came in, and *I* did not see him.

Spanish goes further in the use of this construction than English does:

> **creyó estar soñando**
> he thought he was dreaming

> **creemos poder hacerlo**
> we think we can do it

2. Different subjects

Compare the sentences given above with:

> **quiero que tú lo hagas**
> I want you to do it

There are two people involved here. *I* 'want', but *you* are the person who is 'to do'.

> **entré sin que él me viera**
> I came in without him seeing me
>
> *I* came in, but *he* did not see me.

3. Verbs where the infinitive may take a different subject

There are a small number of verbs with which the subject of a following infinitive may be different from that of the first verb, see page 234:

> **me dejaron entrar**
> they let me come in

4. Infinitives after prepositions

The most obvious exceptions to the general 'rule' are phrases consisting of a preposition followed by an infinitive. In this case the infinitive may have a subject which is different from that of the main verb, but this subject is always placed *after* the infinitive:

quiero hacerlo antes de llegar los otros
I want to do it before the others arrive

However, such expressions are rather literary in style, and even in these cases Spaniards will often prefer to use a subordinate clause:

quiero hacerlo antes de que lleguen los otros
I want to do it before the others arrive

C. THE INFINITIVE

1. verb + preposition + infinitive

A verb used in the infinitive after another verb can either appear on its own, or can be introduced by one of a wide range of prepositions. There are few truly useful rules for predicting which preposition is to be used, and in most cases the preposition required must simply be learned through observation and practice.

For a list of the prepositions required by some common verbs, see pages 230-233.

2. adjective + infinitive

It may be useful at this point to note the following very common construction in Spanish:

(indirect object +) verb + adjective + infinitive

The indirect object may be a pronoun or a noun. The verb may be **ser, parecer, resultar** or similar. A wide range of adjectives is available and any verb can be used in the infinitive after the adjective:

me es difícil creer lo que estás diciendo
it's difficult for me to believe what you're saying

nos parece absurdo proponer tal cosa
it seems absurd to us to suggest such a thing

The same construction can be used with various verbs of 'considering', but in this case there is no indirect object:

encuentro difícil aceptar esto
I find it difficult to accept this

consideramos poco aconsejable continuar así
we consider it inadvisable to continue in this way

3. adjective + *de* + infinitive

If the adjective is not part of an impersonal expression, but relates to an identifiable thing or things already stated in the sentence, it is then followed by **de** + infinitive. The adjective agrees with the thing being described:

estos ejercicios son fáciles de hacer
these exercises are easy to do

encuentro este libro difícil de leer
I find this book difficult to read

4. *que* + infinitive

Note that **que** is placed before the infinitive in expressions such as the following:

tengo una factura que pagar
I've got a bill to pay

nos queda mucho trabajo que hacer
we still have lots of work to do

D. THE SUBORDINATE CLAUSE: INDICATIVE OR SUBJUNCTIVE?

The verb in a subordinate clause will be either in the indicative or in the subjunctive. Since the subjunctive has all but disappeared in English, this can be a difficult concept for the learner of Spanish to grasp.

However, the subjunctive is very widely used in Spanish, and there is really little point in learning 'ways to avoid the subjunctive'. The best approach is to try to understand what the indicative and the subjunctive are used to express.

In general terms the indicative is used to introduce actions which the speaker *believes* to be clear and material statements of fact. The subjunctive, on the other hand, is used if the speaker feels that the statements are untrue, or if he feels unable in some way to guarantee that they will prove to be true, or if, rather than simply stating them, he is expressing an emotional reaction to them. This can be due to a variety of reasons, for example because:

- he doubts, disbelieves or denies the statements;
- the actions have not yet taken place: they belong to the future and therefore cannot be guaranteed;
- the actions are expressed as conditions which are not or cannot be fulfilled;
- the actions are introduced by a statement of emotion.

It is important to realise that there is no single set of rules for the use of the subjunctive in Spanish. For example, different rules apply when referring to future time than when expressing a condition or expressing emotion, and so on. Each case must be dealt with independently.

In general, however, *any* impersonal expression which does not introduce a straightforward statement of fact will be followed by the subjunctive:

> **es posible/probable/una pena que esté allí**
> it's possible/probable/a shame that he'll be there

E. INDIRECT OR REPORTED SPEECH

The indicative is used exclusively for statements and questions in indirect speech in Spanish, since the speaker is simply relating actions which he presents as having actually taken place. The tenses used in Spanish correspond exactly to those used in English.

⚠ Contrary to English usage, *all* indirect statements must be introduced by *que* in Spanish. Omission of the *que* would be confusing for your Spanish listener:

> **dijo que vendría más tarde**
> he said (that) he would come later

> **me explicó que ya lo habían hecho**
> he explained to me that they had already done it

> **le contesté que no sería posible**
> I told him in reply that it wouldn't be possible

8. SOME SPECIAL VERBS

A. TO BE

1. *ser* and *estar*

There are two verbs 'to be' in Spanish, **ser** and **estar**. In general terms it can be said that:

> **ser** is used to *define* things.
> **estar** is used to describe characteristics which could change without affecting the essential definition of the thing.

It is not necessarily the case that **ser** describes characteristics which are permanent and **estar** does not. The question of *definition* is much more important in deciding which verb to use.

The uses of these verbs can be divided into three categories:

> cases where **ser** is obligatory;
> cases where **estar** is obligatory;
> cases where either is possible.

These can be summarized as follows:

a) Cases where *ser* is obligatory

  (i) **When the verb 'to be' is followed by a noun, *ser* must be used, since a noun always provides at least a partial definition of the object in question**

  Typical examples would include professions, nationality or origin, names, statements of possession, materials from which something is made, expressions of time and almost all impersonal expressions:

> **mi padre es minero**
> my father is a miner

  In Spanish, your occupation is considered to be at least part of your 'definition'. The fact that your father may lose his job one day and no longer be a miner (or that it may even be a temporary job) does not alter this in any way.

no somos portugueses, somos españoles
we are not Portuguese, we are Spaniards

España es un país interesante
Spain is an interesting country

Note that **es** goes with the noun **país** and not the adjective
interesante. Your interest in Spain may diminish later, but it will
continue to be a country.

este coche es de mi madre
this car is my mother's

la mesa es de madera
the table is made of wood

¿qué hora es? – son las dos de la tarde
what time is it? – it's two in the afternoon

es necesario hacerlo ahora mismo
it's necessary to do it right now

(ii) **ser** + adjectives describing defining characteristics

yo creo que el español es muy fácil de aprender
I think that Spanish is easy to learn

The fact that others might disagree, or that you might later
change your mind, is irrelevant. For the time being 'easy' is part of
your definition of Spanish.

Note that colour and size are usually considered to be defining
characteristics in Spanish:

la plaza de toros es muy grande
the bull ring is very large

las paredes eran blancas
the walls were white

They may be painted a different colour later, but for the time
being 'being white' is part of their definition.

If the colour is not seen as a defining characteristic, a different
construction (and in some cases a different adjective) is likely to
be used:

tenía los ojos enrojecidos
his eyes were red

(iii) **ser** is used with the past participle to express the passive in Spanish (for an explanation of the passive, see pages 69-70):

>**la cosecha fue destruida por las heladas**
>the crop was destroyed by the frosts

b) Cases where **estar** is obligatory

(i) **estar** must be used when referring to position, whether of persons or things, whether temporary or permanent. The position of an object, however permanent, is not seen as part of its definition in Spanish:

>**estuve en la playa ayer**
>I was at the beach yesterday

>**los pirineos están en la frontera entre España y Francia**
>the Pyrenees are on the frontier between Spain and France

They're likely to remain there for some time, but (in theory at least) the Pyrenees would still be the Pyrenees even if they turned up somewhere else.

Note that **estar** is used to express not only physical position, but also mental position and in fact position of any kind:

>**estamos a favor de las negociaciones**
>we are in favour of negotiations

>**estamos en contra de la política del gobierno**
>we are against the government's policy

>**el problem está en el precio**
>the problem is (lies) in the price

(ii) **estar** is used with the present participle of the verb to form the progressive forms in Spanish:

>**¿qué estás haciendo? – estoy leyendo una revista española**
>what are you doing? – I'm reading a Spanish magazine

>**estábamos escuchando la radio cuando Juan entró**
>we were listening to the radio when Juan came in

(iii) **estar** is typically used with adjectives to express moods and other temporary characteristics:

>**estoy furioso contigo**
>I'm furious with you

estoy muy cansado, he trabajado mucho hoy
I'm very tired, I've worked a lot today

'Being tired' is unlikely to be part of your definition. You will still be the same person when you have recovered your energy.

c) Cases where either is possible

When used with many other adjectives, either **ser** or **estar** may be possible. Which you choose will depend on the extent to which you feel that:

(i) the adjective defines the thing in question, for however short a time this definition might apply, in which case you will use **ser**:

   María es muy guapa
   María is very pretty

(ii) the adjective merely describes a characteristic of the thing in question, in which case you will use **estar**:

   María está muy guapa hoy
   María is looking very pretty today

Compare:

   mi profesor es muy pesado
   my teacher is very boring

   estás muy pesado hoy
   you're being a real bore today

   eres tonto
   you're silly

   estás tonto
   you're being silly

(iii) In a negative command with adjectives like **pesado** and **tonto**, however, only **ser** would be used:

   no seas tonto
   don't be silly

Since silliness is not seen here as a mood in Spanish, **estar** cannot be used. With adjectives of mood, however, **estar** would be used:

   no estés furioso
   don't be furious

d) Some special cases

A few adjectives actually have different meanings when used with **ser** and **estar**:

	ser	*estar*
bueno	good	well (in good health)
cansado	tiring (person)	tired
consciente	aware	conscious (awake, not unconscious)
grave	serious	seriously ill
listo	clever	ready
malo	bad	ill (in poor health)
moreno	dark-haired	suntanned
pesado	heavy (thing)	boring (person)
rico	rich	cute (child), nice (food)
seguro	sure (thing) safe (thing)	sure, certain (person),
verde	green	unripe

Other changes are more subtle. Compare **ser viejo** (to be old) with **estar viejo** (to look older than you are), **ser pequeño** (to be small) with **estar pequeño** (to be small for your age).

Note that, when referring to happiness, Spaniards invariably say **estar contento**, but both **ser feliz** and **estar feliz** are possible, depending on whether it refers to a defining characteristic or a mood.

2. *encontrarse, hallarse, verse, quedar*

encontrarse and **hallarse** can sometimes replace **estar**:

> **el lago se encuentra detrás de la casa**
> the lake is behind the house

> **no me encuentro bien hoy**
> I don't feel well today

Both **verse** and **quedar** can replace **ser** when used with a past participle. **verse** is almost always used in preference to **ser** with **obligado**:

> **el gobierno se vio obligado a retirar su propuesta**
> the government was forced to withdraw its proposal

> **la casa quedó completamente destruida**
> the house was completely destroyed

3. *haber*

'there is' and 'there are' are expressed in Spanish by **hay**. **hay** is in fact the third person singular of the present tense of **haber** – **ha** – with the obsolete word **y** (there) tagged on at the end:

hay mucha gente en la playa
there are lots of people on the beach

It is important to realize that this is in fact part of the verb **haber** since it is the standard parts of **haber** which are used in all other tenses and constructions:

había por lo menos cincuenta personas en la habitación
there were at least fifty people in the room

Note that the singular form is always used, even when referring to a plural noun (**personas**). Note also the following infinitive construction:

debe haber otra manera de abordar el problema
there must be another way of approaching the problem

'there must be' is *never* **debe ser** or **debe estar**, which mean 'it must be'. However, in the following construction the appropriate forms of **ser** and **estar** are indeed used:

¿cuántos sois? – somos siete
how many of you are there? – there are seven of us

estábamos cinco en la cocina
there were five of us in the kitchen

4. *deber*

'is to', 'was to' and the like, indicating that something is due to happen or was supposed to happen, are translated by the present or imperfect of **deber**:

el trabajo debía empezar el día cinco
work was to begin on the fifth

la factura debe pagarse a la entrega de las mercancías
the invoice is to be paid on delivery of the goods

5. General weather conditions

Most descriptions of general weather conditions are made using the verbs **hacer** and **haber**:

¿qué tiempo hace?	what's the weather like?
hace frío/calor	it's cold/warm
hace buen/mal tiempo	the weather is fine/bad
hace mucho sol	it's very sunny
hace/hay mucho viento	it's very windy
hay neblina	it's misty
había luna	the moon was shining

Since Spanish uses nouns here as opposed to the English adjectives, the idea of 'very' is expressed by the appropriate form of **mucho** (or any other appropriate adjective or adjectival clause):

hace mucho calor
it's very hot

está haciendo un frío que pela
it's bitingly cold

Some weather conditions are expressed simply by a verb:

llueve, está lloviendo	it's raining
nieva, está nevando	it's snowing
hiela, está helando	it's freezing
tronaba, estaba tronando	there was a lot of thunder

6. Personal descriptions

Many personal descriptions are made using the verb **tener**:

tengo hambre/sed	I'm hungry/thirsty
tiene sueño/miedo	he's sleepy/afraid
tenemos frío/calor	we're cold/hot
tengo ganas de ir	I'm keen to go
hemos tenido suerte	we were lucky

Again, since Spanish uses nouns here, 'very' is expressed by **mucho** or a similar adjective:

tenemos mucho frío
we are very cold

B. TO BECOME

There is no single verb equivalent to 'to become' in Spanish. How you translate this idea will depend on its context:

a) 'become' with an adjective

With an adjective, 'become' is usually expressed by **hacerse**, **ponerse** or **volverse**. **ponerse** indicates a temporary change, **volverse** indicates a longer-lasting one:

se puso furioso cuando oyó esta noticia
he became furious when he heard this piece of news

se hacía oscuro fuera
it was becoming dark outside

se volvió muy antipático
he became very unfriendly

b) 'become' with a noun

With a noun, 'become' is usually expressed by **hacerse** or **convertirse en**:

esta empresa se ha convertido en la más importante de España
this firm has become Spain's leading company

se hizo diputado a los 30 años de edad
he became an MP at the age of 30

If there is an idea of achievement, **llegar a ser** can also be used:

llegó a ser presidente a pesar de todas las dificultades
he became president despite all the difficulties

c) Other verbs

In many cases where the verb 'become' would be used in English, Spanish would choose a different approach altogether:

España ingresó en el Mercado Común en 1986
Spain became a member of the Common Market in 1986

C. TO HAVE

1. *tener* and *haber*

a) *tener*

tener expresses 'to have' in the sense of 'to possess':

¿tienes coche?
do you have a car?

¿cuánto dinero tienes?
how much money do you have?

contar con and **disponer de** are also often used to express 'to have', less in the sense of 'to own' but 'to have at one's disposal':

España cuenta con nueve centrales nucleares
Spain has nine nuclear power stations

See also the following section.

b) *haber*

haber is used with the participle to form the compound tenses of verbs (see pages 203-4 and 207-8).

⚠ Note that in these constructions the past participle *never* changes its form, irrespective of the number and gender of either the subject or the object of the verb:

¿habéis visto la última película de Almodóvar?
have you seen Almodóvar's latest film?

visto is unaffected by the fact that **habéis** is plural (**vosotros**) or that **película** is feminine.

tener is sometimes used with the participle to express an idea similar to those of the compound tenses. This construction cannot be used unless the verb has an object, and the past participle agrees with the object of the verb:

ya tengo escritas las cartas
I have written the letters

The following two usages are particularly common:

tenemos pensado ir a jugar al tenis
we intend to go and play tennis

tengo entendido que ha sido un éxito
I understand it was a success

2. *hacer*

Note that phrases of the type 'to have a house built', 'to have the room painted' etc are expressed in Spanish using the verb **hacer**. The second verb goes into the infinitive, unlike English where the past participle is used:

se hicieron construir una casa en el campo
they had a house built in the country

haremos ejecutar su pedido cuanto antes
we will have your order carried out as soon as possible

D. TO KNOW

There are two verbs 'to know' in Spanish, **conocer** and **saber**. Conocer means to know in the sense of 'to be familiar with', 'to be acquainted with'. **Saber** is to know in a mental or intellectual sense, to have learned or understood, to know something to be a fact. Compare the following:

¿conoces la teoría de la relatividad?
do you know the theory of relativity?

Have you heard of the theory of relativity? You may be able to answer **sí** to this question without having any idea what the theory means.

¿te sabes la teoría de la relatividad?
do you know the theory of relativity?

Do you understand the theory of relativity? Could you explain it?

conocer is invariably used with people, countries and the like:

conozco muy bien a Pedro
I know Pedro very well

no conozco España
I don't know Spain (I've never been there)

saber is invariably used with noun clauses:

sé lo que estás pensando
I know what you're thinking

no sé como ocurrió esto
I don't know how this happened

E. ACTIONS CONSIDERED IMPERSONAL IN SPANISH

A number of commonly expressed actions take a personal subject in English, but are expressed by an impersonal construction in Spanish. As a result, what is considered to be the object of the verb in English becomes the subject of the Spanish verb, and it is with this subject that the verb agrees. The subject of the English verb is then expressed by an indirect object in Spanish.

The commonest of these verbs are:

verb	meaning	used to translate
faltar	to be absent	not to have enough of, to need, to be left
gustar	to please	to like
parecer	to seem	to think
quedar	to remain	to have ... left
sobrar	to exist in greater amounts than required	to have too much of, to have ... left

a) *faltar*

> **me faltan diez euros**
> I'm ten euros short

> **faltan dos horas**
> there are two hours left

hacer falta is also used with the same meaning:

> **me hace falta más tiempo**
> I need more time

b) *gustar*

⚠ It must always be remembered that *gustar* does not actually mean 'to like', it means 'to please'. Consequently the English object becomes the Spanish subject, and the English subject becomes the Spanish indirect object. *gustar* agrees in number with the thing 'liked':

> **a Juan no le gustan estos caramelos**
> Juan does not like these sweets (literally, the sweets are not pleasing to Juan)

nos gusta mucho la tortilla española
we like Spanish omelette very much

Although forms such as **gusto** or **gustamos** do occur, they are relatively infrequent. If you are tempted to use one of these forms, make sure you have not misunderstood how to use **gustar**.

If 'like' does not include the idea of 'please', **gustar** is not used:

quisiera más información sobre este hotel
I would like more information about this hotel

It is not that this information would be pleasing to you (it might in fact be unpleasant). You are simply asking for information.

c) *parecer*

¿qué te parece mi nuevo coche? – me parece estupendo
what do you think of my new car? – I think it's great

esa idea me parece ridícula
I find that idea ridiculous

d) *quedar*

¿cuánto dinero te queda?
how much money do you have left?

nos quedaban dos horas
we had two hours left

e) *sobrar*

aquí sobran jefes y faltan guerreros
there are too many chiefs here and not enough Indians

me sobran veinte euros
I have twenty euros left

nos sobra tiempo
we've got loads of time

Note also the phrase:

basta y sobra
there's more than enough

9. COMMUNICATING IN SPANISH

A. BELIEF/DISBELIEF/DOUBT/DENIAL

Statements of belief in the positive, however vague, are followed by the verb in the indicative *irrespective of whether the statement is actually true in fact*. The fact that the statement is presented as being true is sufficient to require the indicative to be used:

> **tenía la impresión de que ya te habías marchado**
> I was under the impression you'd already left

The fact that you're still here is irrelevant.

> **supongo que vendrá**
> I suppose he'll come

> **creo que tienes razón**
> I think you're right

Note that Spanish uses **que** in expressions such as the following:

> **creo que sí**
> I think so

> **creo que no**
> I don't think so

1. Direct questions

In the case of a direct question, either the indicative or the subjunctive may be used. The subjunctive expresses actual doubt on the part of the speaker. If the speaker is simply unsure, the indicative is used. In usage the indicative is more common in this construction than the subjunctive.

> **¿crees que Juan vendrá mañana?**
> do you think that Juan will come tomorrow?

> **¿crees que Juan venga?**
> do you think that Juan will come? (I suspect he won't)

2. Verbs of belief in the negative, or verbs of doubting or denying in the affirmative

If a verb of belief is used in the negative, or if a verb of doubting or denying is used in the affirmative, the verb in the subordinate clause is in the subjunctive:

> **no creo que sea justo decir eso**
> I don't think it's fair to say that

> **dudo que consiga hacerlo**
> I doubt that he'll manage to do it

> **niego absolutamente que sea así**
> I absolutely deny that this is the case

It is important to differentiate between statements of opinion and indirect speech. In the latter the indicative is *always* used whether the introductory verb is positive or negative:

> **yo no digo que el Gobierno tenga razón**
> I'm not saying that the Government is right

> **yo no dije que Juan había llegado**
> I didn't say that Juan had arrived

The first of these is a statement of opinion. The second is a narrative of events which happened (or did not happen) in the past.

3. Verbs of doubting or denying in the negative

If a verb of doubting or denying is used in the negative, either the subjunctive or the indicative may be used. The indicative is used if the speaker is very positive about what is being said:

> **no dudo que tengas/tienes razón**

The use of **tengas** implies something like 'I don't doubt that you might be right', whereas the use of **tienes** means 'I am quite sure that you are right'.

> **no niego que sea/es posible hacerlo**
> I don't deny that it might be/is possible to do it

B. CONDITIONS

Conditions in Spanish can be divided into two large groups, each of which requires a different use of the verb:

Type	Definition	Verb
open-ended conditions	those which may or may not be fulfilled, those whose outcome has not yet been decided	indicative
unfulfilled conditions	those which are presented as unfulfilled, those which the speaker believes not to be the case or not to have been carried out	subjunctive

You must be clear which kind of condition you are dealing with, since the rules for expressing the different kinds of conditions are markedly different from each other.

– If the condition is perceived as open-ended in the sense that it may or may not be fulfilled, the indicative is used (with one exception – see open-ended conditions of future time below):

> **si llueve mañana, iré al cine**
> if it rains tomorrow, I'll go to the cinema

– If the condition is perceived as genuinely unreal in the sense that it has not been or cannot be fulfilled, the subjunctive is used in the **si** clause:

> **si fuera rico, no trabajaría**
> if I was rich, I wouldn't work

Do not confuse conditions with the conditional tenses. The *tenses* used in Spanish are in all cases identical to English. The differences between the two languages relate to the uses of the indicative and the subjunctive.

1. Open-ended conditions

Open-ended conditions in Spanish can relate to present, future or past time. They are expressed as follows:

a) Present time

Open-ended conditions relating to present time are expressed in Spanish by the present indicative. The verb in the main clause is usually in the present indicative or sometimes in the imperative:

> **si quieres evitar más problemas, cállate**
> if you want to avoid further problems, keep quiet

ie if you want to avoid problems *now*. You may choose either to avoid the problems or not.

> **si no te gusta éste, puedes tomar otro**
> if you don't like this one, you can take another

You may in fact like this one, in which case you won't take another.

b) Future time

Conditions relating to future time are by definition open-ended since their outcome cannot yet be known. Future conditions are expressed in Spanish by the present indicative. The verb in the main clause is usually future (committed or uncommitted):

> **si vuelves borracho, te mato**
> if you come home drunk I'll kill you

> **si no lo termino a tiempo, no podré salir**
> if I don't finish in time, I won't be able to go out

> **si lo haces, te doy mil euros**
> if you do it, I'll give you a thousand euros

⚠ However, an open-ended condition of future time *may* take the imperfect subjunctive if the speaker wishes to present it as a more remote possibility. The conditional is then used in the main clause:

> **si hicieras eso, los otros se enfadarían**
> if you were to do that, the others would be annoyed

This is a more remote condition than:

> **si haces eso, los otros se enfadarán**
> if you do that the others will be annoyed

but both refer to future time.

c) Past time

Open-ended conditions relating to past time take the same tense of the verb as in English:

> **si no ha hecho sus deberes, no podrá salir**
> if he hasn't done his homework, he won't be able to go out

He may indeed have done it. You are expressing this condition precisely because you are unsure. The condition may indeed have been fulfilled.

si lo utilizó, sabrá como funciona
if he used it, he'll know how it works

You are unable to say for certain whether he used it or not.

si no llovía, ¿por qué estás mojado?
if it wasn't raining, why are you wet?

2. Unfulfilled conditions

Unfulfilled conditions relate only to present time and past time.

a) Present time

Unfulfilled conditions relating to present time are expressed in Spanish by the imperfect subjunctive. Either form of the imperfect subjunctive may be used. The verb in the main clause is usually, though not always, in the conditional:

si Juan estuviera aquí, hablaría con él
if Juan was here I'd speak to him

ie if he was here *now*. You would not be saying this unless you believed that he was *not* there. The fact that he might be there is irrelevant. In your opinion this is an unfulfilled condition.

si tuviera dinero, iría a España
if I had money, I'd go to Spain

si fuera más barato, lo compraríamos
if it was cheaper, we'd buy it

Again, you are only saying this because you do not believe you have enough money.

b) The completed past

Unfulfilled conditions relating to the completed past are expressed in Spanish by the pluperfect subjunctive (either the **hubiera** or the **hubiese** forms). They are unfulfilled in that they refer to events which did not in fact take place. The verb in the main clause is usually in the conditional perfect or less commonly in the pluperfect subjunctive (**hubiera** forms):

si lo hubiéramos sabido, habríamos venido
if we had known, we would have come

We didn't know, so we didn't come.

si hubieras llegado a tiempo, le habrías visto
if you'd arrived on time, you'd have seen him

3. *como* + present subjunctive

In colloquial Spanish, **como** + present subjunctive is frequently used to express a condition of future time. The subjunctive is *always* used in this construction even though the condition is open-ended:

como llegues tarde me enfado
if you arrive late I'll be angry

como is not interchangeable with **si** in all cases. If you are unsure, it is always safer to use **si**.

4. *de* + infinitive

In formal written Spanish, a condition is sometimes expressed by the preposition **de** followed by the infinitive:

de continuar así, suspenderá el examen
if he goes on like this, he'll fail the exam

For past time the perfect infinitive is used:

de haberlo sabido, no habría venido
if I had known I wouldn't have come

5. Negative conditions

Any condition can be made negative by simply placing **no** before the verb in the conditional clause or by using some other negative:

si no haces tus deberes, no podrás salir
if you don't do your homework, you won't be able to go out

However, negative conditions can also be expressed either by **a menos que** or more formally by **a no ser que**. Both mean 'unless', and are always followed by the appropriate tense of the subjunctive:

saldremos mañana a menos que llueva/a no ser que llueva
we'll go out tomorrow unless it rains

6. Conditions introduced by conditional conjunctions

Conditional clauses introduced by conditional conjunctions always have their verb in the subjunctive. The most common of these conjunctions are:

en caso de que	if
a condición de que	on condition that, provided that
con tal que	so long as
siempre que	so long as

en caso de que venga, se lo diré
if he comes, I'll tell him

puedes salir con tal que prometas volver antes de media-noche
you can go out so long as you promise to be home by midnight

los compraremos a condición de que sean baratos
we'll buy them provided they're cheap

7. Points to note

Not all conditions are introduced in English by 'if'. Other forms are sometimes used. This choice is not available in Spanish. If you are translating, you must use **si** (or the **de** + infinitive construction) no matter what the form of the English condition:

had I known, I would have told you
si lo hubiera sabido/de haberlo sabido, te lo habría dicho

were this the case, I would agree with you
si fuera así/de ser así, estaría de acuerdo contigo

If **si** means 'whenever', it introduces a clause of time and only the indicatives are used:

si tenía mucho que hacer, nunca salía antes de las nueve
if I had a lot to do, I never went out before nine

If **si** means 'whether', it introduces an indirect question and again the indicative is used:

me preguntó si lo haría
he asked me if (ie whether) I would do it

no sé si vendrá
I don't know if he'll come

C. CONTRADICTING A PREVIOUS STATEMENT

1. *pero* and *sino*

The idea of 'but' is expressed by two words in Spanish, **pero** and **sino**. **sino** is used to introduce a statement which contradicts a previous one. **pero** *cannot* be used in such situations:

> **el coche es grande pero no cuesta mucho**
> the car is big but it doesn't cost a lot

> **el coche no es verde, sino rojo**
> the car isn't green, but red

> **mi padre no es médico, sino profesor**
> my father isn't a doctor, but a teacher

If the contradiction is contained in a clause, **sino que** is used:

> **no se come, sino que se bebe**
> you don't eat it, you drink it

If the intention is not to contradict, but to emphasise a following affirmation, **pero sí** is used:

> **no conozco a España, pero sí conozco a Portugal**
> I don't know Spain, but I do know Portugal

> **no es moderno, pero sí interesante**
> it isn't modern, but it is interesting

2. *no es que, no porque*

Both of these expressions are followed by a verb in the subjunctive:

> **no es que no tenga confianza en ti**
> it's not that I don't trust you

> **lo hace no porque quiera hacerlo, sino porque no tiene más remedio**
> he does it not because he wants to, but because he has no choice

D. DISCOUNTING A DIFFICULTY

1. 'despite'

The simplest way of discounting a difficulty is to use the compound preposition **a pesar de** followed by the noun. In written Spanish, **pese a** is sometimes used instead of **a pesar de**:

> **decidió continuar a pesar de las dificultades**
> he decided to continue in spite of the difficulties

2. 'although'

The idea of 'although' can be expressed either by **aunque** or **a pesar de que**. In written Spanish **si bien** is a fairly frequent alternative to **aunque**, though it is little used in the spoken language.

aunque may be followed by either the indicative or the subjunctive, depending on the speaker's perception of the difficulty. The indicative suggests a real difficulty, whereas the subjunctive implies a potential difficulty:

> **no se ha puesto el abrigo aunque hace mucho frío**
> he hasn't put on his coat even though it's very cold

> **continuaremos aunque haya problemas**
> we'll continue even though there may be problems

a pesar de que is used mostly with reference to present and past time and is therefore usually followed by the indicative:

> **lo hizo a pesar de que nadie estaba de acuerdo con él**
> he did it even though nobody agreed with him

si bien is always followed by the indicative:

> **se cambiará la ley, si bien hay mucha oposición**
> the law will be changed although there is a lot of opposition

In written Spanish, **con** + infinitive is sometimes used to express the idea of 'although', though this is not a common usage:

> **con ser pobres, viven bien**
> although they're poor, they live well

3. 'however'/'no matter how' + adjective or adverb + verb

This idea is expressed as follows in Spanish: **por** + adjective/adverb + **que** + verb in the subjunctive:

> **las compraremos, por caras que sean**
> we'll buy them, however expensive they are (might be)

> **no dejaré de hacerlo, por difícil que parezca**
> I won't fail to do it, no matter how difficult it might seem

> **por bien que lo haga, no lo aceptaré**
> however well she does it, I won't accept it

4. 'whatever', 'however', 'wherever' etc + verb

There are two ways of expressing this idea in Spanish:

a) verb in the subjunctive + relative + verb in the subjunctive. The same verb is repeated in this construction:

> **lo compraremos, cueste lo que cueste**
> we'll buy it, whatever it costs

> **no quiero verle, sea quien sea**
> I don't want to see him, whoever he is (might be)

> **le encontraremos, esté donde esté**
> we'll find him, wherever he is (might be)

b) indefinite pronoun or adjective + **que** + verb in the subjunctive. The indefinite pronouns and adjectives are formed by adding **-quiera** to the end of the corresponding relative (there is no equivalent form for **lo que**):

> **no quiero verle, quienquiera que sea**
> I don't want to see him, whoever he is (might be)

> **le encontraremos, dondequiera que esté**
> we'll find him, wherever he is (might be)

If the pronoun or adjective is to be made plural, it is the part before the **-quiera** which becomes plural while **-quiera** itself remains unchanged:

> **no quiero verlos, quienesquiera que sean**
> I don't want to see them, whoever they are

E. EMOTION/FEAR/HOPE/REGRET

1. Emotion

a) One subject

An expression of emotion where there is only one subject is followed by the verb in the infinitive:

estamos muy contentos de veros
we are very pleased to see you

We are pleased, and we see you – there is only one subject.

espero poder hablar con él mañana
I hope to be able to speak to him tomorrow

b) More than one subject

However, if more than one subject is involved, the expression of emotion is followed by a verb in the subjunctive. The range of emotions goes from approval to disapproval, pleasure to anger and the like:

me alegra que pienses así
I'm glad you feel that way

le molestó que no estuviéramos de acuerdo con él
it annoyed him that we did not agree with him

The expression of emotion may be implicit in an impersonal construction:

es triste/lógico/natural/una pena que sea así
it's sad/logical/natural/a shame that it should be like this

All of these expressions imply an emotional reaction (however implicit) on the speaker's part rather than a straightforward statement of fact.

Note that the verb is in the subjunctive only if it belongs to a clause introduced by **que** which is *directly* dependent on the expression of emotion. If the clause is introduced by **porque** or if it is dependent on some other verb, the subjunctive is not used:

estaba triste porque todos le habían abandonado
he was sad because everyone had left him

se puso furioso al ver que nadie le escuchaba
he became furious when he saw that no-one was listening to him

In this case the clause is dependent on the verb **ver**, not on the expression of emotion.

2. Fear

a) to fear something/be afraid of something

The simplest way to express fear is to use a phrase such as **tener miedo a**, or less commonly the verb **temer**. Note that the preposition used with **tener miedo** can be either **a** or **de** (as opposed to only 'of' in 'to be afraid of' in English):

tengo miedo a los perros
I'm afraid of dogs

In colloquial Spanish, the phrase **dar miedo** may also be used. However, the object of the English verb becomes the subject of the Spanish verb, and the subject of the English verb becomes the indirect object of the Spanish verb (as with **gustar**, page 104):

me dan miedo las arañas
I'm afraid of spiders

b) 'to fear' + verb

The rules for one or more subjects mentioned earlier (see section E.I) also apply here:

me da miedo salir por la noche
I am afraid of going out at night

temo que surjan problemas imprevistos
I'm afraid that unforeseen problems might crop up

Note that the expression 'I'm afraid' is often used in English to introduce statements of fact or possibility where there is no real suggestion of any fear. **Temer** may also be used in this way in Spanish (it is frequently used reflexively in this context).

In this case **temerse** may be followed by either the indicative or the subjunctive. The indicative is used for a statement of fact. The subjunctive suggests the possibility that something may have happened:

me temo que lo ha/haya perdido
I'm afraid he's lost it/he may have lost it

c) Other expressions

Other expressions indicating genuine fear are also followed by the subjunctive:

> **se escondió por miedo a que se burlasen de él**
> he hid for fear that they would laugh at him

3. Hope

a) to hope for something

This is expressed simply by **esperar**. The idea of 'for' is included in the verb, so that no preposition is used:

> **esperábamos una respuesta más positiva**
> we were hoping for a more positive reply

b) 'to hope' + verb

'to hope' is again usually expressed in this context by the verb **esperar**. With this meaning **esperar** may take either the indicative or the subjunctive (**esperar** meaning 'to wait' is *always* followed by the subjunctive).

When followed by the indicative **esperar** expresses keenness. When followed by the subjunctive it expresses genuine hope. Compare the following:

> **espero que vendrá** (indicative)
> I hope he'll come

I'm counting on him coming. I'll be disappointed/annoyed if he doesn't come.

> **espero que tengas éxito** (subjunctive)
> I hope you succeed

This is genuine hope, and does not have the connotations of 'counting on' mentioned above.

c) Impersonal expressions

Impersonal expressions of hope are followed by the subjunctive:

> **hay pocas esperanzas de que venga**
> there's little hope that he'll come

> **mi ilusión es que un día se resuelva el problema**
> my hope is that one day the problem will be solved

d) *ojalá*

In spoken Spanish **ojalá** is frequently used to introduce an expression of hope. **ojalá** is invariable and never changes its form. It is always followed by the subjunctive:

> **ojalá no llueva mañana**
> I hope it doesn't rain tomorrow

> **ojalá venga**
> I hope he comes

4. Regret

a) Apologising for something

The simplest statements of apology are of course **perdón, perdone** (an imperative) and **lo siento**. They are different in that **perdón** and **perdone** are both requests for forgiveness, whereas **lo siento** is a direct expression of regret:

> **¡ay, perdona! no te vi**
> oh, sorry! I didn't see you

In this case the **tú** form of the imperative (**perdona**) is used.

> **lo siento, pero no será posible terminarlo hoy**
> sorry, but it won't be possible to finish it today

When the thing or action regretted is explicitly stated, the **lo** of **lo siento** is no longer used. The idea of 'for' is included in the verb and is not explicitly stated in Spanish:

> **sentimos la molestia**
> we are sorry/apologise for the inconvenience

In more formal Spanish, **lamentar** is often used in preference to **sentir**:

> **lamentamos la molestia que les hemos causado**
> we regret the inconvenience we have caused

b) 'to regret' + verb

If there is only one subject, the infinitive is used, otherwise a clause with the verb in the subjunctive is required:

> **sentimos tener que molestarle**
> we are sorry to have to bother you

sentimos mucho que no hayas podido hacerlo
we are very sorry that you were not able to do it

Again, the clause must be directly dependent on the verb expressing regret. If it is dependent on any other verb, the indicative will be used:

lamentamos informarles que ya no están disponibles
we are sorry to inform you that they are no longer available

The clause here is dependent on **informar** and not on **lamentamos**.

F. INTENTIONS AND OBJECTIVES

1. Statements of intention

Simple statements of intention are expressed using the verb **pensar** or the phrase **tener la intención de**, both followed by the infinitive. In spoken Spanish, the construction **tener pensado** + infinitive is also widely used.

pensamos ir en coche/tenemos la intención de ir en coche
we intend to go by car

tengo pensado salir esta noche
I intend to go out this evening

2. Statement of objectives

a) One subject

If only one person is involved, objectives are usually expressed by the preposition **para** followed by the infinitive. More formal alternatives are **a fin de**, **con el fin de**, **con la intención de**, **con el objetivo de** or **con la finalidad de**, all followed by the infinitive:

lo hice para ganar un poco de dinero
I did it to earn a little money

me dirijo a Vds. con el objetivo de pedir información
I am writing to you to ask for information

After verbs of motion, intention is usually expressed by the preposition **a** followed by the infinitive, though **para** is also possible:

vine aquí a hablar contigo
I came here to speak to you

Other verbs are followed by different prepositions (see pages 236-241):

luchaban por mejorar sus condiciones de vida
they were fighting to improve their living conditions

b) *Two different subjects*

If more than one subject is involved, **para que** followed by the subjunctive is necessary. A straightforward infinitive will be wrong in Spanish:

les ayudamos para que pudieran acabarlo pronto
we helped them so that they could get it done sooner

The more formal alternatives given earlier can also be used followed by **que** and the subjunctive:

me voy, a fin de que puedan empezar inmediatamente
I'm going, so that they can start immediately

G. OBLIGATION

1. General obligation

A number of constructions exist in Spanish to express obligation on a very general level. The commonest of these are:

hay que + infinitive
es preciso + infinitive
es necesario + infinitive

The degree of obligation can be heightened as follows:

es esencial + infinitive
es imprescindible + infinitive

These expressions are not addressed to any one person in particular. They simply express a general obligation.

hay que tener cuidado
you (ie one) must be careful

¿hay que ser miembro para poder jugar aquí?
do I/you have to be a member to play here?

hay que verificarlo
it'll have to be checked

será necesario verificarlo con él
it will be necessary to check it with him

2. Personal obligation

More personal kinds of obligation (ie those affecting particular people or groups of people) are expressed using the verb **deber** + infinitive or the verb **tener** followed by **que** + infinitive:

tendrás que trabajar mucho
you'll have to work hard

tengo que terminarlo cuanto antes
I have to finish it as soon as possible

debemos salir a las ocho en punto
we must leave at eight on the dot

The sense of obligation can be heightened by using one of the phrases given in section I. (with the exception of **hay que**) followed by **que** and a verb in the subjunctive:

es imprescindible que lo hagas ahora mismo
you absolutely must do it right now

Note that 'have to' in English does not always denote an obligation. For example, in the phrase 'I had to laugh', you were not, of course, obliged to laugh. This simply means that you could not stop yourself from laughing. This idea is expressed in Spanish as follows:

no pudimos por menos de reír
we had to laugh/could not help laughing

3. Moral obligation

Moral obligation is expressed in Spanish by the conditional (or less frequently the imperfect) of **deber** followed by the infinitive. This is usually expressed in English by 'should' or 'ought to':

deberíamos ir a verle
we should go and see him

This is not an obligation in the sense that we are being *forced* to go and see him, but we feel that it is our 'duty'.

⚠ The use of 'should' in English to express moral obligation can *never* be translated into Spanish by the conditional. For example, *haría* can never express the idea of 'I ought to do'. Only *debería hacer* will convey this idea succesfully.

To put this idea into the past, use the perfect infinitive after the conditional of **deber**:

deberíamos haberlo hecho antes
we should have done it sooner

no deberías haber bebido tanto
you shouldn't have drunk so much

4. Obliging someone to do something

This idea is usually expressed by **obligar** or **forzar** + **a** + infinitive. Alternatively, **hacer** + infinitive can be used. The subject of the infinitive will be different from that of **obligar**:

me obligaron a salir   **me hizo levantarme temprano**
they forced me to leave   he made me get up early

When expressing the idea of 'being obliged to do something', **verse** is almost always used in preference to **ser**:

me vi obligado a devolverlo
I was obliged to give it back

H. PROBABILITY/IMPROBABILITY

The adverb **probablemente** (like all adverbs) has no effect on whether the verb is in the indicative or the subjunctive:

probablemente vendrá mañana
he'll probably come tomorrow

However, any impersonal expression of either probability or improbability is followed by a subordinate clause with its verb in the subjunctive:

es probable que salga por la tarde
I'll probably go out this evening (it's probable that I'll go out ...)

es improbable que vuelva
he's unlikely to come back (it's improbable that he'll come back)

me parece increíble que consiga hacerlo
I find it unlikely that he'll manage to do it

tenemos que aceptar la probabilidad de que esto ocurra
we must accept the likelihood that this will happen

I. PERMISSION/PREVENTION/PROHIBITION

1. General permission and prohibition

The most general forms of permission and prohibition are expressed using the verb **poder**:

¿puedo pasar?
may I come in?

¿se puede aparcar por aquí?
can you (ie one) park around here?

no puedes pasar ahora
you may not come in just now

The prohibition corresponding to **se puede** is **se prohíbe, está prohibido** or simply **prohibido**. These are found mostly in official signs:

prohibido/se prohíbe pisar el césped
please do not walk on the grass

This can be emphasised as follows:

queda terminantemente prohibido cruzar la vía
crossing the line is strictly forbidden

2. Personal permission, prevention and prohibition

The commonest verbs of permitting, preventing and prohibiting belong to that group which may be followed by an infinitive with a different subject (see page 234). This usually avoids the need for a subordinate clause:

me dejaron entrar pero me impidieron verle
they let me go in but they prevented me from seeing him

nos prohibieron fumar
they did not allow us to smoke

Note the very common phrase:

¿me permite?
may I?

In many cases a straightforward imperative may be used:

no digas tacos
don't use bad words

J. POSSIBILITY/IMPOSSIBILITY

I. In a personal sense

a) *poder* and related verbs

The simplest way of expressing possibility is to use the verb **poder**:

> **no podré venir mañana**
> I won't be able to come tomorrow

> **no habríamos podido hacerlo sin ti**
> we wouldn't have been able to do it without you

The verbs **conseguir** and **lograr** are used with the same meaning (of these **conseguir** is the more common):

> **no conseguimos llegar a tiempo**
> we didn't manage to arrive on time

> **logramos evitar un conflicto**
> we managed to avoid a conflict

A further alternative is to use the impersonal expression **ser (im)posible**. The person for whom the action is (im)possible becomes the indirect object:

> **no me será posible venir**
> I won't be able (it won't be possible for me) to come

> **nos fue imposible resolver el problema**
> we couldn't solve the problem

resultar is sometimes used instead of **ser**:

> **me resultó imposible hacer lo que quería**
> I could not do what he wanted

b) *saber*

Note that 'to be able' in the sense of 'to know how to' rather than 'to be capable of' is expressed in Spanish by **saber** rather than **poder**:

> **¿sabes tocar la guitarra?**
> can you play the guitar?

> **sí, pero no sé tocar el piano**
> yes, but I can't play the piano

This is a skill rather than a physical ability.

c) Verbs of perception

'to be able' with verbs of perception (seeing, hearing and the like) is not usually expressed in Spanish unless you wish to suggest that there is some kind of obstacle involved:

¿me oyes?
can you hear me?

no podía verle por la niebla
I couldn't see him because of the fog

2. In a general sense

a) *quizá, quizás, tal vez*

Possibility in a more general sense (ie not 'being able to do something', but the possibility that something might happen or not) can be expressed by one of the adverbs **quizás, quizá** or **tal vez. quizás** and **quizá** are more widely used.

These may be followed by either the indicative or the subjunctive, depending on your view of how likely it is that the thing will in fact happen. The indicative expresses a greater degree of confidence than the subjunctive:

quizás venga mañana, no sé (subjunctive)
he may come tomorrow, I don't know

tal vez tienes razón (indicative)
you may be right

b) Verbal forms

poder can also be used to express a general possibility:

puede haber cambios importantes dentro de poco
there may be important changes soon

This idea can also be expressed by the impersonal expressions **es posible que** and **puede que** followed by the appropriate form of the subjunctive:

es posible que venga mañana
he may come tomorrow

puede que no sea verdad
it may not be true

In fact, any impersonal expression of possibility or chance is followed by the subjunctive:

existe la posibilidad de que surjan problemas
there is the possibility that problems will crop up

Note the following expression:

parece mentira que esto haya ocurrido
it seems impossible that this should have happened

K. REQUESTS AND COMMANDS

1. Direct requests

a) Informal requests

Spaniards are rather more direct in their requests than the average English speaker, who tends to introduce most requests with 'would you' and the like. A straightforward question is more likely in Spanish:

¿me pasas esa revista?
would you pass me that magazine?

¿me prestas diez euros?
would you lend me ten euros?

Alternatively, for a slightly less direct request ('could you' in English), the appropriate form of **poder** + infinitive can be used:

¿puedes abrir la ventana?
could you open the window?

¿podría decirme qué hora es?
could you tell me the time, please?

The expression **hacer el favor de** + infinitive is also used if a little more formality is required:

¿me hace el favor de cerrar la ventana?
would you be so kind as to close the window, please

b) Formal requests

There are much more formal ways of introducing a request, particularly in written Spanish. The most common of these are the expressions **tenga(n) la bondad de** + infinitive and **le(s) ruego que** followed by the verb in the subjunctive:

tenga la bondad de cerrar la puerta
be so kind as to close the door

In the very formal Spanish of a business letter, the **que** is sometimes omitted after **le(s) ruego**. This usage should not be imitated in contexts other than commercial correspondence:

les rogamos nos manden dos cajas
please send us two boxes

c) Ultra-formal requests

In very formal Spanish, the old-fashioned form **sírvase** can still be found. This is in fact an imperative. If addressed to more than one person, **sírvanse** is used instead. This construction is restricted to commercial correspondence and official signs:

sírvanse mandarnos más información
please send us more information

2. Indirect requests

Since there are always at least two subjects involved in an indirect request, the verb is always followed by a subordinate clause with its verb in the subjunctive.

The most common verb used to introduce an indirect request is **pedir**. In more formal Spanish, **rogar** is again sometimes used in preference to **pedir**:

le pedí que se callara
I asked him to be quiet

nos rogaron que les ayudáramos
they asked us to help them

⚠️ It is essential not to confuse *pedir* and *preguntar*. *preguntar* means 'to ask a *question*', and is used to introduce an indirect question. It does not involve the idea of a request.

More intense requests can be expressed by verbs such as **suplicar**:

me suplicó que no revelara su secreto
he pleaded with me not to reveal his secret

3. Indirect commands

For direct commands (the imperative) see pages 68, 126, 208.

There are always at least two subjects involved in an indirect command. Normally, this means a subordinate clause with the verb in the subjunctive:

me dijo que lo hiciera inmediatamente
he told me to do it immediately

insistimos en que nos lo devuelvan ahora mismo
we insist that you give it back to us right now

However, the verbs **mandar** and **ordenar** belong to that small group of verbs which can be used with a direct infinitive (see page 234):

me mandó salir del edificio
he ordered me to leave the building

L. SUPPOSITION

1. Future tense

Apart from the usual verbs of supposition (for example **suponer**), the simplest way of expressing supposition in Spanish is to use the future tense for a supposition in the present, and a conditional for a supposition in the past. A similar construction exists in English, though it is less used than its Spanish equivalent:

supongo que vendrá
I imagine he'll come

¿qué hora es? – serán las once
what time is it – it must be about eleven (it'll be about eleven)

la casa estará por aquí
the house must be around here somewhere (will be around here somewhere)

serían las cinco más o menos cuando llegó
it must have been about five (it would be about five) when he arrived

2. *deber de* + infinitive

Supposition can also be expressed by the verb **deber** followed by **de** and the infinitive. Do not confuse this with **deber** followed by a direct infinitive, which expresses an obligation.

> **debes de estar cansado después de tanto trabajo**
> you must be tired after so much work

⚠ Note that the Spanish verb *asumir* does *not* mean 'to assume' in the sense of 'to suppose', but in the sense of 'to take on' as in 'to assume power'. If you need to translate 'assume' in the sense of 'suppose', either use *suponer* or one of the constructions explained above.

M. THANKS

1. Simple expressions of thanks

a) *gracias* and related terms

The simplest expression of thanks is, of course, **gracias**. Since thanking someone always involves the idea of an exchange (you thank someone in exchange for what they have given you, or done for you), the preposition used with **gracias** is always **por**:

> **muchas gracias por el regalo**
> thanks a lot for the present

> **me dio las gracias por el regalo**
> he thanked me for the present

A verb used after **gracias** may be put into either the present or the perfect infinitive:

> **gracias por ayudarme/haberme ayudado**
> thanks for helping me

Likewise, any noun or adjective expressing thanks or gratitude is followed by **por**:

> **queremos expresar nuestro reconocimiento por todo**
> we want to express our gratitude for everything

b) *agradecer*

In more formal Spanish, **gracias** is almost always replaced by the appropriate form of the verb **agradecer**. **agradecer** is an exception to what has been said above in that the idea of 'for' is contained within the verb:

 agradecer **is not followed by any kind of preposition in Spanish:**

> **les agradecemos su cooperación en este asunto**
> we thank you for your cooperation in this matter

> **nos agradecieron nuestra ayuda**
> they thanked us for our help

2. Subordinate clauses

The verb in a subordinate clause following an expression of gratitude goes into the subjunctive. The commonest occurrences of such expressions are the following:

> **agradeceremos mucho que nos ayuden**
> **agradeceríamos mucho que nos ayudasen**

Both of these are Spanish equivalents of 'we would be grateful if you could help us'. Either may be used on any occasion, despite the difference in tenses. Note the idea of 'could' is not expressed in Spanish.

 Note that, unlike English, Spanish does not consider this kind of expression to be a condition, so no *si* clause is used.

In the very formal Spanish of commercial correspondence, the **que** may be omitted from this expression. This should not be imitated in contexts other than commercial correspondence:

> **agradeceremos nos manden diez cajas**
> we would be grateful if you could send us ten boxes

N. WISHES/DESIRES/PREFERENCES

1. One subject

If only one subject is involved, a straightforward infinitive is used:

quiero hablar contigo
I want to speak to you

preferiría salir ahora
I would prefer to leave now

valdría más empezar enseguida
it would be better to start right away

The expression of a wish can always be 'softened' in Spanish by using the imperfect subjunctive of **querer**:

quisiéramos comer ahora
we'd like to eat now

2. Two subjects

In this case the verb of wishing must be followed by a subordinate clause with its verb in the subjunctive:

quiero que lo hagan ellos mismos
I want them to do it themselves

me gustaría que Vds. empezaran enseguida
I would like you to start right away

hubiera preferido que escogieras otra cosa
I would have preferred you to choose something else

10. NUMBERS AND NUMBER-RELATED FUNCTIONS

A. NUMBERS

1. The cardinal numbers

For the forms of the cardinal numbers, see page 245.

Note that, though most numbers are invariable (ie they never change their form), there are feminine forms of **uno** and of all the hundreds between 200 and 900 inclusive. It is a very common error not to make the hundreds agree:

> **me costó quinientas libras**
> it cost me five hundred pounds

uno also agrees in compound numbers:

> **veintiuna ovejas**
> twenty-one sheep

Note that 'one' is not expressed in expressions such as the following:

> **¿qué coche prefieres? – el rojo**
> which car do you prefer? – the red one

> **preferiría uno más grande**
> I'd like a bigger one

No article is used with **cien** or **mil**, or with the adjective **medio**:

> **cien mil soldados**
> one hundred thousand soldiers

> **esperamos media hora**
> we waited for half an hour

Note that both **millón** and **billón** are nouns and *must* be followed by **de**:

> **el gobierno invertirá diez millones de euros**
> the government will invest ten million euros

un billón in Spanish still means one million million (in most other countries the term 'billion' has come to mean one thousand million). In the Spanish press, the word **billón** is frequently written in italics to highlight this difference.

2. The ordinal numbers

For the formation of the ordinal numbers, see page 247.

These are seldom used beyond **décimo**, being usually replaced by the cardinal numbers:

vivo en el tercer piso
I live on the third floor

but

en el siglo veinte
in the twentieth century

en la página treinta y dos
on page thirty-two

3. Approximate numbers

An approximate number can be made from any multiple of ten by dropping the final vowel and adding the ending **-ena**, though such numbers are in fact very rare beyond forty:

una veintena de muchachos
about twenty boys

Some other numbers also formed with this ending have become words in their own right:

| **una docena** | a dozen |
| **una quincena** | a fortnight |

The approximate numbers corresponding to **ciento** and **mil** are **centenar** and **millar**, though **cientos** and **miles** may also be used:

vinieron millares de hinchas
thousands of fans turned up

Approximate numbers can also be expressed by a variety of terms such as **en torno a, alrededor de, aproximadamente, más o menos,** or the plural article **unos** (**a eso de** is limited to expressions of time):

había aproximadamente cincuenta personas en la sala
there were about fifty people in the room

llegaron unos diez hombres
about ten men arrived

cuesta unas dos mil euros
it costs about two thousand euros

Note also the following:

se lo dije hasta veinte veces
I told him as many as twenty times

por lo menos doscientos
at least two hundred

cuarenta y tantos
forty odd

unos pocos, unos cuantos
a few

4. Fractions and decimals

a) Fractions

Note that, when used with another number, the phrase **y medio** comes after the *noun* and not after the number as in English:

dos horas y media
two and a half hours

This also applies in the case of the nouns **millón** and **billón**:

seis millones y medio de turistas británicos
six and a half million British tourists

b) Decimals

Spaniards use a comma to indicate a decimal fraction, and not a point as in English:

dos coma siete por ciento (2,7 por 100)
two point seven per cent

In colloquial Spanish, the word **coma** is often replaced by **con**:

cinco con cuatro millones (5,4 millones)
five point four million

B. TIME

1. There are several words in Spanish for 'time'. They all have different meanings and must not be confused:

la hora	time on the clock
la época	a period of time of unspecified duration but not measured by the clock
el tiempo	time in general
la vez	an occasion

quizás podríamos vernos a una hora conveniente
perhaps we could meet at a convenient time

siempre hay muchos turistas en esta época del año
there are always lots of tourists at this time of year

pasó mucho tiempo en España
he spent a long time in Spain

ya te lo he dicho por lo menos diez veces
I've already told you at least ten times

Note also the following:

de una vez por todas
once and for all

a la tercera va la vencida (Spanish proverb)
third time lucky

2. Time on the clock

Time on the clock is expressed as follows:

¿qué hora es?	**son las tres**
what time is it?	it's three o'clock
es la una	**son las diez**
it's one o'clock	it's ten o'clock

The feminine definite articles are used because the word understood but not expressed is **hora** or **horas**.

Time after the hour is expressed as follows:

son las tres y cinco	it's five past three
son las siete y cuarto	it's a quarter past seven
son las ocho y veinticinco	it's twenty-five past eight
son las once y media	it's half past eleven

Time to the hour:

es la una menos diez	it's ten to one
son las cuatro menos cuarto	it's a quarter to four

'at' is expressed by **a**:

a mediodía, a medianoche	at midday, at midnight
a las seis y diez	at ten past six

Note also:

a las diez en punto	at ten o'clock on the dot
a eso de las ocho	at around eight o'clock
a las tres y pico	just after three
¿qué hora tienes?	what time do you make it?
tengo las ocho	I make it eight o'clock
daban las diez	it was striking ten o'clock

For the purposes of specifying time, the Spanish day is divided into more sections than its English equivalent:

la madrugada	from midnight till dawn
la mañana	from dawn till noon
el mediodía	from noon till early afternoon
la tarde	from early afternoon till dark
la noche	from nightfall till midnight

madrugada can be replaced by **mañana**. The use of **madrugada** emphasises the fact that the speaker considers the time in question to be very early (or very late) from his point of view:

me levanté/me acosté a las dos de la madrugada
I got up/went to bed at two in the morning

a las tres de la madrugada	at three in the morning
a las diez de la mañana	at ten in the morning
a la una del mediodía	at one in the afternoon
a las cinco de la tarde	at five in the evening
a las diez de la noche	at ten in the evening

The twenty-four hour clock is also used in timetables and official announcements, though it is not used conversationally:

a las quince treinta y cinco   at fifteen thirty-five

If no specific time of day is mentioned, broad time of day is expressed using the preposition **por**:

salieron por la mañana
they went out in the morning

volveremos por la tarde
we'll come back in the afternoon

Note also the following:

anoche	last night
ayer	yesterday
antes de ayer/anteayer	the day before yesterday
mañana	tomorrow
pasado mañana	the day after tomorrow
ayer por la mañana	yesterday morning
mañana por la noche	tomorrow evening
dos veces por hora	twice an hour
ochenta kilómetros por hora	eighty kilometres an hour

3. Days of the week

For a list of days, months and seasons, see page 248.

Days of the week are written with a small letter. 'on' is expressed simply by the definite article. No preposition is used:

fuimos al cinema el sábado
we went to the cinema on Saturday

vamos a la playa los domingos
we go to the beach on Sundays

el lunes por la mañana
on Monday morning

los lunes por la mañana
on Monday mornings

Note also:

el miércoles pasado	**el sábado que viene**
last Wednesday	next Saturday

dos veces al día
twice a day

cinco veces a la semana
five times a week

mil euros por semana
a thousand euros per week

4. The date

The months are written with a small letter. 'the first' may be expressed as **el primero** or **el uno**. All other dates are expressed only by the appropriate cardinal number (ie three, four etc not third, fourth etc).

'on' is expressed simply by the definite article, or by placing **el día** in front of the number. The only exception is in the heading to a letter, where no article is used:

¿a cuántos estamos hoy?/¿a qué día del mes estamos?/¿qué día es hoy?
what date is it today?

hoy estamos a dos
today is the second

llegaremos el 12 de febrero
we will arrive on 12 February

salieron el día 9
they left on the 9th

In a full date, both the month and the year are introduced by **de**:

el quince de octubre de mil novecientos ochenta y ocho
the fifteenth of October nineteen eighty-eight

Note also:

el siglo veinte
the twentieth century

el siglo dieciocho
the eighteenth century

en los años treinta
in the thirties

la España de los años ochenta
the Spain of the eighties

a principios/primeros de enero
at the beginning of January

a mediados de marzo
in the middle of March

a finales/fines de octubre
at the end of October

en lo que va de año	**a lo largo del año**
this year so far	throughout the year
dos veces al mes	**cuatro veces al año**
twice a month	four times a year

5. The seasons

The names of the seasons are preceded by a definite article unless used with **en**:

la primavera es muy agradable en España
spring is very pleasant in Spain

iremos a España en otoño
we're going to Spain in the autumn

6. Age

Age is expressed as follows:

¿cuántos años tienes?	**¿qué edad tiene tu hermano?**
how old are you?	what age is your brother?
tengo diecisiete años	
I'm seventeen	

Note also the following:

ronda los cuarenta	**hoy cumplo veinte años**
he's getting on for forty	I'm twenty today
la juventud	**la tercera edad**
youth, young people	senior citizens, OAPs

7. Some useful expressions of time

hoy en día, hoy día	nowadays
hoy por hoy	nowadays
en la actualidad	nowadays
a corto/medio/largo plazo	in the short/medium/long term
hace diez años	ten years ago
diez años antes	ten years earlier
a partir de ahora	from now on
de aquí/hoy en adelante	from now on
en el futuro	in future
en el porvenir	in future
en lo sucesivo (formal)	in future
en lo venidero (formal)	in future
en los años venideros	in the years to come

al día siguiente	the following day
la próxima semana	next week
la semana siguiente	the next week
la semana anterior	the previous week

C. PRICES/MEASUREMENTS/PERCENTAGES

1. Prices

Rate in prices is expressed by the definite article:

este vino cuesta tres euros el litro
this wine costs three euros a litre

lo vendían a seis euros el kilo
they were selling it at six euros a kilo

Note also:

¿cuánto cuestan/valen las manzanas?/¿a cómo se venden las manzanas?
how much are the apples?

2. Measurements

Measurements may be expressed using either the adjective or the noun relating to the measurement in question (length, height, breadth etc):

¿cuál es la altura del muro?
how high is the wall?

el muro tiene dos metros de alto/altura
the wall is two metres high

la calle tiene cien metros de largo/longitud
the street is one hundred metres long

Note that in the following construction the adjective agrees:

una calle de cien metros de larga
a street one hundred metres long

Note also:

¿cuánto pesas? **¿cuánto mides?**
what do you weigh? how tall are you?

mide casi dos metros
he's almost two metres tall

tiene una superficie de cien metros cuadrados
it has a surface area of one hundred square metres

tiene una capacidad de dos metros cúbicos
it has a capacity of two cubic metres

Distance is always indicated by the preposition **a**:

¿a qué distancia está la playa? – a unos cinco kilómetros
how far away is the beach? – about five kilometres

3. Percentages

Percentages in Spanish are invariably preceded by either a definite or an indefinite article. There is no difference in meaning:

la inflación ha aumentado en un diez por ciento
inflation has gone up ten per cent

el treinta por ciento de las personas entrevistadas no contestó
thirty per cent of those interviewed did not give an answer

Percentages are usually written in Spanish as **5 por 100** and the like.
100 por 100 is almost invariably pronounced **cien por cien**.

The amount by which a percentage increases or decreases is indicated in Spanish by the preposition **en**. The commonest verbs used in this connection are:

Increase:

aumentar, incrementar, crecer, subir

Decrease:

caer, bajar, reducir(se)

hemos reducido nuestros precios en un 15 por 100
we have reduced our prices by 15 per cent

If a percentage is not involved, normally no preposition is used:

las acciones han bajado un par de euros
shares have come down by a few euros

11. SENTENCE STRUCTURE

Sentence structure is not the same as word order. Sentence structure concerns the place occupied by the different *component parts* of the sentence, rather than *individual words*. Any of these component parts can consist of a number of words. For example, in a sentence such as the following:

> **el padre del amigo de mi hermano trabaja en Santander**
> my brother's friend's father works in Santander

the words **el padre del amigo de mi hermano** all go together to form the subject of the verb **trabaja**. The verb itself occupies the second *place* in the sentence, although it is the eighth *word*.

The most important elements of any sentence are the verb, the subject of the verb (ie who or what is carrying out the action of the verb), and the object or complement. A transitive verb takes an object, an intransitive verb is followed by a complement. There are other elements – adverbs, prepositional phrases etc – but these are less important and are not dealt with here.

1. English sentence structure

Sentence structure is very predictable in English. Most English sentences follow the order subject – verb – object/complement, eg:

subject	verb	object/complement
the boys	watch	the television (object)
Spanish	is	easy (complement)

The only consistent exception to this order in English is found in questions, where the order verb – subject – object/complement is more common:

verb	subject	object/complement
is	Spanish	easy

2. Spanish sentence structure

Sentence structure is *very* much more flexible in Spanish than it is in English. This is not to suggest that the order subject – verb – object/complement is in any sense uncommon in Spanish. On the contrary, it is probably the commonest pattern in spoken Spanish, and is also commonly used in questions. Nonetheless, it is nowhere near as dominant in Spanish as it is in English, and a Spanish speaker will happily place the verb before the subject, and on occasions will even place the object before the verb.

There are few rules governing sentence structure in Spanish, but in general it could be said that:

- the closer any element of the sentence is to the beginning of the sentence, the more emphasis it receives, the first position in the sentence being obviously the most emphatic;

- it is unusual for the verb not to occupy the first or second *position* in the sentence (see the difference between position and word order given above).

The choice made by a Spanish speaker may be based on reasons of emphasis, but more often it will have to do with the rhythm of the sentence. Rhythms are not something which can be taught. A feeling for such rhythms can be obtained only through exposure to large amounts of genuine spoken Spanish.

3. **Examples of different sentence structures**

a) subject – verb

> **mi hermano está estudiando inglés**
> my brother is studying English
>
> **¿el coche está en el garaje?**
> is the car in the garage?

b) verb – subject

> **llegaron dos tíos y se pusieron a trabajar**
> two fellows came along and started to work
>
> **me lo dijo una vez mi padre**
> my father told me so once

c) object – verb – subject

> **el cuadro lo pintó un amigo mío**
> one of my friends painted the picture
>
> **la moto la compramos Juan y yo**
> Juan and I bought the motorbike

143

Note that when the object is placed before the verb, the corresponding object pronoun *must* also be placed before the verb.

d) use of first position for emphasis

>**a mí no me gusta nada**
>I don't like it at all

>**tal decisión no la apoyaremos nunca**
>we shall never support such a decision

>**a ella no la puede ver**
>he can't stand her

4. Punctuation

Punctuation in Spanish is by and large identical to English. Remember, however, that the upside-down question marks and exclamation marks are written at the beginning of the question and of the exclamation respectively. This is not necessarily at the beginning of the sentence:

>**¿qué quieres tomar?**
>what will you have?

>**y éste, ¿cuánto cuesta?**
>and how much does this one cost?

>**estuviste anoche en la discoteca, ¿verdad?**
>you were at the club last night, weren't you?

>**el público gritó '¡olé!'**
>the crowd shouted 'olé!'

Part II
FORMS

1. ACCENTUATION

Written accents in Spanish relate primarily to *spoken* stress. If you know how a word is pronounced, you can tell by applying a few simple rules if it requires a written accent, and, if so, where the accent should be written.

1. Syllables

In order to know when and where to write an accent, it is important to understand what is meant by a 'syllable'. A syllable is a group of letters within a word at least one of which *must* be a vowel. If there is no vowel, there is no syllable. In many cases, the number of syllables in a word is the same as the number of vowels:

ca-sa (two syllables)   **con-cen-tra-da** (four syllables)

If there are one or more consonants between each vowel, as in the examples just given, the division into syllables is quite straightforward. However, the situation is slightly more complex if two or more vowels are written together.

Vowels in Spanish are divided into strong and weak vowels.

the strong vowels are: A, E and O
the weak vowels are: I and U

The rules regarding whether or not two or more vowels written together form one or more syllables are as follows:

a) When two strong vowels appear together they belong to two distinct syllables:

pa-se-ar (three syllables)
pe-or (two syllables)

b) When a strong and weak vowel appear together and there is no written accent on any of the weak vowels, they form only one syllable, and the strong vowel takes the stress:

fuer-te (two syllables)
vie-jo (two syllables)
an-*cia*-no (three syllables)

If one of the weak vowels is accentuated, it forms a separate syllable:

ha-cí-a (three syllables)
pú-a (two syllables)

146

c) When two or more weak vowels appear together they form only one syllable and the stress falls on the second vowel:

vi*u*-da (two syllables)

fu*i* (one syllable)

These rules apply to *pronunciation* only, and are unaffected by the way a word is written. For example, the **o** and **i** of **prohibir** belong to the same syllable, despite the fact that there is a written (but completely unpronounced) **h** between them. The **e** and **u** of **rehusar** belong to the same syllable for the same reason.

2. Spoken stress

All words in Spanish have one main stressed vowel, and it is the position of this stressed vowel in the word which determines whether or not there is a written accent. The rules for spoken stress are as follows:

a) The stress falls naturally on the second last syllable of the word when:

- the word ends in a vowel
  lla-mo, re-ba-ño, ve-o, va-rio, re-ci-bie-ra

- the word ends in -n or -s
  can-tan, li-bros, jo-ven

b) The stress falls naturally on the last syllable when the word ends in a consonant other than -n and -s:

can-tar, ciu-dad, no-mi-nal

3. Primary use of the written accent

The written accent is mainly used in Spanish to show deviations from the rules for natural spoken stress given above. The pronunciation of the vowel on which the accent is written is not otherwise affected.

If the stress falls where the rules say it should fall, there is no written accent. If it does not, a written accent is placed over the vowel actually carrying the stress. This accounts for the overwhelming majority of cases of written accents in Spanish.

The general rules are, therefore:

- If a word ending in a vowel, -n or -s is *not* stressed on the second last syllable, a written accent is placed on the vowel which is in fact stressed:

menú, región, inglés

– If a word ending in a consonant other than **-n** or **-s** is not stressed on the last syllable, a written accent is placed on the vowel which is in fact stressed:

césped, fácil

More specifically, it can be seen that:

– Any word stressed on the third last syllable carries an accent on the stressed vowel irrespective of its ending:

música, régimen

– Any word ending in a stressed vowel carries an accent on that vowel:

café, rubí

– In any combination of a weak vowel and a strong vowel where it is the weak vowel which carries the stress, this weak vowel will have a written accent:

quería, vacío

Further examples:

stress in 'natural' position *(no accent)*		*stress out of position* *(written accent)*	
varias	several	**varías**	you vary
continuo	continuous	**continúo**	I continue
amar	to love	**ámbar**	amber
fabrica	he manufactures	**fábrica**	factory

Remember again that what counts is pronunciation and not spelling. The written accent on **prohíbo** or **rehúso** is explained by the fact that the weak vowel in the spoken syllables **oi** and **eu** is stressed.

Note also that written accents may have to be omitted from or added to plural forms:

región	**regiones**		**joven**	**jóvenes**

4. **Secondary uses of the written accent**

Other uses of the written accent are:

– to differentiate between two words which have the same spelling:

el (the)	– **él** (he)	**si** (if)	– **sí** (yes)
tu (your)	– **tú** (you)	**de** (of)	– **dé** (give)
mi (my)	– **mí** (me)		

- to identify the interrogative and exclamatory forms of certain pronouns and adverbs:

donde – **¿dónde?**	**quien** – **¿quién?**
where – where?	who – who?

- to differentiate the pronoun forms from the adjectival forms of the demonstratives (the pronouns are written with an accent):

este – **éste**	**aquella** – **aquélla**
this – this one	that – that one

Since the neuter pronouns cannot be confused with any other forms, no accent is required:

esto	**eso**	**aquello**
this (one)	that (one)	that (one)

5. The dieresis

A dieresis is only ever written over the letter **u** in Spanish, in which case it appears as **ü**. The dieresis occurs only in the combinations **güe** and **güi**, and indicates that the **ü** is to be pronounced as a separate vowel. If no dieresis is present, the **u** is not pronounced:

la cigüeña	the stork
la vergüenza	shame
la lingüística	linguistics
el piragüismo	canoeing

Compare these with words such as **la guerra, la guirnalda** and the like, where the **u** is not pronounced.

Note that a dieresis must sometimes be added or indeed omitted in certain forms of certain verbs, to ensure that the pronunciation of the verb is correctly reflected in the spelling, eg:

averiguo (*indicative*: I find out)
averigüe (*subjunctive*)

avergonzarse (*infinitive*: to be ashamed)
me avergüenzo (*first person singular*)

arguyo (*first person singular*)
argüir (*infinitive*: to argue)

2. GENDER

In Spanish all nouns are either *masculine* or *feminine*. There is no equivalent of the English neuter gender for nouns.

All words used with any noun (adjectives, articles etc) take the same gender as the noun.

I. Gender by ending

The gender of a noun can often be deduced from its ending:

a) Most nouns ending in **-o** are masculine:

el libro	**el dinero**	**el piano**
the book	the money	the piano

There are a few common exceptions:

la radio	**la mano**
the radio	the hand

b) Most nouns ending in **-a** are feminine:

la aduana	**la casa**	**la mañana**
the Customs	the house	the morning

Some common exceptions to this:

el día	**el mapa**	**el idioma**	**el clima**
the day	the map	the language	the climate

Also, most nouns ending in **-ema** and a few ending in **-ama** are masculine:

el problema	**el sistema**	**el lema**
the problem	the system	the slogan

el programa	**el drama**	**el telegrama**
the program	the drama	the telegram

c) Almost all nouns ending in **-d** are feminine:

la ciudad	**la vid**	**la juventud**
the city	the vine	youth

la pared	**la dificultad**
the wall	the difficulty

d) Almost all nouns ending in **-ión** are feminine:

⚠️ **la nación**   **la región**
the nation   the region

There are a few common exceptions:

el camión   **el avión**
the lorry   the plane

2. Gender by meaning

a) People and animals

When referring to people and animals, often, though not always, the meaning of the noun decides its gender, eg:

el hombre   **la mujer**   **la vaca**
the man   the woman   the cow

However, there are some exceptions to the above, for example **la víctima** is the Spanish for a victim of either sex.

b) Some nouns are going through a period of transition:

el juez is the Spanish for 'judge' in general, but, as more women judges are appointed in Spain, you will now hear and read both **la juez** and **la jueza**.

Such alternative forms can coexist for some time. For example, Mrs. Thatcher was referred to in the Spanish press as **la Primer Ministro** and **la Primera Ministra**.

c) Words with both genders

There are many words ending in **-ista**, which can be either masculine or feminine, according to the gender of the person referred to:

el socialista, la socialista
the socialist

el periodista, la periodista
the journalist

⚠️ There is no separate 'masculine' form of these nouns – all the masculine forms end in **-ista**, like the feminines.

d)   Nouns with corresponding forms for both genders

Some nouns may have both genders, depending on the gender of the person described:

el camarero the waiter	**la camarera** the waitress
el niño the boy	**la niña** the girl

Sometimes, a more substantial change of spelling is required:

el director the manager	**la directriz** the manageress
el actor the actor	**la actriz** the actress

e)   Nouns with different meanings for different genders

Some nouns may appear with either gender, but their meanings change:

el policía the policeman	**la policía** the police force
el guía the guide (*person*)	**la guía** the guidebook
el capital capital (*money*)	**la capital** the capital city
el cura the parish priest	**la cura** the cure
el pendiente the earring	**la pendiente** the slope
el moral the mulberry bush	**la moral** ethics

3. THE NOUN – PLURAL OF NOUNS

I. Formation

The plural of Spanish nouns is formed as follows:

a) Adding **-s** to nouns ending in an unstressed vowel:

los libros	**las reglas**
the books	the rulers

b) Most nouns ending in a stressed vowel add **-es**:

el rubí	**los rubíes**
the ruby	the rubies

but some common nouns only add **-s**:

los cafés	**las mamás**	**los papás**
the cafes	the mums	the dads

c) Adding **-es** to nouns ending in a consonant other than **-es**:

los señores	**las tempestades**
the men	the storms

d) Nouns already ending in **-s**

If the last syllable is stressed, add **-es**:

el inglés	**los ingleses**
the Englishman	(the) Englishmen

However, if the last syllable is not stressed, the word does not change:

el lunes	**los lunes**
Monday	Mondays

e) Some nouns require a spelling change in the plural

Where nouns end in **-z**, this changes to **-ces**:

la actriz	**las actrices**
the actress	the actresses

f) Changes in written accent

Most singular nouns having a written accent on the last syllable lose this accent in the plural as it is no longer necessary:

la nación the nation	**las naciones** the nations

The few nouns ending in **-n** and which are stressed on the second last syllable in the singular need a written accent in the plural:

el joven the young man	**los jóvenes** the young men
el crimen the crime	**los crímenes** the crimes

g) There are two plurals in Spanish which actually change their accentuation from the singular to the plural form:

el carácter the character	**los caracteres** the characters
el régimen the regime	**los regímenes** the regimes

h) In the case of acronyms, plural forms are indicated by doubling the initials:

EE.UU.	**Estados Unidos** (USA)
CC.OO.	**Comisiones Obreras** (Trade Union)
FF.AA.	**Fuerzas Armadas** (Armed Forces)

i) Most English words used in Spanish keep the form of the English plural:

el camping	**los campings**
el poster	**los posters**
el comic	**los comics**

However, some English words which have been used in Spanish for a long time have also adopted a Spanish plural:

el club	**los clubes**
el bar	**los bares**
el superman	**los supermanes**

2. Special use of the masculine plural

The masculine plural form is frequently used to indicate both genders:

mis padres my parents	**los Reyes** the King and Queen	**mis tíos** my aunt and uncle

4. THE ARTICLES

I. The definite article

a) The standard form

The definite article (the) has both a masculine and a feminine form, each of which can also be put into the plural:

	masculine	*feminine*
singular	**el**	**la**
plural	**los**	**las**

el señor	**la chica**
the man	the girl

los señores	**las chicas**
the men	the girls

b) A special feminine form

Note that the form of the feminine definite article used immediately before nouns which begin with a stressed **a-** or **ha-** is **el** and not **la**:

el agua	**el hambre**
the water	hunger

This change does not affect the *gender* of the noun. Other words accompanying the noun continue to take the feminine form:

el agua está fría
the water is cold

c) Contraction of the definite article

The masculine definite article joins together with the prepositions **a** and **de** to give the following forms:

a + el = al	de + el = del

fui al cine
I went to the cinema

la casa del profesor
the teacher's house

This does not happen if the **el** is part of a title in capital letters:

> **escribí a El Diario**
> I wrote to El Diario

However, feminines and plurals *never* contract.

d) Countries whose names are preceded by the definite article

The names of the following countries are preceded by the appropriate form of the definite article:

el Brasil	Brazil
el Ecuador	Ecuador
la India	India
el Japón	Japan
el Perú	Peru
el Uruguay	Uruguay

2. The indefinite article

a) The standard form

The indefinite article has both a masculine and a feminine form. Unlike English, both of these can also be put into the plural.

	masculine	*feminine*
singular	un	una
plural	unos	unas

un hombre	**una cantidad**
a man	a quantity

b) A special feminine form

Note that the form of the feminine indefinite article used immediately before nouns which begin with a stressed **a-** or **ha-** is **un**:

un hacha	**un ala**
an axe	a wing

This change does not affect the *gender* of the noun. Other words accompanying the noun continue to take the feminine form:

> **construyeron un ala nueva**
> they built a new wing

c) The plural forms are used:

- with nouns which exist only in the plural or are normally used in the plural

- to express the idea of 'some', 'a few'

Otherwise, they are not required:

compré unos pantalones
I bought a pair of trousers

tengo un libro	**tengo unos libros**	**tengo libros**
I have a book	I have some books	I have books

5. THE DEMONSTRATIVES

1. The demonstrative adjectives

The demonstrative adjectives in Spanish are **este** (this) and **ese** and **aquel** (both meaning 'that'). Their forms are as follows:

	masculine	feminine
singular	**este**	**esta**
plural	**estos**	**estas**
singular	**ese**	**esa**
plural	**esos**	**esas**
singular	**aquel**	**aquella**
plural	**aquellos**	**aquellas**

The demonstrative adjectives are placed *before* the noun:

este mes	**ese sillón**	**aquella bicicleta**
this month	that armchair	that bike

See pages 27-9 for their uses.

2. The demonstrative pronouns

The demonstrative pronouns are identical to the demonstrative adjectives with the single exception that they carry a written accent on the stressed vowel:

éste, éstos, ésta, éstas
ése, ésos, ésa, ésas
aquél, aquéllos, aquélla, aquéllas

There is also a neuter form which is *not* written with an accent (see page 28):

esto, eso, aquello

See pages 28-29 for the uses of the demonstrative pronouns.

6. THE POSSESSIVE ADJECTIVES AND PRONOUNS

1. The weak possessive adjectives

The weak possessive adjectives are placed before the noun. Their forms are as follows:

	masc. sing	fem. sing.	masc. plural	fem. plural
my	mi	mi	mis	mis
your	tu	tu	tus	tus
his/her/its/your	su	su	sus	sus
our	nuestro	nuestra	nuestros	nuestras
your	vuestro	vuestra	vuestros	vuestras
their/your	su	su	sus	sus

mi cuchillo
my knife

mi cuchara
my spoon

mis cuchillos
my knives

mis cucharas
my spoons

tu pañuelo
your handkerchief

tu chaqueta
your jacket

tus pañuelos
your handkerchiefs

tus chaquetas
your jackets

su saco
his/her/your sack

su maleta
his/her/your suitcase

sus sacos
his/her/your sack

sus maletas
his/her/your suitcases

nuestro piso
our flat

nuestra casa
our house

nuestros pisos
our flats

nuestras casas
our houses

vuestro coche	**vuestra casa**
your car	your house
vuestros coches	**vuestras casas**
your cars	your houses
su saco	**su maleta**
your/their sack	your/their suitcase
sus sacos	**sus maletas**
your/their sack	your/their suitcases

For a fuller treatment of **su** and **sus**, see page 35.

2. The strong possessive adjectives and pronouns

The strong possessive adjectives and the possessive pronouns are identical in form. They are as follows:

masc. sing.	*fem. sing.*	*masc. plural*	*fem. plural*
mío	**mía**	**míos**	**mías**
tuyo	**tuya**	**tuyos**	**tuyas**
suyo	**suya**	**suyos**	**suyas**
nuestro	**nuestra**	**nuestros**	**nuestras**
vuestro	**vuestra**	**vuestros**	**vuestras**
suyo	**suya**	**suyos**	**suyas**

See pages 34-35 for an explanation of the use of these forms.

7. AUGMENTATIVES AND DIMINUTIVES

1. The augmentatives

a) The following suffixes are added to nouns, adjectives, participles and adverbs as augmentatives (see pages 38-39):

masculine	**-ón**	**-azo**	**-acho**	**-ote**
feminine	**-ona**	**-aza**	**-acha**	**-ota**

b) Any vowel at the end of the original word is dropped.

un muchachazo
a big boy

un hombrote
a big man

2. The diminutives

a) The following suffixes are added to nouns, adjectives, participles and adverbs as diminutives (see pages 38-39):

-ito	longer forms:	**-cito, -ecito**
-illo	longer forms:	**-cillo, -ecillo**
-uelo	longer forms:	**-zuelo, -ezuelo**
-ín	(no longer forms)	
-ucho	(no longer forms)	

All of these endings can be made feminine by changing the **-o** to **-a** (**-ín** becomes **-ina**).

b) When the word ends in a vowel, this is dropped:

Ana	→	**Anita**
señora	→	**señorita**

c) Of the longer forms, **-cito**, **-cillo** and **-zuelo** are used with words of more than one syllable which end in **-n** or **-r**:

salón	→	**saloncito**
calor	→	**calorcito**

d) The forms **-ecito, -ecillo** and **-ezuelo** used with words of one syllable:

| flor | → | florecita, florecilla |
| pez | → | pececito, pececillo |

Note that spelling changes (**z** to **c**) may be necessary.

They are also used with words of two syllables when the first syllable is **-ie** or **-ue**. The final vowel is dropped:

| pueblo | → | pueblecito |
| nieto | → | nietecito |

e) Written accents are dropped from the ending of the original word when a suffix is added:

| salón | → | saloncito |

A written accent is added to the weak vowel of the suffix when the original word ends in an accentuated vowel:

| mamá | → | mamaíta |

8. THE ADJECTIVE

1. Shortened form of adjectives

a) Certain adjectives drop the **-o** from the masculine singular immediately before the noun:

alguno	**¿hay *algún* autobús por aquí?**
	are there any buses around here?
ninguno	**no veo *ningún* tren**
	I don't see any trains
bueno	**un *buen* vino**
	a good wine
malo	**el *mal* tiempo**
	the bad weather
primero	**el *primer* día del año**
	the first day of the year
tercero	**el *tercer* edificio**
	the third building

Note that **ninguno** and **alguno** require a written accent when shortened in this way.

b) **grande** is shortened to **gran** before both masculine and feminine singular nouns:

un gran señor	**una gran señora**
a great man	a great lady

When **grande** refers to physical size, it usually comes after the noun, in which case it is not shortened:

un coche grande	**una cocina grande**
a large car	a large kitchen

c) **cualquiera** becomes **cualquier** before both masculine and feminine singular nouns:

cualquier libro	**cualquier casa**
any book	any house

The plural of this adjective is **cualesquiera**. It is seldom used.

d) **santo** becomes **san** before saints' names, except those beginning with either **Do-** or **To-**:

San Pablo	San Pedro
Santo Domingo	Santo Tomás

2. Forming the feminine of adjectives

a) Adjectives ending in **-o** change to **-a**:

un vuelo corto	**una estancia corta**
a short flight	a short stay

b) Adjectives ending in other vowels or consonants (other than those in sections c and d) have the same form for both masculine and feminine:

un coche verde	**una hoja verde**
a green car	a green leaf
un problema fundamental	**una dificultad fundamental**
a fundamental problem	a fundamental difficulty

c) Those ending in **-án**, **-és**, **-ín**, **-ón**, and **-or** add **-a**:

un niño hablador	**una mujer habladora**
a talkative boy	a talkative woman

The exceptions are the comparative adjectives ending in **-or**, see page 166:

una idea mejor
a better idea

Note also that those ending in **-án**, **-és**, **-ín**, and **-ón** lose their accent in the feminine:

una muchacha muy holgazana
a very lazy girl

d) Adjectives indicating nationality or where someone or something comes from add **-a** if they end in a consonant. Any written accent is also lost:

un hotel escocés
a Scottish hotel

una pensión escocesa
a Scottish boarding house

un vino andaluz
an Andalusian wine

una sopa andaluza
an Andalusian soup

e) Adjectives ending in **-ícola** and **-ista** have the same form for both masculine and feminine:

un país agrícola
an agricultural country

una región vinícola
a wine-growing region

el partido comunista
the communist party

la ideología socialista
socialist ideology

⚠ Note that there is no separate 'masculine' form for these adjectives. The masculine forms end in *-ista* and *-ícola* like the feminines.

3. The plural of adjectives

Adjectives follow the same rules as nouns for the formation of the plural (see pages 153-154):

estos libros son viejos y sucios
these books are old and dirty

unas personas amables
some friendly people

The same spelling and accentuation changes also occur:

feliz – felices   **holgazán – holgazanes**

9. THE COMPARATIVE

See pages 43-46 for uses of the comparative.

1. The standard forms

To form the comparative in Spanish, simply place the word **más** (more), or **menos** (less) before the adjective:

más barato
cheaper

más caro
more expensive

menos guapo
less handsome

menos feo
less ugly

2. Irregular comparatives

There are six irregular comparatives:

bueno	(good)	→	**mejor**	(better)
grande	(big)	→	**mayor**	(bigger)*
malo	(bad)	→	**peor**	(worse)
mucho	(a lot)	→	**más**	(more)
pequeño	(small)	→	**menor**	(smaller)*
poco	(a little)	→	**menos**	(less)

A number of other adjectives are considered to belong to this group, although their comparative meaning has to some extent been lost:

superior (superior)
inferior (inferior)
anterior (previous)
posterior (rear, subsequent)

* **más grande** and **más pequeño** exist, but refer rather to physical size. **mayor** and **menor** refer more to the relative importance of the object or person, or to age.

When referring to age, **mayor** is often treated in spoken Spanish as a simple adjective meaning 'old', 'grown up' and is sometimes itself put into the comparative:

mi hermano más mayor
my older brother

Although fairly widespread, this usage is regarded as ungrammatical and should certainly not be imitated in formal written Spanish.

166

superior and **inferior** are widely used with numbers, amounts, quantities etc:

el paro es superior a tres millones
unemployment is in excess of three million

los beneficios son inferiores a los del año pasado
profits are down on last year's

10. THE SUPERLATIVE

1. The relative superlative

The relative superlative is identical in form to the comparative:

Juan es el estudiante más insolente de la clase
Juan is the most insolent student in class

este coche es el más caro
this car is the dearest

es la peor película que jamás he visto
it's the worst film I've ever seen

2. The absolute superlative

The absolute superlative is formed by adding the ending **-ísimo** to the adjective. If the adjective already ends in a vowel, this is dropped:

alto	altísimo
importante	importantísimo
fácil	facilísimo

When a vowel is dropped from the adjective, spelling changes may be necessary to ensure that the pronunciation of the absolute superlative is properly reflected in the spelling of the word:

rico	riquísimo
feliz	felicísimo
largo	larguísimo

Like any other adjective, the relative superlative agrees with the noun described:

estás guapísima hoy, María
you're looking extremely pretty today, María

estos libros son carísimos
these books are very expensive

11. PREPOSITIONS

A

to	destination	**voy a la escuela/a casa** I am going to school/home
		¿adónde fuiste? where did you go?
at/in	place	**llega a Madrid mañana** he arrives in Madrid tomorrow
at/on	time	**comemos a la una** we eat at one o'clock
		se fue a los quince años he left at the age of fifteen
		al día siguiente murió he died (on) the next day
at/on	place where	**torcieron a la izquierda** they turned to the left
		sentarse a la mesa to sit down at table
on	means of transport	**a pie, a caballo** on foot, on horseback
at	cost	**los vendían a diez euros cada uno** they were selling them at ten euros each
away from	place/time	**a los dos días volvió** he came back two days later
		la casa se sitúa a cien metros de aquí the house is a hundred metres from here
a	frequency	**dos veces al día** twice a day

in	opinion	**a mi ver, a mi juicio, a mis ojos** in my opinion, in my view
purpose	verbs of motion	**fui a comprar pan** I went to buy bread
personal a	see page 58	**he visto a Juan** I saw Juan

ANTE

before	in the presence of	**le llevaron ante el rey** they brought him before the king
before	in the face of	**ante tanto trabajo huyó** in the face of so much work he fled

BAJO

under(neath)	place	**construyeron un túnel bajo el mar** they built a tunnel under the sea
	figuratively	**bajo el reinado de Felipe II** under the reign of Philip II

CON

with	association	**se fueron con su primo** they left with their cousin
	means	**lo cortó con las tijeras** she cut it with the scissors
to		**hablaba con su amigo** he was talking to his friend
towards	figuratively	**no seas cruel conmigo** don't be cruel to me

In this last meaning, **con** is sometimes preceded by **para**:

> **era muy amable para con todos**
> he was very kind to everyone

CONTRA

against	position	**se apoyaba contra la pared** he was leaning against the wall

| | opposition | **los rebeldes luchaban contra el gobierno** |
| | | the rebels were fighting against the government |

In this last meaning, the compound preposition **en contra de** is often preferred:

| | | **votaron en contra de la ley** |
| | | they voted against the bill |

DE

of	possession	**es el coche de mi hermana**
		it's my sister's car
	material	**el vestido es de lana**
		the dress is made of wool
	contents	**un paquete de cigarrillos**
		a packet of cigarettes
(for)	purpose	**una cuchara de café**
		a coffee spoon
from	place	**es de Londres**
		he comes from London
		va de Madrid a Salamanca
		he goes from Madrid to Salamanca
	time	**de año en año vienen aquí**
		they come here year after year
		cenamos de diez a once
		we had dinner from ten to eleven
		se fueron de pequeños
		they left as little children
	number	**el peso es de cien kilos**
		the weight is one hundred kilos
		el total era de mil euros
		the total was a thousand euros
	cost	**un coche de cinco mil libras**
		a car costing five thousand pounds
with	descriptions	**la muchacha de los ojos azules**
		the girl with the blue eyes

el señor de la barba
the man with the beard

¡el bobo del niño!
the silly boy!

to form adjectival phrases   **la comida de siempre**
the usual food

la parte de fuera
the outside part

to form compound prepositions   **además de, alrededor de** etc. See
page 177.

DESDE

from	place	**le vi llegar desde mi ventana** I saw him arrive from my window
from/since	time	**toca la guitarra desde niño** he has been playing the guitar since he was a boy

with **hasta**

from ... to/till	time	**desde las dos hasta las cuatro** from two o'clock till four
from ... to	place	**desde Madrid hasta Barcelona** from Madrid to Barcelona

EN

in/at/on	position	**paró en la puerta** he stopped in the doorway
		quedarse en casa to stay at home
		el ordenador está en la mesa the computer is on the table
		los vimos en la Feria de Muestras we saw it at the Exhibition
	opinion	**en mi opinión sería imprudente** in my opinion it would be unwise
into	numbers	**lo dividió en tres partes** he divided it into three

within	time	**no le he visto en quince días** I haven't seen him in a fortnight
by	increase/ decrease	**los precios han aumentado en un diez por ciento** the prices have gone up by ten per cent
phrases		**en balde, en vano** in vain **en seguida** immediately **en absoluto** absolutely not

ENTRE

between		**entre la puerta y la pared** between the door and the wall **entre tú y yo** between you and me
among		**lo encontré entre tus papeles** I found it among your papers
together		**lo hicimos entre todos** we did it together

HACIA

towards	place	**fue corriendo hacia su padre** he ran towards his father
	figuratively	**muestra hostilidad hacia el jefe** he shows hostility to the boss
about	time	**llegaron hacia las tres** they arrived about three o'clock

HASTA

until	time	**esto continuó hasta el siglo veinte** this continued until the 20th century
up to	number	**vinieron hasta cien personas** as many as a hundred people turned up
as far as	place	**te acompaño hasta tu casa** I'll walk you home

even	figuratively	**hasta los niños quieren acompañarnos** even the children want to come with us

INCLUSO

even		**incluso mi padre está de acuerdo** even my father agrees

MEDIANTE

by means of		**lo consiguió mediante mucho trabajo** he achieved it by hard work

PARA

in order to	purpose	**salió para lavar el coche** he went out to wash the car
		compró una navaja para cortar la cuerda she bought a penknife to cut the rope
		estudió para cura he studied to become a priest
for	in the direction of	**se fueron para Estados Unidos** they left for the USA
by	time by which	**quiero ese trabajo para mañana** I want that work by tomorrow
		para entonces ya me habré marchado I'll have gone away by then
for	as concerns	**el cálculo no es difícil para ella** the calculation isn't difficult for her
for	concession	**para ser español, habla muy bien inglés** for a Spaniard, he speaks very good English
to		**siempre murmuraba para sí** she was always muttering to herself

with **estar**	on the point of	**estábamos todos para salir** we were all ready to go out
idioms		**bastante … para** enough … to/for **demasiado … para** too much … to/for **suficiente … para** enough … to/for
		cuesta demasiado para mí it's too expensive for me

POR

by	agent	**el reparo fue terminado por el jefe** the repair was finished by the boss
for	time during	**habló por dos minutos** he spoke for two minutes
		ocurrió el robo el domingo por la noche the robbery took place on Sunday night
out of		**lo echó por la ventana** she threw it out of the window
through		**pasaron por Valencia** they went through Valencia
about	place	**rodaron por las cercanías** they roamed about the neighbourhood
		vive por aquí he lives around here
by/through	means	**por mí se informaron sobre el desastre** they found out about the disaster through me
		por avión, por teléfono by air, by telephone

in exchange for		**vendió el coche por cien libras** he sold the car for a hundred pounds
per/by	rate/sequence	**cincuenta kilómetros por hora** fifty kilometres per hour
out of/by	cause	**por no estudiar no aprobó el examen** he failed the exam through not having studied
for the sake of/ through		**por amor le siguió a España** she followed him to Spain out of love
times	multiplication	**dos por dos son cuatro** two times two are four
for	to get	**voy a por hielo** I am going to get some ice
idioms	tomar ... por	**¿me tomas por idiota?** do you take me for a fool?
	pasar por	**pasa por buen conductor** he is considered a good driver
	estar por	**los platos están por lavar** the dishes still have to be washed
		estoy por salir I feel like going out

SEGÚN

according to	**según él, es peligroso** according to him, it's dangerous
	los precios varían según la época del año the prices vary according to the time of year

SIN

without	**continuaremos sin su ayuda** we will go on without your help
	sin saber without knowing

SOBRE

on/over	place	**las tazas están sobre la mesa** the cups are on the table
		el avión voló sobre las montañas the plane flew over the mountains
around	time	**vendrá sobre las siete** he will come around seven o'clock
on/about	concerning	**he leído un artículo sobre la guerra** I read an article about the war

TRAS

after	time	**tras una reunión de tres horas** after a three hour meeting
	succession	**uno tras otro** one after the other

COMPOUND PREPOSITIONS

acerca de	about/ concerning	**me habló el jefe acerca del empleado** the boss spoke to me about the employee
a causa de	because of	**no salimos a causa de la tormenta** we are not going out because of the storm
a favor de	in favour of/for	**¿estás a favor de la energía nuclear?** are you in favour of nuclear energy?
a fuerza de	by dint of	**consiguió terminar a fuerza de trabajar noche y día** he managed to get finished by dint of working both night and day
a pesar de	in spite of	**salieron a pesar de la lluvia** they went out in spite of the rain

a lo largo de	along	**hay flores a lo largo del río** there are flowers all along the riverside
	throughout	**a lo largo del mes de agosto** throughout the month of August
a través de	across/through	**la luz entra a través de la ventana** the light comes in through the window
además de	besides/as well as	**compré pan además de mantequilla** I bought bread as well as butter
alrededor de	about/around	**gana alrededor de veinte libras al día** he earns around twenty pounds a day
		las casas están situadas alrededor de la iglesia the houses are situated around the church
antes de	before (time)	**antes de entrar dejen salir** let people off before getting on
cerca de	near	**la casa está cerca del colegio** the house is near the school
	around	**tiene cerca de mil ovejas** he has nearly a thousand sheep
debajo de	under	**se pararon debajo del árbol** they stopped under the tree
delante de	in front of	**el coche se detuvo delante del hotel** the car stopped in front of the hotel
dentro de	inside	**encontró un regalo dentro del paquete** she found a gift inside the parcel
después de	after	**salió después de terminar su trabajo** he went out after finishing his work
		después de las dos after two o'clock
		después de todo after all
detrás de	behind	**el bar se encuentra detrás del mercado** the bar is behind the market

en lugar de / en vez de	instead of	**en lugar de telefonear, les escribió** instead of phoning, he wrote to them
en medio de	in the midst of	**paró en medio de tocar la sonata** he stopped in the midst of playing the sonata
encima de	on (top of)	**colocó el vaso encima de la mesa** she put the glass on the table
enfrente de	opposite	**la iglesia está enfrente del Ayuntamiento** the church is opposite the Town Hall
fuera de	apart from	**fuera de los de al lado, no conozco a nadie** apart from the next-door neighbours, I don't know anyone
	outside	**la granja está situada fuera de la aldea** the farm is outside the village
lejos de	far from	**la iglesia no está lejos de la escuela** the church is not far from the school
		lejos de acatar la ley far from respecting the law
por medio de	by (means of)	**consiguió obtener el dinero por medio de un embuste** he managed to get the money by means of trickery

12. RELATIVE PRONOUNS

For a detailed explanation of the use of relative pronouns, see pages 48-51.

1. Simple relative pronouns

a) *que* (who, whom, which, that)

que relates to either persons or things, singular or plural. Note that it is invariable.

b) *quien/quienes* (who, whom, that)

quien (singular), **quienes** (plural) relate exclusively to people and are normally used after prepositions.

2. Compound relative pronouns

The compound relative pronouns have separate forms for masculine singular and plural, and feminine singular and plural. They also have a neuter form.

a) *el que* (who, whom, which, that)

	masculine	feminine	neuter
singular	el que	la que	lo que
plural	los que	las que	

b) *el cual* (who, whom, which, that)

	masculine	feminine	neuter
singular	el cual	la cual	lo cual
plural	los cuales	las cuales	

13. PRONOUNS

1. Subject pronouns

	singular	*plural*
1st person	**yo** (I)	**nosotros, nosotras** (we)
2nd person	**tú** (you)	**vosotros, vosotras** (you)
3rd person	**él** (he, it)	**ellos** (they)
	ella (she, it)	**ellas** (they)
	ello (it)	
	usted (you)	**ustedes** (you)

usted and **ustedes** are commonly abbreviated to **Vd.** and **Vds.** (or occasionally to **Ud.** and **Uds.**). They are followed by the *third* person forms of the verb. For the difference between **Vd.** and **tú**, see page 54. For the use of **ello** see pages 53-4.

2. Weak object pronouns

For the use of the weak object pronouns, see pages 58-60.

a) Direct object pronouns

	singular	*plural*
1st person	**me** (me)	**nos** (us)
2nd person	**te** (you)	**os** (you)
3rd person	**le** (him, you)	**les** (them, you)
	la (her, it, you)	**las** (them, you)
	lo (it)	**los** (them)

le and **les** are the masculine pronouns used for people

lo and **los** are the masculine pronouns used for things

la and **las** are the feminine pronouns for either people or things

b) Indirect object pronouns

	singular	*plural*
1st person	**me** (to me)	**nos** (to us)
2nd person	**te** (to you)	**os** (to you)
3rd person	**le** (to him/her/it/you)	**les** (to them/you)

c) Reflexive pronouns (myself etc)

	singular	*plural*
1st person	**me**	**nos**
2nd person	**te**	**os**
3rd person	**se**	**se**

3. Strong object pronouns

For the use of the strong object pronouns, see pages 60-61.

	singular	*plural*
1st person	**mí**	**nosotros, nosotras**
2nd person	**ti**	**vosotros, vosotras**
3rd person	**él, ella, ello**	**ellos, ellas**
	Vd.	**Vds.**
(reflexive)	**sí**	**sí**

mí, ti and **sí** combine with **con** to give the following forms:

conmigo	with me
contigo	with you
consigo	with himself/herself/yourself/
	themselves/yourselves

4. Position of the pronouns

The weak object pronouns normally come before the verb. In the compound tenses they are placed before the auxiliary verb:

él lo hizo	**yo le he visto**
he did it	I saw him

nos hemos levantado	**Vd. se despierta**
we got up	you wake up

In the following three cases the pronouns come after the verb and are joined to it:

a) when the verb is in the infinitive:

quiero verla	**salió después de hacerlo**
I want to see her	he went out after doing it

However, if the infinitive immediately follows another verb, the pronoun may precede the first verb:

querían encontrarnos   they wanted to meet us

OR   **nos querían encontrar**

b)   when the verb is in the present participle:

estoy pintándolo	**estaba cantándola**
I am painting it	he was singing it

Again, in the case of a progressive form of the verb, the pronoun may precede the first verb:

están llevándolo   they are carrying it

OR   **lo están llevando**

c)   when giving a positive command:

¡déjalo!	**¡date prisa!**
leave it!	hurry up!
¡quédese aquí!	**¡espéreme!**
stay here!	wait for me!

However, the pronoun precedes the verb in a negative command:

¡no lo hagas!	**¡no te muevas!**
don't do it!	don't move!

5.   Changes in accentuation and spelling

a)   Accents

Note that when more than one pronoun is added to an infinitive, a present participle or an imperative, a written accent is usually required on the original verb to indicate spoken stress if this has moved to the third last syllable (see page 148):

¿quieres pasarme el vino?	**¿quieres pasármelo?**
will you pass me the wine?	will you pass me it?
está explicándome la lección	**está explicándomela**
he is explaining the lesson to me	he is explaining it to me

dame el libro
give me the book

dámelo
give me it

ponga el libro en la mesa
put the book on the table

póngalo en la mesa
put it on the table

dígame
hello (on the phone)

b) Changes in spelling

When **-se** is joined to the verb, any final **s** of the verb ending is dropped:

vendámoselo
let's sell it to him

The final **s** of the first person plural is dropped before the reflexive pronoun **nos**:

sentémonos
let's sit down

The **d** of the second person plural imperative is dropped before the reflexive pronoun **os**:

sentaos, por favor
have a seat, please

With third conjugation verbs, an accent is then required on the **i**:

vestíos
get dressed

The only exception is the verb **ir**, where the **d** of the imperative is in fact retained:

idos
go away

6. Order of pronouns

When two or more pronouns are being used together they come in the following order:

a) The reflexive **se** must always come first:

se me ha ocurrido
it occurred to me

se le olvidó
he forgot

b) When a direct and an indirect object pronoun are both being used, the indirect comes first:

me lo dio **nos la mostraron**
he gave me it they showed it to us

c) If there are both a third person direct object pronoun (**la, lo, le, los, las, les**) and a third person indirect object pronoun (**le, les**), the indirect **le** and **les** are both replaced by **se** before the direct object pronoun:

se la vendieron (a ella) **se los mandó (a Vd.)**
they sold it to her he sent them to you

The addition of **a él, a ella, a Vd.** or **a Vds.** and the like can clarify to whom the **se** refers.

d) In those cases where the direct object pronouns **me, te, nos** or **os** are used with another indirect object pronoun, the direct object pronoun stands before the verb, and the indirect pronoun is replaced by **a** + the corresponding strong pronoun after the verb:

me mandaron a ti
they sent me to you

nos acercamos a ellos
we approached them

14. ADVERBS

Adverbs are used with verbs, adjectives and other adverbs. When used with a verb, they describe:

how an action is done	adverbs of manner
when an action is done	adverbs of time
where an action is done	adverbs of place
to what *degree* an action is done	adverbs of degree

1. Adverbs of manner

a) Most of these adverbs can be formed by adding **-mente** to the feminine singular form of the adjective:

lenta	slow	**lentamente**	slowly
extensa	wide	**extensamente**	widely

Accents appearing on the adjective are retained on the adverb:

lógica	logical	**lógicamente**	logically
rápida	quick	**rápidamente**	quickly

b) When two or more adverbs are used to describe the same verb, only the last one takes **-mente**, but the initial ones retain the feminine form of the adjective:

caminaron nerviosa y rápidamente
they travelled anxiously and fast

c) The following adverbs of manner do not have a form in **-mente**:

bien	well	**mal**	badly
adrede	on purpose	**así**	in this way
despacio	slowly	**deprisa**	quickly

caminaban despacio por el calor que hacía
they travelled slowly because of the heat

tú has trabajado bien, Juanito
you've done a good job, Juanito

2. Adverbs of time

Most of these adverbs are not formed from adjectives. The commonest are:

ahora	now
anoche	last night
anteanoche	the night before last
anteayer/antes de ayer	the day before yesterday
antes	before
ayer	yesterday
después	after
entonces	then
hoy	today
luego	presently
mañana	tomorrow
nunca	never
pasado mañana	the day after tomorrow
primero	firstly
pronto	soon
prontísimo	very soon
siempre	always
tarde	late
tardísimo	very late
temprano	early
tempranísimo	very early
todavía	still/yet
ya	already/now/presently

Some common adverbial phrases of time:

a continuación	next
acto seguido	immediately after
algunas veces	sometimes
a menudo	often
a veces	sometimes
dentro de poco	soon
de vez en cuando	from time to time
en breve	soon
muchas veces	often
nunca más	never again
otra vez	again
pocas veces	rarely
rara vez	seldom
repetidas veces	again and again
una y otra vez	again and again

quiero empezar ahora, no espero hasta mañana
I want to start now, I'm not waiting until tomorrow

siempre va en tren hasta el centro, luego coge el autobús
she always takes the train into the centre and then catches a bus

quedamos en vernos pasado mañana, no mañana
we agreed to meet the day after tomorrow, not tomorrow

Points to note

a) As well as meaning 'already', **ya** is used in everyday speech to mean 'right away':

¡ya voy!
I'm coming right away!

There are times when **ya** has no clear translation into English as it is often used as a filler:

ya me lo decía yo
I thought so

In the negative **ya no** means 'no longer':

siempre iba a ver a su tía el sábado, pero ya no va
he always used to visit his aunt on Saturdays, but he no longer goes

⚠ **It should not be confused with *todavía no*, which means 'not yet':**

todavía no han llegado
they haven't arrived yet

b) **luego** can also mean 'therefore':

pienso luego existo
I think therefore I am

c) **recientemente** is shortened to **recién** before past participles. **recién** is invariable and does not change its form whatever the gender or number of the past participle:

una niña recién nacida
a new-born baby girl

los recién casados
the newly-weds

3. Adverbs of place

The commonest of these are:

abajo	down/below
ahí/allí	there
allá	over there
aquí	here
arriba	up/above
cerca	near
debajo	below/beneath
delante	forward/in front
dentro	inside
detrás	behind/back
donde	where
encima	over/above/on
enfrente	opposite
fuera	outside
lejos	far

Some adverbial phrases:

en alguna parte	somewhere
en otra parte	somewhere else
en/por todas partes	everywhere

la aldea donde nací
the village where I was born

¿dónde está Juan? – está dentro
where's Juan? – he's inside

¿hay alguna tienda por aquí cerca?
is there a shop hereabouts?

se me cayeron encima
they fell on me

Points to note

a) **aquí, allí** and **allá** express the same relationships as the demonstrative adjectives **este, ese** and **aquel** (see page 27):

aquí	means 'here, near me'
allí	means 'there, near you'
allá	means 'there, far from both of us'

b) The forms **arriba**, **abajo**, **adelante** and **atrás** can be used immediately after a noun in adverbial phrases such as:

> **andábamos calle abajo**
> we walked down the street

> **aquello sucedió años atrás**
> that event took place years later

adentro and **a través** also appear in set phrases:

> **mar adentro**
> out at sea

> **campo a través**
> cross country

4. Adverbs of degree

The commonest of these are:

algo	somewhat
apenas	hardly
bastante	fairly/rather/enough
casi	almost
como	about
cuánto	how/how much
demasiado	too much
más	more
menos	less
mitad/medio	half
mucho	very much
muy	very much
nada	not at all
poco	little
qué	how
suficientemente	enough
tan	so/as
tanto	so much/as much
todo	entirely
un poco	a little

> **la casa es muy vieja pero es bastante grande**
> the house is very old but it is fairly big

me gusta mucho la tortilla, pero no me gustan nada los calamares
I like tortilla very much, but I don't like squid at all

tiene casi tres años, todavía es demasiado pequeño para ir solo
he is almost three, still too little to go by himself

hoy se siente un poco mejor
he is feeling a little better today

Points to note

a) This use of **qué** is restricted to exclamations:

¡qué inteligente eres!
how clever you are!

b) **muy** is used with adjectives and adjectival phrases, and adverbs:

estoy muy cansado
I am very tired

me parece muy temprano
it seems very early to me

In a few exceptional cases, it can be used with a noun:

es muy amigo mío
he's a very good friend of mine

When used as an adverb, **mucho** goes with verbs, comparative adverbs, and comparative adjectives:

me gustó mucho
I liked it a lot
está mucho mejor
he's much better

c) When used as an adverb, **medio** never changes its form:

María estaba medio dormida
María was half asleep

d) Note the common construction with **suficientemente**:

no es lo suficientemente inteligente como para entender esto
he isn't clever enough to understand this

15. THE VERB

DIFFERENT CATEGORIES OF VERBS: THE CONJUGATIONS

There are three conjugations of verbs in Spanish. The infinitive of a verb indicates which conjugation it belongs to.

> all verbs ending in **-ar** belong to the first conjugation
> all verbs ending in **-er** belong to the second conjugation
> all verbs ending in **-ir** belong to the third conjugation

Some verbs are irregular, and others have minor deviations from the rules. These will be treated separately.

Spanish has many 'radical changing verbs' where changes are made to the stressed vowel of the stem, although the endings of these verbs are perfectly normal. These verbs will be dealt with in a separate section.

All newly coined verbs automatically go into the first conjugation and adopt its endings and forms, eg **informatizar** (to computerize).

A. THE TENSES OF THE INDICATIVE – THE SIMPLE TENSES

Tenses may be either simple – consisting of one word only – or compound, where an auxiliary verb is used with a participle of the main verb.

1. THE PRESENT TENSE

The stem for the present tense of the verb is found by removing the endings **-ar**, **-er** or **-ir** from the infinitive. The present tense itself is then formed by adding the following endings to the stem:

1st conjugation	**-o, -as, -a, -amos, -áis, -an**
2nd conjugation	**-o, -es, -e, -emos, -éis, -en**
3rd conjugation	**-o, -es, -e, -imos, -ís, -en**

cant-ar	beb-er	recib-ir
canto	bebo	recibo
cantas	bebes	recibes
canta	bebe	recibe
cantamos	bebemos	recibimos
cantáis	bebéis	recibís
cantan	beben	reciben

a) Irregularities in the present tense

For **ser** and **estar**, and the irregular verbs **haber**, **dar**, **ir**, **tener** and **venir** see pages 223–229. For radical changing verbs see pages 210–217.

b) First conjugation verbs ending in -iar and -uar

Most of these verbs have the spoken accent and also a written accent on the final **i** and **u** of the stem in all but the first and second persons plural:

enviar	continuar
envío	continúo
envías	continúas
envía	continúa
enviamos	continuamos
enviáis	continuáis
envían	continúan

The commonest exceptions are the verbs **cambiar** (to change) and **averiguar** (to ascertain).

c) Second conjugation verbs ending in -ecer

The ending of the first person singular is **-ezco**. All other forms are regular:

parecer	parezco, pareces …
crecer	crezco, creces …

d) Third conjugation verbs ending in **-uir**, and the verb **oír**

These verbs add **y** to the stem *unless* the stem is followed by a stressed **i**, ie in all but the first and second persons plural. Note that **oír** also has an irregular first person singular (see below):

construir	oír
construyo	oigo
construyes	oyes
construye	oye
construimos	oímos
construís	oís
construyen	oyen

e) Third conjugation verbs ending in **-ucir**

The ending of the first person singular is **-uzco**. All other forms are regular:

conducir	conduzco, conduces ...
producir	produzco, produces ...

f) Second and third conjugation verbs whose stem ends in **c** or **g**

Such verbs change the **c** to **z** and the **g** to **j** in the first person singular. All other forms are regular:

vencer	venzo, vences ...
esparcir	esparzo, esparces ...
escoger	escojo, escoges ...
rugir	rujo, ruges ...

g) Third conjugation verbs whose stem ends in **qu** or **gu**

Such verbs change the **qu** to **c** and the **gu** to **g** in the first person singular. All other forms are regular:

delinquir	delinco, delinques ...
distinguir	distingo, distingues ...

h) Third conjugation verbs whose infinitive ends in **-güir**

These verbs drop the dieresis except in the first and second persons plural:

argüir	arguyo, arguyes, arguye, argüimos, argüís, arguyen

i) Verbs with an irregular first person singular

The following verbs have largely unpredictable irregularities in the first person singular:

caber	to fit	quepo
caer	to fall	caigo
conocer	to know	conozco
decir	to say	digo
estar	to be	estoy
hacer	to do/make	hago
ir	to go	voy
oír	to hear	oigo
saber	to know	sé
salir	to go out/leave	salgo
ser	to be	soy
tener	to have	tengo
traer	to bring	traigo
valer	to be worth	valgo
venir	to come	vengo

Any compound form of these verbs shares the same irregularities.

contradecir	to contradict	contradigo
obtener	to obtain	obtengo

Note that **satisfacer** behaves in the same way as **hacer**:

satisfacer	to satisfy	satisfago

2. THE FUTURE TENSE

The future tense of all conjugations is formed by adding the following endings to the infinitive of the verb, irrespective of its conjugation:

-é, -ás, -á, -emos, -éis, -án

cantaré	beberé	recibiré
cantarás	beberás	recibirás
cantará	beberá	recibirá
cantaremos	beberemos	recibiremos
cantaréis	beberéis	recibiréis
cantarán	beberán	recibirán

Irregularities in the future tense

A number of verbs add these endings to an irregular stem:

caber	to fit	cabré
decir	to say	diré
haber	to have	habré
hacer	to do/make	haré
poder	to be able	podré
poner	to put	pondré
querer	to want	querré
saber	to know	sabré
salir	to go out/leave	saldré
tener	to have	tendré
valer	to be worth	valdrá
venir	to come	vendré

Again, any compounds share the same irregularities:

deshacer	to undo	desharé
convenir	to agree/suit	convendré

3. THE IMPERFECT TENSE

The imperfect tense is formed by adding the following endings to the stem of the infinitive:

1st conjugation   **-aba, -abas, -aba, -ábamos, -abais, -aban**

2nd &3rd conjugations   **-ía, -ías, -ía, -íamos, -íais, -ían**

cantaba	bebía	recibía
cantabas	bebías	recibías
cantaba	bebía	recibía
cantábamos	bebíamos	recibíamos
cantabais	bebíais	recibíais
cantaban	bebían	recibían

Irregularities in the imperfect tense

There are only three irregular imperfects in Spanish:

ser	ir	ver
era	iba	veía
eras	ibas	veías
era	iba	veía
éramos	íbamos	veíamos
erais	ibais	veíais
eran	iban	veían

4. THE PRETERITE TENSE

The preterite is formed by adding the following endings to the stem of the infinitive:

1st conjugation   -é, -aste, -ó, -amos, -asteis, -aron
2nd &3rd conjugations -í, -iste, -ió, -imos, -isteis, -ieron

canté	bebí	recibí
cantaste	bebiste	recibiste
cantó	bebió	recibió
cantamos	bebimos	recibimos
cantasteis	bebisteis	recibisteis
cantaron	bebieron	recibieron

Irregularities in the preterite tense

a) The so-called **pretérito grave**

This group comprises a sizable number of mostly second and third conjugation verbs which all add the following endings to irregular stems:

-e, -iste, -o, -imos, -isteis, -ieron

Note in particular that the first and third person singular endings are not stressed (the term **grave** in **pretérito grave** means 'stressed on the *second last* syllable').

If the stem itself ends in **j**, the third person plural ending is shortened to **-eron**.

andar	anduve, anduviste, anduvo, anduvimos, anduvisteis, anduvieron
caber	cupe, cupiste, cupo, cupimos, cupisteis, cupieron
decir	dije, dijiste, dijo, dijimos, dijisteis, dijeron
estar	estuve, estuviste, estuvo, estuvimos, estuvisteis, estuvieron
haber	hube, hubiste, hubo, hubimos, hubisteis, hubieron
hacer	hice, hiziste, hizo, hicimos, hicisteis, hicieron
poder	pude, pudiste, pudo, pudimos, pudisteis, pudieron
poner	puse, pusiste, puso, pusimos, pusisteis, pusieron
querer	quise, quisiste, quiso, quisimos, quisisteis, quisieron
tener	tuve, tuviste, tuvo, tuvimos, tuvisteis, tuvieron
traer	traje, trajiste, trajo, trajimos, trajisteis, trajeron
saber	supe, supiste, supo, supimos, supisteis, supieron
venir	vine, viniste, vino, vinimos, vinisteis, vinieron

All compounds of these verbs share the same irregularities:

| contraer | contraje … |
| componer | compuse … |

This group also comprises all verbs ending in **-ucir**, with the exception of **lucir**, which is regular. Their stem for the preterite ends in **uj**:

| producir | produje, produjiste, produjo, produjimos, produjisteis, produjeron |

b) Other verbs

The following verbs are also irregular:

dar	di, diste, dio, dimos, disteis, dieron
ir	fui, fuiste, fue, fuimos, fuisteis, fueron
ser	fui, fuiste, fue, fuimos, fuisteis, fueron
ver	vi, viste, vio, vimos, visteis, vieron

As can be seen, the preterites of **ir** and **ser** are identical. However, the context always indicates clearly which one is involved.

c) Spelling changes

First conjugation verbs whose stems end in **c** or **g** change these to **qu** and **gu** in the first person singular of the preterite. All other forms are regular:

explicar	expliqué, explicaste ...
llegar	llegué, llegaste ...

Verbs ending in **-aer**, **-eer**, **-oer** and **-uir**

In these verbs, the **i** of the third person singular and plural ending changes to **y**. All other forms are regular:

caer	cayó	cayeron
construir	construyó	construyeron
leer	leyó	leyeron
roer	royó	royeron

oír also belongs to this group:

oír	oyó	oyeron

Third conjugation verbs ending in **-güir** drop the dieresis in the third persons singular and plural:

argüir	argüí, argüiste, arguyó, argüimos, argüisteis, arguyeron

Second and third conjugation verbs whose stems end in **ñ** drop the **i** from the third person singular and plural endings:

gruñir	gruñó	gruñeron
tañer	tañó	tañeron

5. THE CONDITIONAL

The conditional is formed for all conjugations by adding the following endings to the infinitive of the verb:

-ía, -ías, -ía, -íamos, -íais, -ían

cantaría	bebería	recibiría
cantarías	beberías	recibirías
cantaría	bebería	recibiría
cantaríamos	beberíamos	recibiríamos
cantaríais	beberíais	recibiríais
cantarían	beberían	recibirían

Irregularities in the conditional

Any verb with an irregular stem in the future uses the same stem for the formation of the conditional (see page 196):

hacer	haría
venir	vendría

and so on.

B. COMPOUND TENSES

Compound tenses are formed by using an auxiliary verb with either the present or the past participle.

I. THE PRESENT PARTICIPLE

a) The regular forms

The present participle is formed by adding the following endings to the stem of the infinitive:

1st conjugation   -ando
2nd & 3rd conjugations   -iendo

b) Irregular present participles

Verbs ending in **-aer**, **-eer**, **-oer** and **-uir**, and the verb **oír**.

In these verbs the **i** of the ending is changed to **y**:

caer	cayendo
construir	construyendo
creer	creyendo
oír	oyendo
roer	royendo

Verbs ending in **-güir** drop the dieresis in the present participle:

argüir	arguyendo

Second and third conjugation verbs whose stems end in **ñ** drop the **i** from the ending:

gruñir	gruñendo
tañer	tañendo

Third conjugation radical changing verbs of groups 3, 4 and 5 also have irregular present participles (see pages 213-217):

dormir	durmiendo
pedir	pidiendo
sentir	sintiendo

2. THE PAST PARTICIPLE

a) The regular forms

To form the past participle of a regular verb remove the infinitive ending and add:

1st conjugation	**-ado**	**cantado**
2nd & 3rd conjugations	**-ido**	**bebido, recibido**

b) Irregular past participles

Some verbs have irregular past participles. The most common are:

abrir	to open	**abierto**	opened
cubrir	to cover	**cubierto**	covered
decir	to say	**dicho**	said
escribir	to write	**escrito**	written
hacer	to make/to do	**hecho**	made/done
morir	to die	**muerto**	dead
poner	to put	**puesto**	put
resolver	to solve	**resuelto**	solved
ver	to see	**visto**	seen
volver	to return	**vuelto**	returned

Compounds of these verbs have the same irregularities in their past participles, eg:

descubrir	to discover	**descubierto**	discovered
describir	to describe	**descrito**	described

The verb **satisfacer** behaves in the same way as **hacer**:

satisfacer	to satisfy	**satisfecho**	satisfied

3. THE PROGRESSIVE FORMS OF THE TENSES

A progressive form of any tense can be formed by using **estar** (or one of an associated group of verbs) with the present participle. For the full conjugation of **estar**, see page 224:

> **estamos trabajando**
> we are working

yo estaba estudiando cuando Juan entró
I was studying when Juan came in

For a full discussion of the progressive tenses, see pages 72-74.

4. THE PERFECT TENSE

The compound past tenses are formed with the appropriate tense of the verb **haber** together with the past participle of the verb. For the full conjugation of **haber**, see page 225.

The perfect tense is formed by using the present tense of **haber** with the past participle of the main verb:

he cantado	he bebido	he recibido
has cantado	has bebido	has recibido
ha cantado	ha bebido	ha recibido
hemos cantado	hemos bebido	hemos recibido
habéis cantado	habéis bebido	habéis recibido
han cantado	han bebido	han recibido

5. THE PLUPERFECT TENSE

The pluperfect tense is formed by using the imperfect of **haber** with the past participle of the main verb:

había cantado	había bebido	había recibido
habías cantado	habías bebido	habías recibido
había cantado	había bebido	había recibido
habíamos cantado	habíamos bebido	habíamos recibido
habíais cantado	habíais bebido	habíais recibido
habían cantado	habían bebido	habían recibido

6. THE FUTURE PERFECT TENSE

The future perfect tense is formed by using the future of **haber** with the past participle of the main verb:

habré cantado	habré bebido	habré recibido
habrás cantado	habrás bebido	habrás recibido
habrá cantado	habrá bebido	habrá recibido
habremos cantado	habremos bebido	habremos recibido
habréis cantado	habréis bebido	habréis recibido
habrán cantado	habrán bebido	habrán recibido

7. THE PAST ANTERIOR TENSE

The past anterior tense is formed by using the preterite of **haber** with the past participle of the main verb:

hube cantado	hube bebido	hube recibido
hubiste cantado	hubiste bebido	hubiste recibido
hubo cantado	hubo bebido	hubo recibido
hubimos cantado	hubimos bebido	hubimos recibido
hubisteis cantado	hubisteis bebido	hubisteis recibido
hubieron cantado	hubieron bebido	hubieron recibido

8. THE CONDITIONAL PERFECT

The conditional perfect is formed by using the conditional of **haber** with the past participle of the main verb:

habría cantado	habría bebido	habría recibido
habrías cantado	habrías bebido	habrías recibido
habría cantado	habría bebido	habría recibido
habríamos cantado	habríamos bebido	habríamos recibido
habríais cantado	habríais bebido	habríais recibido
habrían cantado	habrían bebido	habrían recibido

C. THE TENSES OF THE SUBJUNCTIVE MOOD

1. THE PRESENT SUBJUNCTIVE

With the exception of a few irregular verbs (**estar, ser, ir, dar**) the stem for the present subjunctive of a verb is found by removing the **-o** from the ending of the first person singular of the present tense. The subjunctive is then formed by adding the following endings to that stem.

1st conjugation	-e, -es, -e, -emos, -éis, -en
2nd & 3rd conjugations	-a, -as, -a, -amos, -áis, -an

cant-o	beb-o	recib-o
cante	beba	reciba
cantes	bebas	recibas
cante	beba	reciba
cantemos	bebamos	recibamos
cantéis	bebáis	recibáis
canten	beban	reciban

Irregularities in the present subjunctive:

(For radical changing verbs see pages 210-217.)

a) Verbs in **-iar** and **-uar**

Such verbs have the same pattern of accentuation in the subjunctive as they do in the indicative, ie a written accent on the **i** or **u** of the stem in all but the first and second persons plural:

enviar	envíe, envíes, envíe, enviemos, enviéis, envíen
continuar	continúe, continúes, continúe, continuemos, continuéis, continúen

b) Irregular stems

Since the stem of the subjunctive is based on the first person singular of the indicative, any irregularities there appear throughout the present subjunctive, for example:

infinitive	1st pers pres	subjunctive
decir	digo	diga, digas, diga, digamos, digáis, digan
coger	cojo	coja, cojas, coja, cojamos, cojáis, cojan
parecer	parezco	parezca, parezcas, parezca, parezcamos, parezcáis, parezcan
poner	pongo	ponga, pongas, ponga, pongamos, pongáis, pongan
vencer	venzo	venza, venzas, venza, venzamos, venzáis, venzan

c) Spelling changes

buscar busque, busques, busque, busquemos, busquéis, busquen

llegar llegue, llegues, llegue, lleguemos, lleguéis, lleguen

First conjugation verbs ending in **-guar** require a dieresis throughout the present subjunctive.

averiguar averigüe, averigües, averigüe, averigüemos, averigüéis, averigüen

2. THE IMPERFECT SUBJUNCTIVE

The stem for the imperfect subjunctive is found by removing the ending **-ron** from the third person plural of the preterite of the verb. The imperfect subjunctive has two possible forms, formed by adding the following endings to that stem:

1st conjugation	-ara, -aras, -ara, -áramos, -arais, -aran
	-ase, -ases, -ase, -ásemos, -aseis, -asen
2nd & 3rd conjugations	-iera, -ieras, -iera, -iéramos, -ierais, -ieran
	-iese, -ieses, -iese, -iésemos, -ieseis, -iesen

cantara/cantase	bebiera/bebiese
cantaras/cantases	bebieras/bebieses
cantara/cantase	bebiera/bebiese
cantáramos/cantásemos	bebiéramos/bebiésemos
cantarais/cantaseis	bebierais/bebieseis
cantaran/cantasen	bebieran/bebiesen

recibiera/recibiese
recibieras/recibieses
recibiera/recibiese
recibiéramos/recibiésemos
recibierais/recibieseis
recibieran/recibiesen

In general, the first form of each pair is more common in spoken Spanish.

Verbs whose preterites are irregular display the same irregularity in the imperfect subjunctive:

infinitive	preterite	imperfect subjunctive
decir	dijeron	dijera/dijese
tener	tuvieron	tuviera/tuviese
venir	vinieron	viniera/viniese

Compounds of these verbs display the same irregularities:

convenir	conviniera/conviniese
obtener	obtuviera/obtuviese

3. THE PERFECT SUBJUNCTIVE

The perfect tense of the subjunctive is formed by using the present subjunctive of **haber** with the past participle of the main verb:

haya cantado	haya bebido	haya recibido
hayas cantado	hayas bebido	hayas recibido
haya cantado	haya bebido	haya recibido
hayamos cantado	hayamos bebido	hayamos recibido
hayáis cantado	hayáis bebido	hayáis recibido
hayan cantado	hayan bebido	hayan recibido

FORMS

4. THE PLUPERFECT SUBJUNCTIVE

The pluperfect of the subjunctive is formed by using the imperfect subjunctive of **haber** with the past participle of the main verb:

hubiera cantado	hubiera bebido	hubiera recibido
hubieras cantado	hubieras bebido	hubieras recibido
hubiera cantado	hubiera bebido	hubiera recibido
hubiéramos cantado	hubiéramos bebido	hubiéramos recibido
hubierais cantado	hubierais bebido	hubierais recibido
hubieran cantado	hubieran bebido	hubieran recibido
hubiese cantado	hubiese bebido	hubiese recibido
hubieses cantado	hubieses bebido	hubieses recibido
hubiese cantado	hubiese bebido	hubiese recibido
hubiésemos cantado	hubiésemos bebido	hubiésemos recibido
hubieseis cantado	hubieseis bebido	hubieseis recibido
hubiesen cantado	hubiesen bebido	hubiesen recibido

5. THE IMPERATIVE

The imperative proper exists only for the **tú** and **vosotros** forms of the verb, and is used *only* in positive commands. It is formed as follows:

tú — Remove the **s** from the second person singular of the present indicative of the verb. This applies for all conjugations.

vosotros — First and second conjugations: remove the **áis/éis** from the second person plural of the present indicative of the verb and replace it with **ad/ed**. Third conjugation: remove the **ís** from the second person plural of the present indicative of the verb and replace it with **id**.

hablar	habla	hablad
comer	come	comed
escribir	escribe	escribid

Note that, since the **tú** form is based on the second person singular of the verb, any radical changes will also be present in the singular, but not in the plural form of the imperative:

cerrar	cierra	cerrad
torcer	tuerce	torced
pedir	pide	pedid

There are a number of irregular imperatives in the **tú** form:

decir	di	decid
hacer	haz	haced
ir	ve	id
poner	pon	poned
salir	sal	salid
ser	sé	**sed** (also irregular in plural)
tener	ten	tened
valer	val	valed
venir	ven	venid

Commands addressed to all other persons – **Vd.**, **Vds.**, third and first person (ie 'let's') commands – and *all* negative commands are formed using the subjunctive. See pages 68-69 for details.

D. THE RADICAL CHANGING VERBS

Some verbs have spelling changes to their stem when the latter is stressed. The endings are not affected unless the verb itself is irregular.

1. **e** changes to **ie** (first and second conjugations only)

The commonest of these verbs are:

acertar	to guess correctly
alentar	to encourage
apretar	to squeeze
ascender	to go up, come to
atender	to attend to
aterrar	to terrify
atravesar	to cross
calentar	to heat
cerrar	to close
comenzar	to begin
concertar	to agree to
condescender	to condescend
confesar	to confess
defender	to defend
desalentar	to discourage
desatender	to disregard
descender	to come down
desconcertar	to disconcert
despertar	to waken
desplegar	to unfold
discernir	to discern
empezar	to begin
encender	to light, switch on
encerrar	to enclose
encomendar	to entrust
entender	to understand
enterrar	to bury
extender	to extend
fregar	to scrub
gobernar	to govern
helar	to freeze
manifestar	to show
merendar	to have tea
negar	to deny

nevar	to snow
pensar	to think
perder	to lose
quebrar	to break
recomendar	to recommend
regar	to irrigate
reventar	to burst
sembrar	to sow
sentarse	to sit
sosegar	to calm
temblar	to tremble
* tener	to have
tender	to stretch out
tentar	to attempt
tropezar	to stumble
verter	to pour

The change occurs in the present indicative and the present subjunctive only, wherever the **e** is stressed, ie the three persons of the singular and the third person plural:

PRESENT INDICATIVE	PRESENT SUBJUNCTIVE
atravieso	atraviese
atraviesas	atravieses
atraviesa	atraviese
atravesamos	atravesemos
atravesáis	atraveséis
atraviesan	atraviesen

Note that if the stressed **e** is the first letter in the word, it changes to **ye** and not **ie**:

errar to wander yerro, yerras, yerra, erramos, erráis, yerran

* tener has an irregular first person singular: **tengo**

The subjunctive of **tener** is based on this irregular first person singular:

tenga, tengas, tenga, tengamos, tengáis, tengan

2. o changes to **ue** (first and second conjugations only)

The commonest verbs in this group are:

absolver	to absolve
acordarse	to remember

acostarse	to go to bed
almorzar	to lunch
apostar	to bet
aprobar	to approve
avergonzarse	to be ashamed
cocer	to cook
colarse	to slip in
colgar	to hang
comprobar	to check
concordar	to agree
conmover	to move
consolar	to console
contar	to count, tell
costar	to cost
demostrar	to demonstrate
desaprobar	to disapprove
descolgar	to take down
descontar	to deduct
desenvolverse	to get by
despoblar	to depopulate
devolver	to give back
disolver	to dissolve
doler	to hurt
encontrar	to meet, find
envolver	to wrap
esforzarse	to endeavour
forzar	to force
holgar	to be idle
* jugar	to play
llover	to rain
moler	to grind
morder	to bite
mostrar	to show
mover	to move
** oler	to smell
probar	to try, taste
promover	to promote
recordar	to remember
renovar	to renew
resolver	to resolve
resollar	to wheeze

resonar	to resound
revolver	to revolve
rodar	to prowl
rogar	to ask
soldar	to weld
soler	to be in the habit of
soltar	to let go
sonar	to ring, sound
soñar	to dream
torcer	to twist, turn
tostar	to toast
trocar	to exchange
tronar	to thunder
volar	to fly
volcar	to tip over
volver	to return

The pattern of change is identical to that of group I:

PRESENT INDICATIVE	PRESENT SUBJUNCTIVE
vuelvo	**vuelva**
vuelves	**vuelvas**
vuelve	**vuelva**
volvemos	volvamos
volvéis	volváis
vuelven	**vuelvan**

* **jugar**: the **u** changes to **ue** when stressed: **juego**.

** **oler**: **h** is added to all forms where the change occurs: **huele** etc.

3. e changes to **ie** and **i** (third conjugation only)

The commonest verbs in this group are:

adherir	to join
***adquirir**	to acquire
advertir	to notice
arrepentirse	to repent
asentir	to agree
conferir	to confer
consentir	to agree
convertir	to convert
digerir	to digest
divertir	to amuse

** erguir	to raise
herir	to wound
hervir	to boil
inferir	to infer
* inquirir	to enquire into
invertir	to invest
mentir	to tell lies
pervertir	to pervert
preferir	to prefer
presentir	to foresee
proferir	to utter
referir	to refer
requerir	to require
resentirse	to resent
sentir	to feel
subvertir	to subvert
sugerir	to suggest
transferir	to transfer
*** venir	to come

When stressed, **e** changes to **ie** in the present indicative, present subjunctive, and imperative singular.

Also, unstressed **e** changes to **i** in:
- the 1st and 2nd persons plural of the present subjunctive
- the present participle
- the 3rd persons singular and plural of the preterite
- all of the imperfect subjunctive:

PRESENT

PRETERITE

siento	sentí
sientes	sentiste
siente	sintió
sentimos	sentimos
sentís	sentisteis
sienten	sintieron

PRESENT SUBJUNCTIVE	IMPERFECT SUBJUNCTIVE
sienta	sintiera/sintiese
sientas	sintieras/sintieses
sienta	sintiera/sintiese
sintamos	sintiéramos/sintiésemos
sintáis	sintierais/sintieseis
sientan	sintieran/sintiesen

IMPERATIVE	PRESENT PARTICIPLE
siente	sintiendo

* In the case of **adquirir** and **inquirir** it is the **i** of the stem which changes to **ie**.

** When stressed, the **e** of **erguir** changes to **ye** and not **ie**:

yergo, yergues, yergue, erguimos, erguís, yerguen

*** **venir** has an irregular first person singular: **vengo**

The subjunctive of **venir** is based on this irregular first person singular:

venga, vengas, venga, vengamos, vengáis, vengan

4. e changes to **i** (third conjugation only)

The commonest verbs in this group are:

colegir	to collect
competir	to compete
concebir	to design
conseguir	to manage
corregir	to correct
derretir	to melt
despedir	to sack
elegir	to elect
expedir	to dispatch
gemir	to groan
impedir	to prevent
invertir	to invest
medir	to measure
pedir	to ask for
perseguir	to persecute
proseguir	to continue
regir	to govern
rendir	to yield

repetir	to repeat
seguir	to follow
servir	to serve
vestir	to dress

When stressed, **e** changes to **i** in the present indicative, present subjunctive, and imperative singular.

Also, unstressed **e** changes to **i** in:

- the 1st and 2nd persons plural of the present subjunctive
- the present participle
- the 3rd persons singular and plural of the preterite
- all of the imperfect subjunctive:

PRESENT	PRETERITE

pido	**pedí**
pides	**pediste**
pide	**pidió**
pedimos	**pedimos**
pedís	**pedisteis**
piden	**pidieron**

PRESENT SUBJUNCTIVE	IMPERFECT SUBJUNCTIVE

pida	**pidiera/pidiese**
pidas	**pidieras/pidieses**
pida	**pidiera/pidiese**
pidamos	**pidiéramos/pidiésemos**
pidáis	**pidierais/pidieseis**
pidan	**pidieran/pidiesen**

IMPERATIVE	PRESENT PARTICIPLE

pide	**pidiendo**

Verbs in this group which end in **-eír** and **-eñir** make an additional change: if the ending begins with an unstressed **i**, this **i** is dropped if it comes immediately after the **ñ** or **i** of the stem. This occurs only in the present participle, the third persons singular and plural of the preterite, and in the imperfect subjunctive.

The commonest verbs in this group are:

ceñir	to fit closely	**desteñir**	to fade
freír	to fry	**reír**	to laugh

reñir	to scold	**sonreír**	to smile
teñir	to dye		
reír		**ceñir**	
riendo		**ciñendo**	
rio		**ciñó**	
rieron		**ciñeron**	

5. o changes to ue and u (third conjugation only)

The pattern of changes is identical to that of group 3 above. In other words:

When stressed, **o** changes to **ue** in the present indicative, present subjunctive, and imperative singular.

Unstressed **o** changes to **u** in:

- the 1st and 2nd persons plural of the present subjunctive
- the present participle
- the 3rd persons singular and plural of the preterite
- all of the imperfect subjunctive.

The commonest verbs in this group are

dormir	to sleep	**morir**	to die

and their compounds.

PRESENT	PRETERITE
duermo	**dormí**
duermes	**dormiste**
duerme	**durmió**
dormimos	**dormimos**
dormís	**dormisteis**
duermen	**durmieron**

PRESENT SUBJUNCTIVE	IMPERFECT SUBJUNCTIVE
duerma	**durmiera/durmiese**
duermas	**durmieras/durmieses**
duerma	**durmiera/durmiese**
durmamos	**durmiéramos/durmiésemos**
durmáis	**durmierais/durmieseis**
duerman	**durmieran/durmiesen**

IMPERATIVE	PRESENT PARTICIPLE
duerme	**durmiendo**

E. CONJUGATION TABLES

The following verb tables provide the main conjugation patterns, including the conjugation of the most common irregular verbs:

-ar verbs	*(see page 192)*	HABLAR
-er verbs	*(see page 192)*	COMER
-ir verbs	*(see page 192)*	VIVIR
Reflexive verbs	*(see pages 66-7)*	BAÑARSE
Auxiliaries:	*(see pages 93-97)*	SER
	(see pages 93-97)	ESTAR
	(see page 101)	HABER
Common irregular verbs:		DAR
		IR
		TENER
		VENIR

'**Harrap Spanish Verbs**', a fully comprehensive list of Spanish verbs and their conjugations, is also available in this series.

HABLAR   to speak

PRESENT	IMPERFECT	FUTURE
1. hablo	hablaba	hablaré
2. hablas	hablabas	hablarás
3. habla	hablaba	hablará
1. hablamos	hablábamos	hablaremos
2. habláis	hablabais	hablaréis
3. hablan	hablaban	hablarán

PRETERITE	PERFECT	PLUPERFECT
1. hablé	he hablado	había hablado
2. hablaste	has hablado	habías hablado
3. habló	ha hablado	había hablado
1. hablamos	hemos hablado	habíamos hablado
2. hablasteis	habéis hablado	habíais hablado
3. hablaron	han hablado	habían hablado

PAST ANTERIOR	FUTURE PERFECT
hube hablado etc	habré hablado etc

CONDITIONAL		*IMPERATIVE*
PRESENT	**PAST**	
1. hablaría	habría hablado	
2. hablarías	habrías hablado	(tú) habla
3. hablaría	habría hablado	(Vd) hable
1. hablaríamos	habríamos hablado	(nosotros) hablemos
2. hablaríais	habríais hablado	(vosotros) hablad
3. hablarían	habrían hablado	(Vds) hablen

SUBJUNCTIVE		
PRESENT	**IMPERFECT**	**PLUPERFECT**
1. hable	habl-ara/ase	hubiera hablado
2. hables	habl-ara/ases	hubieras hablado
3. hable	habl-ara/ase	hubiera hablado
1. hablemos	habl-áramos/ásemos	hubiéramos hablado
2. habléis	habl-arais/aseis	hubierais hablado
3. hablen	habl-aran/asen	hubieran hablado

PERFECT   haya hablado etc

INFINITIVE	*PARTICIPLE*
PRESENT	**PRESENT**
hablar	hablando
PAST	**PAST**
haber hablado	hablado

COMER   to eat

PRESENT	IMPERFECT	FUTURE
1. como	comía	comeré
2. comes	comías	comerás
3. come	comía	comerá
1. comemos	comíamos	comeremos
2. coméis	comíais	comeréis
3. comen	comían	comerán

PRETERITE	PERFECT	PLUPERFECT
1. comí	he comido	había comido
2. comiste	has comido	habías comido
3. comió	ha comido	había comido
1. comimos	hemos comido	habíamos comido
2. comisteis	habéis comido	habíais comido
3. comieron	han comido	habían comido

PAST ANTERIOR	FUTURE PERFECT
hube comido etc	habré comido etc

CONDITIONAL		IMPERATIVE
PRESENT	PAST	
1. comería	habría comido	
2. comerías	habrías comido	(tú) come
3. comería	habría comido	(Vd) coma
1. comeríamos	habríamos comido	(nosotros) comamos
2. comeríais	habríais comido	(vosotros) comed
3. comerían	habrían comido	(Vds) coman

SUBJUNCTIVE		
PRESENT	IMPERFECT	PLUPERFECT
1. coma	com-iera/iese	hubiera comido
2. comas	com-ieras/ieses	hubieras comido
3. coma	com-iera/iese	hubiera comido
1. comamos	com-iéramos/-iésemos	hubiéramos comido
2. comáis	com-ierais/ieseis	hubierais comido
3. coman	com-ieran/iesen	hubieran comido

PERFECT	haya comido etc

INFINITIVE	PARTICIPLE
PRESENT	PRESENT
comer	comiendo
PAST	PAST
haber comido	comido

VIVIR   to live

PRESENT	IMPERFECT	FUTURE
1. vivo	vivía	viviré
2. vives	vivías	vivirás
3. vive	vivía	vivirá
1. vivimos	vivíamos	viviremos
2. vivís	vivíais	viviréis
3. viven	vivían	vivirán

PRETERITE	PERFECT	PLUPERFECT
1. viví	he vivido	había vivido
2. viviste	has vivido	habías vivido
3. vivió	ha vivido	había vivido
1. vivimos	hemos vivido	habíamos vivido
2. vivisteis	habéis vivido	habíais vivido
3. vivieron	han vivido	habían vivido

PAST ANTERIOR	FUTURE PERFECT
hube vivido etc	habré vivido etc

CONDITIONAL		*IMPERATIVE*
PRESENT	**PAST**	
1. viviría	habría vivido	
2. vivirías	habrías vivido	(tú) vive
3. viviría	habría vivido	(Vd) viva
1. viviríamos	habríamos vivido	(nosotros) vivamos
2. viviríais	habríais vivido	(vosotros) vivid
3. vivirían	habrían vivido	(Vds) vivan

SUBJUNCTIVE

PRESENT	IMPERFECT	PLUPERFECT
1. viva	viv-iera/iese	hubiera vivido
2. vivas	viv-ieras/ieses	hubieras vivido
3. viva	viv-iera/iese	hubiera vivido
1. vivamos	viv-iéramos/-iésemos	hubiéramos vivido
2. viváis	viv-ierais/ieseis	hubierais vivido
3. vivan	viv-ieran/iesen	hubieran vivido

PERFECT   haya vivido etc

INFINITIVE	*PARTICIPLE*
PRESENT	**PRESENT**
vivir	viviendo
PAST	**PAST**
haber vivido	vivido

FORMS

BAÑARSE   to have a bath

PRESENT	IMPERFECT	FUTURE
1. me baño	me bañaba	me bañaré
2. te bañas	te bañabas	te bañarás
3. se baña	se bañaba	se bañará
1. nos bañamos	nos bañábamos	nos bañaremos
2. os bañáis	os bañabais	os bañaréis
3. se bañan	se bañaban	se bañarán

PRETERITE	PERFECT	PLUPERFECT
1. me bañé	me he bañado	me había bañado
2. te bañaste	te has bañado	te habías bañado
3. se bañó	se ha bañado	se había bañado
1. nos bañamos	nos hemos bañado	nos habíamos bañado
2. os bañasteis	os habéis bañado	os habíais bañado
3. se bañaron	se han bañado	se habían bañado

PAST ANTERIOR	FUTURE PERFECT
me hube bañado etc	me habré bañado etc

CONDITIONAL		*IMPERATIVE*
PRESENT	**PAST**	
1. me bañaría	me habría bañado	
2. te bañarías	te habrías bañado	(tú) báñate
3. se bañaría	se habría bañado	(Vd) báñese
1. nos bañaríamos	nos habríamos bañado	(nosotros) bañémonos
2. os bañaríais	os habríais bañado	(vosotros) bañaos
3. se bañarían	se habrían bañado	(Vds) báñense

SUBJUNCTIVE

PRESENT	IMPERFECT	PLUPERFECT
1. me bañe	me bañ-ara/ase	me hubiera bañado
2. te bañes	te bañ-aras/ases	te hubieras bañado
3. se bañe	se bañ-ara/ase	se hubiera bañado
1. nos bañemos	nos bañ-áramos/-ásemos	nos hubiéramos bañado
2. os bañéis	os bañ-arais/aseis	os hubierais bañado
3. se bañen	se bañ-aran/asen	se hubieran bañado

PERFECT   haya bañado etc

INFINITIVE	*PARTICIPLE*
PRESENT	**PRESENT**
bañarse	bañándose
PAST	**PAST**
haberse bañado	bañado

SER   to be

PRESENT	IMPERFECT	FUTURE
1. soy	era	seré
2. eres	eras	serás
3. es	era	será
1. somos	éramos	seremos
2. sois	erais	seréis
3. son	eran	serán

PRETERITE	PERFECT	PLUPERFECT
1. fui	he sido	había sido
2. fuiste	has sido	habías sido
3. fue	ha sido	había sido
1. fuimos	hemos sido	habíamos sido
2. fuisteis	habéis sido	habíais sido
3. fueron	han sido	habían sido

PAST ANTERIOR	FUTURE PERFECT
hube sido etc	habré sido etc

CONDITIONAL		*IMPERATIVE*
PRESENT	PAST	
1. sería	habría sido	
2. serías	habrías sido	(tú) sé
3. sería	habría sido	(Vd) sea
1. seríamos	habríamos sido	(nosotros) seamos
2. seríais	habríais sido	(vosotros) sed
3. serían	habrían sido	(Vds) sean

SUBJUNCTIVE		
PRESENT	IMPERFECT	PLUPERFECT
1. sea	fu-era/ese	hubiera sido
2. seas	fu-eras/eses	hubieras sido
3. sea	fu-era/ese	hubiera sido
1. seamos	fu-éramos/-ésemos	hubiéramos sido
2. seáis	fu-erais/eseis	hubierais sido
3. sean	fu-eran/esen	hubieran sido

PERFECT   haya sido etc

INFINITIVE	*PARTICIPLE*
PRESENT	PRESENT
ser	siendo
PAST	PAST
haber sido	sido

ESTAR   to be

PRESENT	IMPERFECT	FUTURE
1. estoy	estaba	estaré
2. estás	estabas	estarás
3. está	estaba	estará
1. estamos	estábamos	estaremos
2. estáis	estabais	estaréis
3. están	estaban	estarán
PRETERITE	**PERFECT**	**PLUPERFECT**
1. estuve	he estado	había estado
2. estuviste	has estado	habías estado
3. estuvo	ha estado	había estado
1. estuvimos	hemos estado	habíamos estado
2. estuvisteis	habéis estado	habíais estado
3. estuvieron	han estado	habían estado
PAST ANTERIOR		**FUTURE PERFECT**
hube estado etc		habré estado etc

CONDITIONAL		*IMPERATIVE*
PRESENT	**PAST**	
1. estaría	habría estado	
2. estarías	habrías estado	(tú) está
3. estaría	habría estado	(Vd) esté
1. estaríamos	habríamos estado	(nosotros) estemos
2. estaríais	habríais estado	(vosotros) estad
3. estarían	habrían estado	(Vds) estén

SUBJUNCTIVE		
PRESENT	**IMPERFECT**	**PLUPERFECT**
1. esté	estuv-iera/iese	hubiera estado
2. estés	estuv-ieras/ieses	hubieras estado
3. esté	estuv-iera/iese	hubiera estado
1. estemos	estuv-iéramos/-iésemos	hubiéramos estado
2. estéis	estuv-ierais/ieseis	hubierais estado
3. estén	estuv-ieran/iesen	hubieran estado
PERFECT haya estado etc		

INFINITIVE	*PARTICIPLE*
PRESENT	**PRESENT**
estar	estando
PAST	**PAST**
haber estado	estado

224

HABER   to have (auxiliary)

PRESENT	IMPERFECT	FUTURE
1. he	había	habré
2. has	habías	habrás
3. ha/hay*	había	habrá
1. hemos	habíamos	habremos
2. habéis	habíais	habréis
3. han	habían	habrán

PRETERITE	PERFECT	PLUPERFECT
1. hube		
2. hubiste		
3. hubo	ha habido	había habido
1. hubimos		
2. hubisteis		
3. hubieron		

PAST ANTERIOR	FUTURE PERFECT
hubo habido etc	habrá habido etc

CONDITIONAL		IMPERATIVE
PRESENT	PAST	
1. habría		
2. habrías		
3. habría	habría habido	
1. habríamos		
2. habríais		
3. habrían		

SUBJUNCTIVE		
PRESENT	IMPERFECT	PLUPERFECT
1. haya	hub-iera/iese	
2. hayas	hub-ieras/ieses	
3. haya	hub-iera/iese	hubiera habido
1. hayamos	hub-iéramos/-iésemos	
2. hayáis	hub-ierais/ieseis	
3. hayan	hub-ieran/iesen	

PERFECT   haya habido etc

INFINITIVE	PARTICIPLE	NOTE
PRESENT	PRESENT	This verb is an auxiliary used for compound tenses (eg he bebido – I have drunk)
haber	habiendo	
PAST	PAST	*'hay' means 'there is/are'.
haber habido	habido	

DAR   to give

PRESENT	IMPERFECT	FUTURE
1. doy	daba	daré
2. das	dabas	darás
3. da	daba	dará
1. damos	dábamos	daremos
2. dais	dabais	daréis
3. dan	daban	darán

PRETERITE	PERFECT	PLUPERFECT
1. di	he dado	había dado
2. diste	has dado	habías dado
3. dio	ha dado	había dado
1. dimos	hemos dado	habíamos dado
2. disteis	habéis dado	habíais dado
3. dieron	han dado	habían dado

PAST ANTERIOR	FUTURE PERFECT
hube dado etc	habré dado etc

CONDITIONAL		IMPERATIVE
PRESENT	PAST	
1. daría	habría dado	
2. darías	habrías dado	(tú) da
3. daría	habría dado	(Vd) dé
1. daríamos	habríamos dado	(nosotros) demos
2. daríais	habríais dado	(vosotros) dad
3. darían	habrían dado	(Vds) den

SUBJUNCTIVE

PRESENT	IMPERFECT	PLUPERFECT
1. dé	di-era/ese	hubiera dado
2. des	di-eras/eses	hubieras dado
3. dé	di-era/ese	hubiera dado
1. demos	di-éramos/-ésemos	hubiéramos dado
2. deis	di-erais/eseis	hubierais dado
3. den	di-eran/esen	hubieran dado

PERFECT   haya dado etc

INFINITIVE	PARTICIPLE
PRESENT	PRESENT
dar	dando
PAST	PAST
haber dado	dado

IR   to go

PRESENT	IMPERFECT	FUTURE
1. voy	iba	iré
2. vas	ibas	irás
3. va	iba	irá
1. vamos	íbamos	iremos
2. vais	ibais	iréis
3. van	iban	irán

PRETERITE	PERFECT	PLUPERFECT
1. fui	he ido	había ido
2. fuiste	has ido	habías ido
3. fue	ha ido	había ido
1. fuimos	hemos ido	habíamos ido
2. fuisteis	habéis ido	habíais ido
3. fueron	han ido	habían ido

PAST ANTERIOR	FUTURE PERFECT
hube ido etc	habré ido etc

CONDITIONAL		*IMPERATIVE*
PRESENT	PAST	
1. iría	habría ido	
2. irías	habrías ido	(tú) ve
3. iría	habría ido	(Vd) vaya
1. iríamos	habríamos ido	(nosotros) vamos
2. iríais	habríais ido	(vosotros) id
3. irían	habrían ido	(Vds) vayan

SUBJUNCTIVE		
PRESENT	IMPERFECT	PLUPERFECT
1. vaya	fu-era/ese	hubiera ido
2. vayas	fu-eras/eses	hubieras ido
3. vaya	fu-era/ese	hubiera ido
1. vayamos	fu-éramos/-ésemos	hubiéramos ido
2. vayáis	fu-erais/eseis	hubierais ido
3. vayan	fu-eran/esen	hubieran ido

PERFECT	haya ido etc

INFINITIVE	*PARTICIPLE*
PRESENT	PRESENT
ir	yendo
PAST	PAST
haber ido	ido

TENER to have

PRESENT	IMPERFECT	FUTURE
1. tengo	tenía	tendré
2. tienes	tenías	tendrás
3. tiene	tenía	tendrá
1. tenemos	teníamos	tendremos
2. tenéis	teníais	tendréis
3. tienen	tenían	tendrán
PRETERITE	**PERFECT**	**PLUPERFECT**
1. tuve	he tenido	había tenido
2. tuviste	has tenido	habías tenido
3. tuvo	ha tenido	había tenido
1. tuvimos	hemos tenido	habíamos tenido
2. tuvisteis	habéis tenido	habíais tenido
3. tuvieron	han tenido	habían tenido
PAST ANTERIOR		**FUTURE PERFECT**
hube tenido etc		habré tenido etc

CONDITIONAL		*IMPERATIVE*
PRESENT	**PAST**	
1. tendría	habría tenido	
2. tendrías	habrías tenido	(tú) ten
3. tendría	habría tenido	(Vd) tenga
1. tendríamos	habríamos tenido	(nosotros) tengamos
2. tendríais	habríais tenido	(vosotros) tened
3. tendrían	habrían tenido	(Vds) tengan

SUBJUNCTIVE		
PRESENT	**IMPERFECT**	**PLUPERFECT**
1. tenga	tuv-iera/iese	hubiera tenido
2. tengas	tuv-ieras/ieses	hubieras tenido
3. tenga	tuv-iera/iese	hubiera tenido
1. tengamos	tuv-iéramos/-iésemos	hubiéramos tenido
2. tengáis	tuv-ierais/ieseis	hubierais tenido
3. tengan	tuv-ieran/iesen	hubieran tenido
PERFECT haya tenido etc		

INFINITIVE	*PARTICIPLE*
PRESENT	**PRESENT**
tener	teniendo
PAST	**PAST**
haber tenido	tenido

228

VENIR   to come

PRESENT	IMPERFECT	FUTURE
1. vengo	venía	vendré
2. vienes	venías	vendrás
3. viene	venía	vendrá
1. venimos	veníamos	vendremos
2. venís	venías	vendréis
3. vienen	venían	vendrán

PRETERITE	PERFECT	PLUPERFECT
1. vine	he venido	había venido
2. viniste	has venido	habías venido
3. vino	ha venido	había venido
1. vinimos	hemos venido	habíamos venido
2. vinisteis	habéis venido	habíais venido
3. vinieron	han venido	habían venido

PAST ANTERIOR	FUTURE PERFECT
hube venido etc	habré venido etc

CONDITIONAL		*IMPERATIVE*
PRESENT	**PAST**	
1. vendría	habría venido	
2. vendrías	habrías venido	(tú) ven
3. vendría	habría venido	(Vd) venga
1. vendríamos	habríamos venido	(nosotros) vengamos
2. vendríais	habríais venido	(vosotros) venid
3. vendrían	habrían venido	(Vds) vengan

SUBJUNCTIVE

PRESENT	IMPERFECT	PLUPERFECT
1. venga	vin-iera/iese	hubiera venido
2. vengas	vin-ieras/ieses	hubieras venido
3. venga	vin-iera/iese	hubiera venido
1. vengamos	vin-iéramos/-iésemos	hubiéramos venido
2. vengáis	vin-ierais/ieseis	hubierais venido
3. vengan	vin-ieran/iesen	hubieran venido

PERFECT   haya venido etc

INFINITIVE	*PARTICIPLE*
PRESENT	**PRESENT**
venir	viniendo
PAST	**PAST**
haber venido	venido

16. VERBS AND THEIR OBJECTS

A number of verbs in Spanish cannot be used without a specific preposition if their object is expressed.

1. Verbs taking *a* before an object

acercarse a	to approach
aproximarse a	to approach
asistir a	to attend
asomarse a	to lean out of
dar a	to look out onto
faltar a	not to fulfil/keep
jugar a	to play at (*game*)
llegar a	to arrive at/in
oler a	to smell of
oponerse a	to oppose
parecerse a	to resemble
renunciar a	to give up
resistir a	to resist
saber a	to taste of
sobrevivir a	to outlive

faltó a su promesa
he didn't keep his promise

la ventana de mi cuarto daba a un matadero
the window of my room looked out onto an abattoir

la pequeña se parece a su padre
the little girl looks like her father

2. Verbs taking *de* before an object

abusar de	to misuse
acordarse de	to remember
apoderarse de	to seize
asombrarse de	to wonder at
burlarse de	to make fun of
cambiar de	to change
carecer de	to lack
compadecerse de	to take pity on
depender de	to depend on
desconfiar de	to distrust
despedirse de	to say goodbye to

disfrutar de	to enjoy
dudar de	to doubt
enamorarse de	to fall in love with
enterarse de	to find out
gozar de	to enjoy
maravillarse de	to wonder at
mudar de	to change
ocuparse de	to attend to
olvidarse de	to forget
pasar de	to exceed
prescindir de	to do without
reírse de	to make fun of
responder de	to answer for
saber de	to know of
salir de	to leave (*a place*)
servirse de	to use
sospechar de	to distrust
tirar de	to pull
tratarse de	to be about
variar de	to change
vengarse de	to take revenge for/on

se trata de mi primo
it's about my cousin

afortunadamente gozamos de buena salud
fortunately we enjoy good health

dudar can be used with the direct object **lo** in cases like:

lo dudo	**no lo dude Vd.**
I doubt it	don't you doubt it

Otherwise it takes **de**:

dudo de su testimonio
I doubt his testimony

3. Verbs taking *con* before an object

acabar con	to put an end to
casarse con	to marry
contar con	to rely on
dar con	to come across
divertirse con	to be amused by
encontrarse con	to meet
hablar con	to talk to
portarse con	to behave towards
soñar con	to dream about

¡acabemos con estas mentiras!
let's put an end to these lies!

cuento contigo
I'm counting on you

4. Verbs taking *en* before an object

consentir en	to agree to
consistir en	to consist of
convenir en	to agree to
entrar en	to enter/go into
fijarse en	to look at
ingresar en	to enter
penetrar en	to penetrate
* pensar en	to think about
reparar en	to notice

consintió en ello
he agreed to it

¡fíjate en aquel edificio!
just look at that building!

* do not confuse **pensar en** with **pensar de** which means 'to have an opinion of'.

pensaba en sus vacaciones en España
she was thinking about her holidays in Spain

¿qué piensas de esta idea?
what do you think of this idea?

5. **Verbs taking *por* before an object**

asomarse por	to lean out of
felicitar por	to congratulate on
interesarse por	to take an interest in
preguntar por	to ask after

el cura preguntó por mi tía que está enferma
the priest asked after my aunt who is ill

6. **Verbs which take no preposition before the object in Spanish though they do in English**

agradecer	to be grateful for
aguantar	to put up with
aprobar	to approve of
aprovechar	to take advantage of
buscar	to look for
cuidar	to look after
escuchar	to listen to
esperar	to wait for
extrañar	to wonder at
lamentar	to be sorry about
mirar	to look at
pagar	to pay for
recordar	to remind of
regalar	to make a present of
rumiar	to ponder over
sentir	to be sorry about
soportar	to put up with

aprovecharon la ocasión para felicitar a Juan
they took advantage of the opportunity to congratulate Juan

la agradezco mucho el regalo
thank you very much for the gift

su historia me extraña
your story surprises me

17. VERBS FOLLOWED BY AN INFINITIVE

1. Verbs followed immediately by the infinitive

The direct infinitive is used after the following verbs, though they may also be followed by a clause with its verb in the subjunctive:

a) Verbs of making, advising, ordering, preventing and permitting

aconsejar	to advise to
amenazar	to threaten to
conceder	to concede to
dejar	to let/allow to
hacer	to make
impedir	to prevent from
mandar	to command/order to
ordenar	to command/order to
permitir	to permit/allow to
prohibir	to prohibit from/forbid to

mis padres no me dejan poner la radio después de medianoche
my parents don't allow me to have the radio on after midnight

me mandó salir
he ordered me to leave

b) Verbs of the senses: *sentir, ver* and *oír*

oír	to hear
sentir	to feel
ver	to see

no te vi llegar
I didn't see you come in

le oí roncar
I heard him snoring

c) Impersonal verbs, where the verb used in the infinitive is the subject of the impersonal verb

alegrarse	**me alegra verte de nuevo** I am happy to see you again
gustar	**nos gusta mucho pasear en el campo** we love walking in the country

hacer falta	**te hace falta estudiar** you need to study
olvidarse	**se me olvidó ir al banco** I forgot to go to the bank
parecer	**¿te parece bien salir ahora?** do you think it's a good idea to leave now?
convenir	**no me conviene partir mañana** it doesn't suit me to leave tomorrow

d) After the following verbs when the subject is the same as that of the infinitive

acordar	to agree to
ansiar	to long to
concertar	to agree to
confesar	to confess to
conseguir	to succeed in -ing, manage to
creer	to believe
deber	to have to
decidir	to decide to
decir	to say, tell
descuidar	to neglect to
desear	to wish/want to
esperar	to hope/expect to
evitar	to avoid -ing
figurarse	to suppose, imagine
fingir	to pretend to
imaginar	to imagine -ing
intentar	to try to
lograr	to succeed in -ing, manage to
merecer	to merit -ing
necesitar	to need to
negar	to deny -ing
ofrecer	to offer to
olvidar	to forget to
osar	to dare to
parecer	to appear to
pedir	to ask to
pensar	to intend to
poder	to be able to
preferir	to prefer to

presumir	to presume to
pretender	to try/claim to
procurar	to endeavour to
prometer	to promise to
querer	to wish to
recordar	to remember to
resistir	to resist -ing
resolver	to resolve to
resultar	to turn out to (be)
saber	to know how to
sentir	to regret to/-ing
soler	to be accustomed to -ing
temer	to be afraid to

debemos pagar la cuenta ahora
we must pay the bill now

nuestro equipo consiguió ganar el partido
our team managed to win the match

el niño resultó ser el hijo del rey
the boy turned out to be the king's son

solemos merendar en el bosque los domingos
we usually go for a picnic in the woods on Sundays

2. Verbs followed by *a* + infinitive

The verbs given below take the preposition **a** before a following infinitive. In most cases the idea of 'in order to' is involved.

a) Verbs of motion

acercarse a	to come forward to
acudir a	to come to
adelantarse a	to go towards
andar a	to go to
apresurarse a	to hurry to
bajar a	to go down to
correr a	to run to
dirigirse a	to go towards ... to
entrar a	to go in to
enviar a	to send to
ir a	to go to
lanzarse a	to rush to
mandar a	to send to

precipitarse a	to rush to
salir a	to go out to
sentarse a	to sit down to
subir a	to go up to
traer a	to bring to
venir a	to come to
volver a	to do … again

el mecánico se acercó a hablar conmigo
the mechanic came forward to speak to me

la chica se apresuró a hacer las camas
the maid rushed off to make the beds

el jefe mandó al chico a recoger las cartas
the boss sent the boy to pick up the mail

volveré a llamarte mañana
I'll call you again tomorrow

b) Verbs of forcing, compelling, inviting

animar a	to encourage to
conducir a	to lead to
convidar a	to invite to
empujar a	to push into
excitar a	to excite to
exhortar a	to exhort to
forzar a	to force to
impulsar a	to impel to
incitar a	to incite to
inducir a	to induce to
invitar a	to invite to
llamar a	to call to
llevar a	to bring/lead to
obligar a	to oblige to
persuadir a	to persuade to

animaron a la niña a montar al caballo
they encouraged the little girl to get on the horse

el dueño forzó al camarero a limpiar los platos
the owner forced the waiter to clean the plates

me invitó a pasar el fin de semana
he invited me to spend the weekend

FORMS

c) Verbs of beginning

comenzar a	to begin to
echarse a	to start -ing
empezar a	to begin to
ponerse a	to begin to, set about -ing
romper a	to break into, do suddenly

el bebé se echó a llorar
they baby burst into tears

todos los alumnos se pusieron a trabajar
all the pupils started to work

d) Verbs used reflexively to mean deciding or refusing

decidirse a	to decide to
negarse a	to refuse to
resolverse a	to resolve to

el niño se negó a comer
the little boy refused to eat

e) The following verbs

acostumbrarse a	to get used to -ing
aguardar a	to wait to
alcanzar a	to manage to
aprender a	to learn to
arriesgarse a	to risk -ing
aspirar a	to aspire to
atreverse a	to dare to
autorizar a	to authorise to
aventurarse a	to venture to
ayudar a	to help to
comprometerse a	to undertake to
condenar a	to condemn to
contribuir a	to contribute to -ing
dedicarse a	to devote oneself to
detenerse a	to stop to
disponerse a	to get ready to
enseñar a	to teach to
entregarse a	to devote oneself to
exponerse a	to expose oneself to
habituarse a	to get used to -ing
limitarse a	to limit oneself to -ing

ofrecerse a	to offer oneself to
oponerse a	to object to -ing
prepararse a	to prepare to
pararse a	to stop to
quedarse a	to stay and
renunciar a	to give up -ing
resignarse a	to resign oneself to -ing
tender a	to tend to

los chicos no se arriesgaron a cruzar el río
the boys didn't dare cross the river

después del accidente, Juan se dedicó a cuidar de su mujer
after the accident, Juan devoted himself to looking after his wife

se detuvo a hablar conmigo
he stopped to speak to me

3. Verbs followed by *de* + infinitive

In these cases **de** is required before a following infinitive:

a) Verbs of stopping or leaving off an action

abstenerse de	to abstain from -ing
acabar de	to finish -ing, have just
cansarse de	to become tired of -ing
cesar de	to cease -ing
dejar de	to leave off -ing
desistir de	to desist from -ing
disuadir de	to dissuade from -ing
excusar de	to excuse from -ing
fatigarse de	to grow tired of -ing
guardarse de	to take care not to
hartarse de	to grow tired of -ing
librarse de	to escape from -ing
parar de	to stop -ing
saciarse de	to grow tired of -ing
terminar de	to finish -ing

When **dejar de** is used in the negative, it expresses the idea of 'not to fail to':

no dejes de devolverme los discos la semana que viene
make sure you give me back the records next week

b) Also the following verbs

acordarse de	to remember to
acusar de	to accuse of -ing
alegrarse de	to be glad to
arrepentirse de	to repent of -ing
avergonzarse de	to be ashamed of -ing
consolarse de	to console oneself for -ing
cuidar de	to be careful to
desconfiar de	to mistrust
desesperar de	to despair of -ing
dispensar de	to excuse from -ing
encargarse de	to undertake to, see to -ing
jactarse de	to boast of -ing
maravillarse de	to marvel at
olvidarse de	to forget to
no poder por menos de	not to be able to help -ing
tratar de	to try to
tratarse de	to be a question of

yo me encargo de hacer eso
I'll see to doing that

el joven se olvidó de acudir a la cita
the young man forgot to keep his appointment

se trata de trabajar más
it's a question of working more

no pude por menos de reírme
I couldn't help laughing

4. Verbs followed by *en* + infinitive

complacerse en	to take pleasure in -ing
consentir en	to consent to
consistir en	to consist in -ing
convenir en	to agree to
dudar en	to hesitate to
empeñarse en	to insist on -ing
entretenerse en	to amuse oneself in -ing
esforzarse en	to try hard to
hacer bien en	to do well/right to
hacer mal en	to do badly/wrong in
insistir en	to insist on -ing
interesarse en	to be interested in -ing

obstinarse en	to be determined to
pensar en	to think of -ing
persistir en	to persist in -ing
quedar en	to agree to
soñar en	to have in mind to
tardar en	to take (a long) time to
vacilar en	to hesitate to

la niña se esforzaba en montar en bicicleta
the little girl was trying hard to ride the bicycle

haces bien en aydar a tu madre
you do well to help your mother

los amigos quedaron en verse a los ocho
the friends agreed to meet at eight o'clock

el tren tardó treinta minutos en llegar
the train took thirty minutes to come

5. Verbs followed by *con* + infinitive

amenazar con	to threaten to
contentarse con	to content oneself with -ing
soñar con	to dream of

el hombre de negocios soñaba con ir a Río de Janeiro
the business man dreamed of going off to Rio

6. Verbs followed by *por* + infinitive

a) Verbs of beginning and ending, with the sense of English 'by'

acabar por	to end up by -ing
comenzar por	to begin by -ing
empezar por	to begin by -ing

acabó por comprarse el traje azul
she finished up buying the blue suit

b) Verbs of longing/trying to etc

esforzarse por	to make an effort to
luchar por	to struggle to
morirse por	to be dying to
rabiar por	to be dying to

la niña se moría por abrir los paquetes
the little girl was dying to open the parcels

18. CONJUNCTIONS

1. Simple conjunctions

Simple conjunctions consist of one word only. The commonest are:

aunque	although
como	as (reason)
conforme	as (in proportion as)
conque	so, so then
cuando	when
e	and
* mas	but
mientras	while
ni	neither/nor
o	or
pero	but
porque	because
pues	since, so
que	that, for (because)
según	according to
si	if, whether
sino	but
siquiera	if only
u	or
y	and

* mas is old-fashioned nowadays, the everyday word for 'but' being **pero**.

me fui al cine porque creía que ya no venías
I went to the cinema because I thought you weren't coming

sabremos pronto si hemos ganado el premio
we'll soon know whether we've won the prize

se puso triste cuando se murió su perro
he became sad when his dog died

no grites tanto, que ya te oigo
don't shout so much, I can hear you

2. Compound conjunctions

These conjunctions consist of two or more words, the last one usually being **que**:

a condición de que	on condition that
a fin de que	so that
a medida que	as
a menos que	unless
a no ser que	unless
antes de que	before
a pesar de que	despite
así que	so (that)
con tal (de) que	provided that
de manera que	so (that)
de modo que	so (that)
desde que	since
después de que	after
en caso de que	in case
hasta que	until
luego que	as soon as
mientras	while
mientras que	whereas
para que	in order that
por lo que	for which reason
por si	in case
puesto que	since
salvo que	except that
siempre que	whenever, so long as
sino que	but
tan pronto como	as soon as
ya que	since

vamos a preparar la comida por si vienen pronto
let's get the meal ready in case they come soon

los niños jugaban mientras su madre se ocupaba de la casa
the children played while their mother took care of the house

llevo el paraguas por si llueve
I'll take my umbrella in case it rains

 Note that, whereas *puesto que* and *ya que* refer to cause, *desde que* refers *only* to time in Spanish:

todo marcha bien desde que él llegó
everything has been fine since he arrived

puesto que las mercancías ya no están disponibles
since the goods are no longer available

3. Coordinating conjunctions

Coordinating conjunctions come in pairs and are used to link two closely associated ideas:

apenas ... (cuando)	hardly... when
bien ... bien	either... or
o ... o	either... or
o bien ... o bien	either... or
ni ... ni	neither... nor
no sólo ... sino también	not only... but also
que ... o que	whether... or
ya ... ya	sometimes ... sometimes
tanto ... como	both ... and
no ... sino	not ... but
no ... pero sí	not ... but

ni los sindicatos ni los empresarios están contentos
neither the unions nor the employers are happy

tanto tú como yo
both you and I

19. NUMBERS

I. THE CARDINAL NUMBERS

0	cero	10	diez
1	uno, una	11	once
2	dos	12	doce
3	tres	13	trece
4	cuatro	14	catorce
5	cinco	15	quince
6	seis	16	dieciséis
7	siete	17	diecisiete
8	ocho	18	dieciocho
9	nueve	19	diecinueve
20	veinte	21	veintiuno
22	veintidós	23	veintitrés
24	veinticuatro	25	veinticinco
26	veintiséis	27	veintisiete
28	veintiocho	29	veintinueve
30	treinta	31	treinta y uno/una
40	cuarenta	42	cuarenta y dos
50	cincuenta	53	cincuenta y tres
60	sesenta	64	sesenta y cuatro
70	setenta	75	setenta y cinco
80	ochenta	86	ochenta y seis
90	noventa	97	noventa y siete
100	ciento	101	ciento uno/una
105	ciento cinco	115	ciento quince
120	ciento veinte	123	ciento veintitrés
150	ciento cincuenta	176	ciento setenta y seis
200	doscientos/as	202	doscientos dos
300	trescientos/as	317	trescientos diecisiete
400	cuatrocientos/as	428	cuatrocientos veintiocho
500	quinientos/as	539	quinientos treinta y nueve
600	seiscientos/as	645	seiscientos cuarenta y cinco
700	setecientos/as	754	setecientos cincuenta y cuatro
800	ochocientos/as	863	ochocientos sesenta y tres
900	novecientos/as	971	novecientos setenta y uno/una

1,000	mil	2,000	dos mil
3,000	tres mil	4,000	cuatro mil
5,000	cinco mil	6,000	seis mil
7,000	siete mil	8,000	ocho mil
9,000	nueve mil	10,000	diez mil

200,000	doscientos mil
300,000	trescientos mil
600,000	seiscientos mil
1,000,000	un millón
2,000,000	dos millones

a) Alternative forms

There are alternative forms for 16 to 19 which are written as three separate words:

diez y seis, diez y siete etc

b) Shortened forms of certain numbers

uno is shortened to **un** when followed by a noun or adjective + noun:

treinta y un meses	**doscientos un días**
thirty-one months	two hundred and one days

ciento is shortened to **cien** when followed by (1) a noun, (2) an adjective + noun, (3) the numeral **mil**:

cien panes	**cien mil hojas**
a hundred loaves	a hundred thousand leaves

cien millones de euros	**cien buenos días**
a hundred million euros	a hundred good days

c) Agreement

Cardinal numbers are invariable except for the plural hundreds and numbers ending in **-uno**:

doscientas personas	**quinientas cincuenta libras**
two hundred people	five hundred and fifty pounds

veintiuna páginas	**ciento una cosas**
twenty-one pages	a hundred and one things

d) Accents

Written accents are necessary for some of the twenties:

22 **veintidós** 23 **veintitrés** 26 **veintiséis**

also: **veintiún años** twenty-one years

e) Counting by hundreds stops at 900:

1966	**mil novecientos sesenta y seis**
	nineteen hundred and sixty-six
1200 euros	**mil doscientos euros**
	twelve hundred euros

2. THE ORDINAL NUMBERS

primero	first	**sexto**	sixth
segundo	second	**séptimo**	seventh
tercero	third	**octavo**	eighth
cuarto	fourth	**noveno**	ninth
quinto	fifth	**décimo**	tenth

a) Ordinals are adjectives and as such agree with their noun:

la segunda esquina **la séptima semana**
the second corner the seventh week

b) **primero** and **tercero** are shortened to **primer** and **tercer** before a masculine singular noun:

el primer tren **el tercer coche**
the first train the third coach

c) Ordinals are rarely used beyond the tenth, when cardinals are used instead:

el siglo once **Luis XIV – Luis catorce**
the eleventh century Louis the fourteenth

20. DAYS, MONTHS AND SEASONS

The names of the days of the week, the months and the seasons are written with small letters in Spanish.

Days of the week

el lunes	Monday
el martes	Tuesday
el miércoles	Wednesday
el jueves	Thursday
el viernes	Friday
el sábado	Saturday
el domingo	Sunday

Months

enero	January
febrero	February
marzo	March
abril	April
mayo	May
junio	June
julio	July
agosto	August
se(p)tiembre	September
octubre	October
noviembre	November
diciembre	December

Seasons

primavera	spring (21 March to 21 June)
verano	summer (21 June to 21 September)
otoño	autumn (21 September to 21 December)
invierno	(21 December to 21 March)

INDEX

INDEX

INDEX

INDEX